Handbook of Children's Religious Education

Handbooks in this series:

Handbook of Preschool Religious Education

Handbook of Children's Religious Education

Handbook of Youth Ministry

Handbook of Adult Religious Education

Handbook
of
Children's Religious Education

Edited by
Donald Ratcliff

Religious Education Press
Birmingham, Alabama

Library of Congress Cataloging-in-Publication Data

Handbook of children's religious education / edited by Donald Ratcliff.
    Includes bibliographical references and index.
    ISBN 0-89135-085-3
    1. Christian education of children—Handbooks, manuals, etc.
  I. Ratcliff, Donald.
  BV1475.2.H339   1992
  268'.432—dc20   91-43038
                                                  CIP

Religious Education Press, Inc.
5316 Meadow Brook Road
Birmingham, Alabama 35242
10 9 8 7 6 5 4 3 2

Religious Education Press publishes books exclusively in religious education
and in areas closely related to religious education. It is committed to enhancing and professionalizing religious education through the publication of
serious, significant, and scholarly works.

PUBLISHER TO THE PROFESSION

Contents

Introduction

The *Handbook of Children's Religious Education* is a concise, comprehensive guide to providing quality religious education for school-aged children. Top scholars in religious education and closely allied fields have combined their talents to produce this multifaceted work. No one theoretical perspective is championed; several alternative viewpoints are substantiated by empirical research. Each chapter summarizes the major theories and best research on each topic, then practical implications, teaching methods, and suggestions are detailed. Leaders and educators will find here the resources for developing grounded, quality religious education programs. Like its predecessors, this handbook probably will be used in colleges and seminaries as well. While the emphasis is upon serious scholarship, care has been taken to make the contents readable and practical.

SUMMARY

The cognitive, social, and physical aspects of child development are summarized in the first chapter. While the various areas are considered separately, domains are interwoven so that a more holistic perspective predominates. The chapter opens with a brief survey of physical development in middle childhood. Special emphasis is placed upon Jean Piaget's concrete operations stage and how recent research supports some aspects of that stage and calls for refinement of other aspects. The social interaction of children is also considered, including the importance of games and rules in games.

Chapter two surveys Fowler's faith development theory, but branches out to consider alternative perspectives of faith development including that of Fritz Oser. The theoretical concepts of each view are described while empirical support for and against each theory is noted. Strengths and weaknesses are summarized and applications for children are suggested. The language of faith is also considered. The author's own research of religious language in play is summarized, as well as how and when formal religious language should be initiated.

The third chapter considers the important topic of children's religious concepts. The primary authors, prominent Italian and Finnish researchers, outline the major findings of their extensive research of children in this area. They consider children's concepts of God, prayer and immanent justice, understandings of the Bible, death and life after death, and how personal religion has its genesis in late childhood. Implications for curricular decisions are noted, as well as important contrasts and similarities of other research on the topic.

The moral and affective dimensions of childhood are considered in chapter four. While Kohlberg's theory is summarized, the author takes a broad, inclusive approach that incorporates other theories as well. As with other chapters, research evidence for and against the various perspectives is considered and applications recommended. Particular emphasis is placed upon the child's feelings, emotions, attitudes, values, and love, and how these characteristics impinge upon religious education methods and content. The aesthetic dimension of affectivity is included, such as music, dance, painting, and sculpting.

The religious lifestyle dimension is highlighted in chapter five, particularly as it relates to the family. Ways of teaching the Christian lifestyle to children are noted, such as participation in the life of the congregation, play, community service work, children's liturgy, and so on. A major section of the chapter concentrates upon the importance of the family in lifestyle content, with emphasis upon how religious educators can train and encourage families to educate their children through daily experiences. A summary of the research on how the family influences the religion of the child is included.

Chapter six describes the social contexts of religious education. Primarily sociological in his orientation, the author summarizes research and theory on socialization as well as culture and ethnicity, and culls ideas from the sociologies of education and religion that have a bearing on religious education of children. The chapter includes a survey of various contexts of that education, including the Sunday school, catechismal classes, camping, parochial schools and Christian dayschools, weekly Bible meetings, released time instruction, and boarding schools for missionary children.

Religious educators often wonder what kind of discipline is best in religious education settings. Gallup polls also indicate that discipline is consistently the number one concern of parents and teachers of elementary-aged children. Chapter seven surveys various theories and strategies of discipline and how each relates to spiritual growth.

A chapter addresses what is sometimes described as the general method of religious education. This involves establishing the general conditions for teaching and learning, such as encouraging a warm socio-emotional climate. Principles and procedures of motivation are analyzed. The improvement of teaching by in-service and pre-service training is considered, as well as the use of audio visuals.

Specific methods are comprehensively summarized in chapter nine. These methods are related to cognitive, behavioral, and affective theories of educational pedagogy. Not only are these methods described in detail, but the author also considers when it is appropriate and inappropriate to make use of each. Lecture, peer teaching, role playing, simulation, discussion, questions and answers, and other methods are surveyed.

Assessment, placement, and evaluation are the topics of the final chapter, with a strong emphasis upon readiness for religion. Assessment of competencies prior to instruction involves the measurement of cognitive abilities, attitudes, and other factors. Age-graded placement is contrasted with ability placement and nongraded, intergenerational placement in light of both social and personal consequences to children. Instruction and postinstructional evaluation should be integrally related to the child's readiness as well as the teacher's preparation.

THE AGE RANGE

Children are defined as youngsters between six and twelve, an age span sometimes referred to as "middle and late childhood" or "school-aged." The initiation of this period of life is marked by the beginning of formal schooling. While preschoolers increasingly are being given formal schooling, this is considered at best an unwise practice, as David Elkind notes in *Miseducation*. A key difference between preschoolers and school-aged children is their tolerance for, and ability to profit from, formal instruction. There is also neurological evidence noted by researchers in this area that certain parts of the brain mature at about age six, give or take a couple of years. Finally, many preindustrial cultures distinguish infancy and childhood (for example, several indulge children until about age five, then teach infant care and survival skills after that point).

The end point of childhood is marked by a number of events. The biological marker is the onset of puberty, generally accompanied by the development of formal operational reasoning. Erik Erikson's theory notes that socially the adolescent is quite different from the child, and the full range of adult emotions becomes possible. Neurologically, areas of the brain mature that were less functional in earlier years. Many students enter junior high at about twelve. Cross-culturally, rites of passage often occur at about this time, in which children are initiated into adulthood. In some churches confirmation is celebrated as such a rite of passage.

An in-depth analysis of younger children is provided by *The Handbook of Preschool Religious Education*, while adolescence is detailed in the *Handbook of Youth Ministry*, both of which are companion volumes to this book. However, younger children and adolescents are occasionally considered in the present work for the purpose of contrasting skills and abilities.

WHY IS THIS BOOK NEEDED?

Demographic data indicate that the decade of the 1990s will be a decade of children. The baby bust, the downturn in number of children born during the 1970s, emptied and forced the closure of some schools in the 1980s. However, during the 1980s there was a substantial increase in the number of children born, particularly in the second half of the decade. For several years the birth rate has been higher than at any time since the baby boom of the 1950s and 1960s, although it never equaled baby boom levels. As a result we can expect to see a major increase in the number of school-aged children in the 1990s. It is too soon to tell if the increase will continue beyond this decade.

Another reason for increased religious education is that more parents desire that instruction for their children. The popular *Megatrends 2000* predicts a major return to religion in the years ahead, spurred by the New Age movement, evangelicalism, fundamentalism, and the emergence of emotional religion within mainline denominations. The authors note that baby boomers are increasingly bringing their children to church to receive a religious education. *Newsweek* (December 17, 1990, pp.51-52) confirms this trend, noting "couples with children are twice as likely to join a religious congregation." *Christianity Today* (April 3, 1987) concludes a "bull market for religion" is directly tied to the provision of religious education for baby boomers' children.

Likewise, pollster George Gallup in his book *The People's Religion* (1990) notes that 90 percent of adults with school-aged children want some kind of religious training for their offspring, but only 69 percent are providing it either at home or church. This gap is wider for single, separated, and divorced parents. Researcher George Barna, in his 1991 study *User Friendly Churches*, found that healthy, growing churches inevitably have a strong children's program. Perhaps it is not too much to suggest that there is tremendous potential for the religious education of children in the last decade of this century.

DEDICATION

I dedicate this book to one of the finest religious educators I have ever known, my wife Brenda. She has done more than her share in influencing our three children toward a productive, living faith. This has been accomplished not just by formal instruction but by modeling attitudes that reflect the Presence of God in her life. In the midst of the full-time job of raising and educating our children, she has also written church curricula and offered invaluable suggestions as she critiqued my writing. My greatest hope is that my children will emulate her by being consistent and faithful religious educators of their children.

Chapter One

Characteristics of School-Aged Children

CARY A. BUZZELLI

*The first grader slinked down the hallway of the church education-
al center. His frown seemed ready to break into tears at any moment.
The dreaded hour was soon to begin. From another direction his teacher reluctantly shuffled to the room, also dreading the moments ahead.
As usual the class began, with the teacher reading out of the teacher's
book and the youngsters staring out windows. The only break from
boredom was an occasional spitball thrown by the class clown, which
was followed by angry scolding. "God doesn't like nonsense," the
teacher bellowed. Later the teacher paused to explain a theological
term, but no one cared in the slightest. Everyone, including the teacher, kept wondering why the minutes passed so slowly. The first indication
of delight from the children came when the teacher concluded his
monologue. "Is this really what religious education is all about?" he
wondered.*

*Just down the hall, children ran for a hug from another teacher.
Her class had been an exciting experience for everyone involved. The
bright, colorful classroom clearly related to the children's age and
interests. The hour was spent with many games and activities. Each lesson was carefully crafted to meet the needs of six-year-olds. As the
children departed, the teacher overhead her youngsters excitedly telling
their smiling parents about the day's lesson. "I think those kids really
understood," the teacher thought. Meanwhile more than one of her
students thought, "I can't wait for next week."*

The above account, written by the editor and taken from actual situations, clearly indicates the necessity of religious educators understanding

1

the developmental characteristics of school-aged children. Between the years of five and seven children show marked changes in their abilities. This coincides with a new level of responsibility and independence that adults give children, a level far different from that accorded the preschool child (Whiting & Whiting, 1975).

Children are able to meet the increasing expectations of adults because of increased physical, cognitive, and social abilities. Greater strength and better overall body coordination permit complex physical tasks such as household chores or caring for younger siblings. Changes in cognitive abilities enable children to formulate goals and complex strategies to attain them (Cole & Cole, 1989). Advanced ability in taking others' perspectives leads children to a greater understanding of the thoughts and feelings of others. This chapter examines the research documenting changes in children's development from the time they leave the preschool years until they enter early adolescence and considers how these changes should be taken into account in the religious education of school-aged children.

PHYSICAL DEVELOPMENT

The physical development of children during middle childhood is marked by 1) slow and steady physical growth and 2) increased refinement of motor skills used in games and sports. Children's increased size, strength, and physical coordination contribute to their feelings of physical well-being, self-esteem, self-competence, and to aspects of their cognitive development.

The slow, steady rate of children's physical growth during middle childhood is apparent when compared to the rapid growth spurts during the preschool and adolescent years. By age six the average child weighs 43 pounds, is 44 inches tall, and has reached about two-thirds his or her adult height. In about six years, at age twelve, average weight will be around 80 pounds and average height about 5 feet. As most of the weight gain during this period is in muscle rather than fat, there is a large increase in physical strength. Boys at the end of middle childhood have reached 80 percent of adult height while girls have attained about 90 percent of adult height (Tanner, 1978).

Changes in height and weight are accompanied by changes in body proportion. Limbs tend to grow more than the trunk of the body. The roundish body of the preschool child gives way to the leaner, slimmer body of the school-aged child. It is not until the end of the school-aged period, during the preadolescent growth spurt, that children's bodies once again undergo major changes in size and shape.

The basic motor skills learned during early childhood are further refined during middle childhood. Skills such as running, jumping, throwing, and hitting are combined and used in simple games. For example, tag and dodge ball require running, balance, and advanced body movements like dodging. Childhood games also require advanced cognitive skills such as turn-taking and the social understanding necessary to coordinate multiple players in a mutual activity. As we will see later in the chapter these cognitive skills are also developing at this time.

Participation in organized activities brings with it concerns about injury. Children may have the motor and cognitive skills necessary to engage in sports, yet the immaturity of their bones and muscles makes them prone to injury. Because school-aged children's bones grow faster than their muscles they are less flexible than preschool-aged children (Teitz, 1982). Therefore, warm-up activities are particularly important for preventing injury.

Changes are likewise occurring in children's fine motor abilities, especially the ability to use pencil or pen. However, as development of individual children varies considerably, care should be taken when planning activities requiring writing skills. Forcing children to write or draw in specified ways or in restricted areas, such as on lines or on small papers, may dampen their enthusiasm and creativity.

Children's feelings about their competence in large and small motor activities and their perceptions of body characteristics become increasingly important dimensions of children's self-understanding and self-concept (Damon & Hart, 1982). Children competent at large motor activities, like running and jumping, are often more popular with peers and express more self-confidence (Harter, 1982). Difficulty mastering fine motor activities such as writing, printing, and drawing may lead to early school problems and to children feeling less cognitively competent (Denkla, 1984).

Children's physical abilities greatly increase as does their coordination. They move from participants in games with simple rules to complex games with intricate rules of their own making. However, the immature nature of their developing bones and muscles needs to be considered when planning physical activities. Thus, consideration should be given to the physical demands of liturgical activities and being required to sit or stand during lengthy services. Likewise, they progress from rudimentary drawing and writing skills to sophisticated artistic and writing abilities through which they express their deepening relations with others and their experience of faith and God. Yet, parents and teachers need to realize that each child has an individual rate and course of development.

PIAGET'S THEORY OF COGNITIVE DEVELOPMENT

Piaget's central belief is that development, specifically cognitive development, is the result of children's interactions with objects and persons within their environment. The innumerable interactions children have with people and objects are the elements that contribute to the general ways in which they understand the world. Through seeking to master and adapt to their surroundings children construct higher levels of understanding. As children's cognitive level of understanding changes so does their understanding of the world.

A second fundamental claim of Piaget is that knowledge is a process rather than a state. Children come to know objects by acting upon them physically or mentally. They "construct" knowledge of an object and its properties. The infant knows an object, such as a nipple or rattle, by physically acting upon it. An older child knows an object by mentally acting upon it. An example from Miller (1989) illustrates how children develop concepts of spatial relations. Infants construct knowledge of near and far, up and down by crawling and trying to obtain objects. Older children understand the concepts in more abstract ways by constructing cognitive maps, that is, by manipulating mental representations of the room and the objects in it.

Religious educators often believe that their job is to fill children's heads with religious facts. Clearly there needs to be more acting upon religious ideas for adequate comprehension. For younger children to understand such concepts as love, sharing, and forgiveness, they need to experience these firsthand through relationships with significant people in their lives. Younger children learn religious meaning through experience. For older children, religious meaning is constructed through mental actions such as discussion, debates, and the application of principles to firsthand experiences.

Cognitive Structures, Assimilation, and Accommodation

Knowledge is the result of changes in children's cognitive structures. For Piaget the basic mental structure is the *schema*. A schema "can be thought of as a psychological structure that provides an organism with a template for action in similar or analogous circumstances" (Piaget & Inhelder, 1969). It serves as a basis for how one interacts with the environment. Schemes have their beginning in the inborn reflexes of infants, such as the grasping reflex. Through interactions and experience, schemes become more differentiated and are transformed into new schemes. Thus babies develop schemes to classify objects as "squeezable" or "nonsqueezable."

The changes in schemes and the development of new schemes occur as adaptations to the environment. For Piaget, intelligence is adaptation to the environment. Through his training as a biologist Piaget believed that the concepts and principles of biology could also apply to the development of human thought and intelligence. Just as humans adapt physically to their environment, intelligence develops through adaptation at the psychological level (Piaget, 1976). Adaptation for Piaget involves two complementary processes: assimilation and accommodation. Through *assimilation* one attempts to understand experiences with current cognitive structures. For example, a baby given a new toy will investigate it using behaviors which reflect her level of cognitive development, that is, by using schemes such as grasping or sucking. Thus, new experiences are understood by being assimilated or fit into existing schemes. The new toy is assimilated as something that can be sucked or grasped.

In religious education, for example, a child asked to tell God what was on his mind, responded by saying the Lord's Prayer. It was a new idea for him, but he assimilated it into his existing bedtime ritual.

However, not all that is new to the child can be fit into existing schemes. The baby must change existing schemes to understand certain new objects; the baby must *accommodate* to them. Schemes are modified in order to be applied to new experiences. According to Piaget, though, only events or experiences that are moderately discrepant from previous experiences can be accommodated; those too discrepant are neither assimilated nor accommodated. An example from Miller (1989) illustrates this point. Suppose children of various ages were given a magnet. An infant might accommodate to the shape, the sound it makes when dropped, and perhaps its taste. But the infant cannot accommodate to the magnetic properties. A three-year-old could accommodate the observation that some objects stick to the magnet. The child might offer explanations relating to the scheme "stickiness." The eight- or nine-year-old may hypothesize about the characteristics of objects that are attracted to the magnet. A child of this age could also formulate tests to check the hypotheses. It is not until adolescence that the ability to accommodate by formulating an abstract theory of magnetism occurs.

For a child with the concept of God as person, the concept of God as Spirit may be too discrepant for accommodation. As such an understanding develops over time, the religious educator can present stories portraying God as more than a person, yet not necessarily introduce God as Spirit until later. Thus, the child can construct her concept of God as Spirit through experiences only mildly discrepant with her present schemes.

Equilibration

The complementary processes of assimilation and accommodation are present in every action. As every encounter with the environment involves some degree of novelty, it is not possible to understand it entirely, or assimilate it. Some accommodations, or adjustments in cognitive structures must be made. Resolution of the discrepancy between the child's cognitive structures and new environmental experiences through assimilation and accommodation brings about a balance or equilibrium. Piaget believed that all organisms strive toward equilibrium (Piaget & Inhelder, 1969). However, each new understanding only leads to the awareness of new discrepancies in experiences, thus producing new assimilations or accommodations. Through these processes during endless encounters with the environment, developmental change occurs. Although the cognitive structures (schemes) change, the processes do not.

Stages of Development

According to Piaget, developmental change in children's cognitive structures proceeds through a series of four qualitatively different stages. Piaget outlined four major developmental stages which roughly correspond to the periods of infancy, early childhood, middle childhood, and adolescence (Piaget, 1983). Each stage represents the individual's predominant way of cognitively adapting to the environment because each stage reflects the underlying global structure during that particular time. Piaget described four necessary characteristics of stages: 1) Each stage reflects the nature of child-environment interaction and, subsequently, how one understands and views the world. Movement from one stage to the next involves change that is qualitative (change of kind) rather than quantitative (change in degree). 2) Each stage subsumes the previous stage and prepares for the subsequent stage. Old skills become integrated into new, more complex skills. 3) Stages form an invariant sequence. Stages proceed in an order; no stage can be skipped. 4) The stages are universal. The same stages, in the same order, appear in all individuals across cultures (Piaget, 1983).

Religious educators and theologians have theorized that the development of religious understanding and faith may occur through a similar series of stages in the development of faith. These will be considered in chapter two.

CONCRETE OPERATIONS

During the transition to concrete operations, from about age five to seven, a major shift in children's cognitive abilities occurs. Preoperational children can manipulate objects but do so physically, not mentally. This accounts for their dependence on how things look rather than on how things are. However, around the age of six to seven years, most children develop the ability to transform, combine, and otherwise manipulate information mentally in a truly logical system. Piaget referred to this ability as an operation—an internalized mental action that is part of a coherent and reversible logical system (Piaget & Inhelder, 1969). This stage, lasting from roughly age seven to about age eleven, is called concrete operations because children can manipulate information about concrete objects such as glasses of water, clay, and other physical objects. It is not until the stage of formal operations, usually beginning around age twelve, that the adolescent can manipulate abstract ideas and symbols. Concrete operations stage is characterized by three developments in children's reasoning: 1) reversibility, the ability to think through an action and then reverse it; 2) decentration, the ability to focus on all relevant information in a task, and 3) focusing on transformations of objects rather than on static states (Flavell, 1985). These three factors provide the necessary cognitive skills for the development of another crucial aspect of concrete operational thought, conservation. *Conservation* is the understanding that properties of an object, such as quantity, remain constant (are "conserved") despite changes in appearance.

With the new powers of reversibility, understanding of transformations, and decentration, children's thinking becomes more flexible. Children can consider alternative ways to solve problems and when necessary are able to retrace their steps (reverse their actions). Children can understand that through transformations objects and events change from one state to another, rather than limiting their attention to the present static condition. Finally, phenomena in the world are more predictable because children can consider all relevant perceptual data in solving problems (decenter) rather than focusing on a single interesting feature to the neglect of other task-important information (Flavell, 1985). As noted above, the three abilities are necessary for the understanding that the quantities and qualities of objects remain constant (are conserved) despite changes in superficial appearance.

Reversibility

Piaget elaborated upon two types of reversible mental actions: 1) *inversion*, the existence of reverse actions; and 2) *compensation*, actions that counterbalance or compensate for the effects of another action (Piaget & Inhelder, 1969). Inversion means that children understand that actions and thought processes occurring in one direction can be reversed, that is, repeated in the opposite direction. For example, the pouring of water into a tall, thin glass can be undone by the reverse action of pouring the water back into the original container. Children realize the existence of an inverse action which reverses the process returning the water to its original state in its original container. Similarly, in two rows of objects where each row has the same number but the objects in one row are separated so that it is longer, concrete operational children will say that the number remains unchanged. When asked why, they say that the row could be put back to the way it was when the objects were moved.

Using inversion, school-aged children recognize that one action can compensate for or counterbalance another action. Rather than an inverse action which undoes a previous action, compensation achieves a balance through changes in another dimension. In the above experiment, although one row of objects is longer, there are bigger gaps between objects in the row. The overall length of the row is compensated for by the larger gaps between the objects. Similarly, in Piaget's classic pouring task, the child notes that while the second container is taller it is also thinner. The change in height is exactly compensated for by a change in width, leaving the quantity unchanged.

An appreciation for the nature of reversibility and how it structures children's thought is crucial for the religious educator. Reversibility, both as inversion and compensation, is central to children's understanding of forgiveness. By having a concept of reversibility that includes inversion, children come to understand that as part of forgiveness they are relieved of the wrong they have done. In a manner of speaking they are as they were before they committed the wrong-doing, or before they sinned. Through forgiveness they are returned to a union with God, to a state of grace. Through an understanding of compensation, they also understand the role of penance, reparation, or restitution; actions that do not undo what was done but are necessary for forgiveness.

States and Transformations

Preschool children focus their attention on the state of objects rather than the state-producing transformations. Similarly, when attempting to solve a problem they are more likely to use the present condition of things and less likely to call to mind pertinent previous states or to anticipate future ones (Flavell, 1985). It is as though they have a type of "temporal centration." They center on present conditions to the exclusion of state-altering transformations. Concrete operational children, on the other hand, have the ability to consider both states and their transformations.

This difference in abilities is most evident in the pouring task. The task involves the consideration of two states, the initial and the final state, and the intervening transformation linking the two states. Because preoperational children ignore the transformation of pouring the water from the shorter wider beaker to the taller narrower one, they note that the beaker with the higher level has more. Concrete operational children comprehend the pouring as an intervening transformation and that since no liquid was added nor lost, the quantity is the same despite a different appearance. It is because of this understanding of real and potential states and transformations that the conservation task is a conceptual rather than perceptual problem (Flavell, 1985).

Children's understanding of relationships between states and intervening transformations has important implications for religious educators. Central to the worship practices of several denominations is the Eucharist. During the service a transformation is believed to occur through which ordinary bread and wine become sacramental elements. Concrete operational children will have difficulty fully comprehending theological explanations of the mystery of the transformation. Further, the explanation of the nature of the transformation as transubstantiation or consubstantiation is dependent upon denominational doctrine. But what is of significance is that concrete operational children are better able to understand the relationship of the initial state of the bread and wine to the transformational act of consecration and then ultimately to the body and blood of Christ.

Younger children being perception-bound focus only on initial and end states. No change in appearance indicates no change in state. However older children, because of their understanding of transformations, can focus on the process itself and the changes between initial and end states that result from the process. But they may also understand that changes can occur because of a process even if appearances remain the same. Thus younger children may not understand the changes in the bread and wine because of failing to consider the transformational process of consecration, but older children with better understanding of the nature of the transformations realize that although the bread and wine did not change in appearance, a much more significant change occurred as a result of a transformation.

Decentration

Preschool children tend to rely heavily on the perceptual features of objects when solving problems. They "center" their attention on a single feature, usually the most salient or interesting to the neglect of other relevant data. They appear to understand the solution of the task as requiring a perceptual rather than a conceptual judgment. To "decenter" means that children have a broader, more inclusive approach to a problem. Thus, older children consider all relevant perceptual data when attempting to solve a problem or understand a situation. For example, in the conservation task, concrete operational children are able to notice not only the lesser width but also the greater height of the liquid in the narrower but taller beaker (Flavell, 1985).

For the religious educator, as school-age children are able to "decenter" they not only understand the central beliefs of the Christian faith, belief in God, Jesus, and the Bible, but now can also appreciate the features unique to their own faith community (Ratcliff, 1988). However, younger children may focus on the clothing and beard to identify the distinctiveness of Jesus rather than his unique spiritual identity.

In concrete operations the child uses operations to order, classify, and reverse objects and events. With the advent of formal operations, beginning about age eleven, the adolescent is now able to "operate" on abstract thoughts and ideas. The adolescent can generate hypotheses, propositions, and statements, and formulate logical relationships among them. They now perform operations on operations. Thought becomes fully logical, abstract, and hypothetical (Miller, 1989).

NEO-PIAGETIAN VIEWS

Piaget was constantly at work on his theory, refining and expanding certain aspects (Piaget, 1980, 1985). Likewise a group of developmental psychologists labeled "neo-Piagetians" (such as Case, 1978, 1985) began to address what they perceived as the limitations and problems of the theory. Case attempts to integrate Piagetian and information processing theory. Thus his theory incorporates the constructs of stages, sequences, and structural change but also includes executive processing space which he defines as "the maximum number of independent schemes a child can activate at any one time" (1985, p. 289).

Perhaps the best way to compare the views of Case and Piaget is to examine the metaphors they use to describe children. To Piaget the child is a scientist at work, continuously constructing increasingly sophisticated models of the world or "logico-mathematical structures." Piaget's research focused on delineating the structures underlying children's thought through the use of symbolic logic.

For Case, the child is a problem solver "capable of formulating its own objectives, and actively pursuing them in the face of such obstacles as the world may interpose" (Case, 1985, p. 59). In solving simple problems first encountered early in life children become capable of conceiving more complex problems. It is in the pursuit of solving these later problems and challenges that cognitive development occurs. Like Piaget, Case views the child as having innate processing abilities which are used for the construction of more advanced structures. However, Case and Piaget differ on the major mechanism of development. In Case's view, limits in processing capacity limit logical reasoning thus limiting what children can learn at any particular developmental level. Increases in capacity resulting from greater efficiency of processing make available more capacity and new opportunities for development of logical reasoning.

For religious educators, Case's theory points to the importance of considering children's current level of cognitive development when presenting information as well as noting their efficiency in processing information and the amount of information presented in any one lesson. Specifically, he would suggest that the child cannot learn as many things as quickly as an adolescent or adult.

SOCIAL PERSPECTIVE-TAKING

Another hallmark in the development of school-aged children is the ability to put themselves in another's place. In a classic experiment by Piaget and Inhelder (1956) children were shown a model of three mountains. Using a doll placed at different positions around the model, children were asked to select from several pictures the one that portrayed how the mountains looked to the doll. Children under six chose the picture depicting their own rather than the doll's perspective. Piaget and Inhelder concluded that because of their egocentrism, preoperational children have difficulty taking a perspective other than their own (Piaget & Inhelder, 1956). Although recent studies (for example, Borke, 1975) contradict Piaget's claim, it is evident that children's perspective-taking abilities change over time.

Social perspective-taking is the ability to comprehend the inner psychological characteristics of oneself and others, thereby anticipating what that person might think, feel, or do (Selman, 1980). As in cognitive tasks where children are able to consider changes in two dimensions or variables simultaneously, they can now more easily keep two perspectives in mind, their own and that of another person. Thus it is now possible to relate and coordinate one's social perspective with those of others for use as a framework to understand social relationships (Selman, 1980).

Selman (1976, 1980) has delineated five levels of social perspective-taking. At the first level, Level 0, *Undifferentiated Egocentric Role Taking* (about ages 3-6), children have an egocentric or undifferentiated perspective. They are unable to distinguish their perspective from that of others. There is no recognition that another person could understand or interpret the same social event differently.

In Level 1, *Differentiated and Subjective Perspective Taking* (about ages 5-9), children can differentiate physical from psychological characteristics of others. Children understand that others can have a different perspective but the difference is thought to be the result of different information. There is still no realization of different perspectives on the same event.

The conceptual advance of Level 2, *Self-reflective Reciprocal Perspective Taking* (about ages 7-12), is children's growing ability to step outside of themselves and take a second-person perspective on their own thoughts and feelings. Children also realize that others can do the same. Thus, children can think about their own thoughts and feelings and those of others by putting themselves in others' shoes. With this ability children see the endless possibilities of perspective-taking ("I know he knows that I know that he knows . . ." and so on). However, children still do not have a full understanding of the relationship that exists between them and others.

With the transition to Level 3, *Third Person, Mutual Perspective Taking* (about ages 10-15), children can simultaneously coordinate and consider their own perspective with that of others from a third-person or generalized perspective. Selman states that children develop an "observer ego" allowing them to see themselves simultaneously as actor and object. They are aware of their actions in the relationship and can reflect on the effects of the actions on themselves. For children at this level, relationships are viewed as ongoing systems requiring the mutual coordination and sharing of thoughts and feelings.

Two new abilities appear at Level 4, *Societal-Symbolic Perspective Taking* (about ages 12 to adult). First, the recognition of a societal view of social relations, a "generalized other" perspective, allows for the acknowledgement of societal, conventional, and moral systems which all individuals can share. Second, there is the understanding of personality as a system of traits, beliefs, and values. Together these advances signify the appreciation of a shared social system necessary for communication between individuals, each having a complex personality, only part of which is accessible to another.

It is likely that in any one religious education class two or more levels will be represented. Religious educators should choose curricular content at the children's level as well as a slightly more advanced level. This will stimulate children to consider different perspectives and thus move them toward more complex levels of perspective taking.

CHILDREN'S CONCEPTIONS OF FRIENDSHIP

The manner in which developments in social perspective-taking underlie children's relationships with others is best illustrated by examining changes in children's understanding of friendship.

One major task of childhood is development of positive peer relations. Friendships mark a high point in this development. Friendship is a social relation; it does not reside within one individual but is formed by two partners. Maintaining a friendship involves continuous contact and the sharing of feelings, concerns and interests (Ginsberg, Gottman, & Parker, 1986). Friendships are also described as an orientation or attitude composed of beliefs, feelings, and behaviors (Allen, 1981). Friendships provide companionship and mutual support (Damon, 1983). They are governed by a reciprocity rule system the type and characteristics of which change throughout childhood and adolescence (Berndt & Ladd, 1988). Friendships are volitional and have no safeguards from termination.

The answers children give to the questions, "What is a friend?" and "How do you know someone is your friend?" reflect their understanding of friends, friendship, and the rule systems which govern relationships. Researchers have interpreted the changes in children's responses in different ways. Selman (1980) draws parallels between children's conceptions of friendship and levels of social perspective-taking. Selman (1980) has proposed a sequence of stages in children's conceptions of friendship. The stages are closely related to levels of social perspective-taking. Developing an awareness of another's perspective helps children better understand the meaning of their actions within a relationship. Through this process children move from a physical to a psychological orientation of friends and friendship.

At Level 0 of Selman's sequence, children's friendships are dominated by physicalistic thinking. Children are unable to separate the physical qualities of an individual from psychological attributes. The duration of a friendship is also defined in physical, momentary, here and now terms. Friendships are determined by physical acts and physical contact. Friends share material resources, such as candy and toys. Friends are children who play together, sit near, or live nearby each other. Friendship is maintained by acts of goodwill and is terminated if the friend acts in an unkind manner.

Friendships at Level 1 are characterized by a new awareness of internal psychological phenomena. There is the realization that psychological perspectives are differentiated as the self and other. Children are capable of understanding that another person thinks differently and may have different interests. Children are unable, however, to coordinate the two perspectives, that of self and of the other. Friendship has gone beyond demographics as friends are rated by how closely they match the self's interests.

A rudimentary understanding of reciprocal relations marks the next level of friendship conceptions. Children are now able to take into account the perspectives of others. This ability means cooperation is now possible within a context-specific setting. Children at this stage believe people want and need companionship but that this is only possible if each partner does what the other wants. Disagreements lead to dissolution of the friendship. Friendships are not understood as transcending the present, therefore failure to act in the best interest of the partner may end the friendship. Selman has called this stage "fair-weather cooperation."

The relationship itself becomes the focus at Level 3. Children are now able to step outside themselves and the relationship. Emphasis is now on mutual sharing and support over a period of time. Effort has shifted to maintaining the relationship beyond the present. Each partner discovers the personality of the other and is willing to share "psychological" information such as interests, thoughts, and feelings. Friends select each other because of their "psychological make-up" and compatibility. Friends help others by being mutually understanding and forgiving. Friendship is considered a long-term relation which is maintained over time. It survives minor conflicts but can be threatened by a breach of trust.

At the last level of friendship there is an appreciation that a person's psychological needs can be met by different types of relationships. Friendships as relationships are open to change and transformation just as are individuals. Through friendships individuals develop a sense of identity; an identity which is autonomous yet interdependent upon friends. There is the understanding of friendship as a process which one may grow into, as well as out of.

The religious educator can help children realize that playing together is an act of caring and sharing which helps meet the needs of oneself and others. Within the acts of caring and sharing children can come to see how they may have qualities and interests similar to those of their friends. Likewise, when children have disagreements with one another which end a play session or friendship, the religious educator can help them reconcile and thereby illustrate that friendships can be maintained despite difficulties. The Bible offers many such instances.

Youniss (1980) has formulated a view of friendship development based upon the work of Sullivan (1953) and Piaget (1965). Youniss stresses the importance of direct reciprocity in the development of children's peer relations. Direct reciprocity involves the equal participation and contribution of each person in the relationship. It is through reciprocal relations that children develop an understanding of how their behavior influences the behavior of others. Through this process peers also develop a rule system, mutually agreed upon, which directs their relationship. If either partner violates a rule the relationship may cease. The key to the relationship is cooperation based upon direct reciprocity. Youniss has labeled the respective levels as cooperation, mutual respect, and interpersonal sensitivity.

Children from six to eight years of age have an understanding of the dual nature of direct reciprocity. A child's offer to share is likely to be returned with a similar offer. Likewise, when one child hurts another, the second is likely to retaliate. Direct reciprocity is thus used in both positive and negative ways. This may bring peers closer together or separate them, thus discouraging stable interpersonal relations. Cooperation at this level is based on concrete situation-specific actions. The behavior of a person takes precedence over the characteristics of the person.

The nature of reciprocity changes as children begin to differentiate friends and non-friends on the basis of their personal qualities rather than their actions. There is a developing appreciation for the various interests and individuality of another. Friends are able to make adjustments for differences in interests. Cooperation as mutual respect is now seen as a principle of the relationship. Respect is given because the other person is a friend.

Respect for another individual as a separate person marks another change in the understanding of direct reciprocity. This may appear around ten to twelve years of age. Partners in a friendship now feel able to exchange personal information without fear of losing respect from the other person. There is the obligation to respond to self-disclosure with emotional support and sensitivity. This is important as it benefits the other person. Offering support and assistance to make the other person feel better is an important feature of reciprocity at this level.

How children respond to others and their understanding of "love thy neighbor as thyself" are related to children's level of perspective-taking and conceptions of friendship. Thus, these developmental changes have important implications for religious educators. By gauging children's understanding of relationships with others through careful listening, religious educators can better nurture and guide children's development by setting realistic expectations for children's behavior. Younger children should not be expected to respond to others in the same way or for the same reasons as older children. The more self-centered reasoning of younger children is a reflection of their egocentrism rather than selfishness and should be regarded as a developmental phenomenon, not a lack of virtue. Children develop relationships based upon direct, mutual reciprocity. Those relationships are marked by deep caring and love through positive relations with their peers and adults who play a significant role in their lives.

GROUP GAMES

For the religious educator, group games offer opportunities to promote learning and perspective taking. School-aged children now have the cognitive and social abilities necessary for playing group games. Children must be able to keep in mind the ultimate goal of the game while considering specific procedures and strategies of the moment. Likewise, they need social perspective-taking skills necessary for turn-taking and understanding the relationship between their actions and the thoughts of others ("If I move here she will probably move there and block my next move").

Group games are games "in which children play together according to conventional rules specifying: 1) some preestablished climax (or series of climaxes) to be achieved, and 2) what players should try to do in roles which are interdependent, opposed, and collaborative" (Kamii & DeVries, 1980, p. 2). Hide and Seek is an example. In this game the roles of "hider" and "seeker" are interdependent because neither can exist without the other. The roles are opposed because each is trying to prevent the other from achieving a goal, either remaining hidden or being found. Such opposition allows for the development and use of strategies. Finally, the roles are collaborative because players must abide by the rules, such as accepting the consequences, for the game to continue (Kamii & DeVries, 1980).

Group games also provide children with crucial opportunities to learn about and use rules. Piaget believed that "all morality consists of a system of rules, and the essence of all morality is to be sought for in the respect which the individual acquires for these rules" (1965, p. 13). Children develop a sense of morality through their understanding of rules and from the standards with which they are raised.

During the early school-age years children believe that rules of games have been made and handed down by authority figures such as adults, older children, or even God. Young children, therefore, treat rules as sacred and unchangeable. As children get older they come to understand that rules are the result of mutual consent among the game players. Through the give and take of negotiating, compromising, changing, reiterating, and enforcing the rules, children discover that rules provide a social structure enabling cooperation among individuals thus making the playing of games possible. Rules are seen as social conventions whose value and utility arise from children's realization that to play a game, rules must be respected and followed by all participants. Rules can be changed "as long as opinion is on your side" (Piaget, 1965, p. 28).

For Kamii and DeVries the long-term objective of playing group games must be seen within the context of learning as development and that nurturing children's development rather than the learning of specific, isolated facts is the aim of education (1980). Children's cognitive, social-cognitive, and social-perspective-taking abilities are enhanced through participation in group games. Group games provide experiences which nurture development because learning which occurs is "personally meaningful, useful, and interesting" (Kamii & DeVries, 1980, p. 12). It goes beyond mere facts. Similarly in religious education, a child's experiences with others must be "personally meaningful," for within such experiences a child can see others as children of God. Personally meaningful encounters with others are the basis of Buber's "I-Thou" relationships.

Kamii and DeVries (1980) cite three specific objectives for the use of group games with children: 1) to help children develop the intellectual and moral autonomy whereby they think for themselves, not relying on the dictates of others to determine what is "correct" or "right" in a particular situation; 2) to facilitate children's ability to coordinate the viewpoints of others with their own by decentration; and 3) to help children take the initiative in formulating interesting ideas, problems, questions, and the means to solve them by being alert, curious, and confident in their abilities to do so.

For group games to fulfill these three objectives and thereby be of educational value, they must meet not only the guidelines of the definition but three other criteria. First, does the game offer something interesting and challenging for children to figure out? Good games elicit reasoning, such as strategies, as part of the game. Teachers must analyze the content of games by asking what is possible for the children to think about and do. This is best done by considering, from the children's perspective, how the game might challenge children's reasoning while affording opportunities to cooperate with peers. Games where children are divided into two teams and engage in fact-naming competitive contests where points are given for the correct answers should be avoided. Whereas children may learn facts during such games, they are of questionable educational value as they do not inspire advanced reasoning or cooperation with peers. Such games do not meet the criteria outlined above. Likewise, within the religious education classroom such games may foster a spiritual "elitism" as losers might reject religion because of an association of winning as being of more spiritual value.

Second, does the game allow the children to evaluate the results of their actions? This means that children do not need another's help to know whether or not they have been successful. Games in which the teachers must "check" or overly guide children force children to rely on the authority of others and accept their word as correct or "true." On the other hand, when results of their actions are clear to children it is more likely that they will find the game more interesting because they can discover the direct relation between their efforts and the outcomes. For example one might have children discuss and debate the answers to questions with one another, and then provide them with resources such as concordances, Bible dictionaries, and so on, to verify and substantiate the answers.

Third, do all players participate actively throughout the game? Active participation means "mental activity and a feeling of involvement from the child's point of view" (Kamii & DeVries, 1980, p. 8). Teachers must be very aware of the developmental level of all the children. For younger children (some 5- and 6-year-olds) participation may mean more reliance on physical activity because thought may not yet be fully differentiated from action. Thus, mental activity is closely linked to physical activity. For older children, active participation means offering opportunities for mental activities such as outlining strategies to solve problems.

UNDERSTANDING OF TIME

School-age children also have a better understanding of time. Preoperational children's sense of time is fleeting at best. These children are caught in the present moment. They are aware of what has happened in the past, but "long ago" may mean last week, or when they were little babies. Similarly, future events will happen "tomorrow." Time is collapsed into what has happened (the past), what is happening now (the present), and what will happen (the future).

With increased cognitive abilities, along with a growing understanding of number concepts, school-aged children are developing a more realistic sense of time. They can differentiate between several years ago and hundreds of years ago. This allows a better appreciation of historical events. Although their understanding of time grows progressively more accurate during the years from six to twelve, most six year-olds may understand "a long time ago" but be unable to comprehend differences between several hundred and several thousand years ago. By the age of twelve, children can easily make such distinctions. Religious educators can present Bible stories as events that occurred in distant times and places but this should be done with careful attention to individual children's abilities to place events within an historical time frame.

MEMORY

Most educators and parents readily recognize the differences between preschoolers' and school-aged children's abilities to follow directions and perform complex tasks. One explanation is that younger children may simply forget the directions or necessary information. Recent research points to four factors which may account for these differences in children's memory: 1) increased memory capacity; 2) development of memory strategies; 3) greater knowledge of the topic being considered; and 4) knowledge of one's own memory processes (Siegler & Richards, 1982).

Although research studies have established that school-aged children have increased memory ability, there are differing explanations to account for the difference. One view holds that the greater ability is related to children's increased capacity in short-term memory. Older children are better able to hold information in short-term memory while executing the necessary actions for the task (Pascual-Leone, 1970). A different explanation is offered by Case (1985). As noted above, the absolute size of memory capacity does not increase, rather children become more efficient in using their memory. Older children use less information processing capacity, thus making more processing space available to perform the task.

Increased memory may also result from conscious use of memory strategies. School-aged children employ memory strategies such as rehearsal and the repetition of material more often than do younger children (Weissberg & Paris, 1986). A second strategy is memory organization. School-aged children are more likely than younger children to organize information to be memorized in categories that are easy to remember, such as vehicles or animals. Younger children may use rhyming or situational associations to remember words (Kail, 1984).

REFERENCES

Allen, V.L. (1981). Self, social group and social structure: Surmises about the study of children's friendships. In S.R. Asher & J.M. Gottman (Eds.), *The development of children's friendships*. Cambridge: Cambridge University Press.

Berndt, T., & Ladd, G. (1988). *Peer relationships in child development*. New York: Wiley.

Borke, H. (1975). Piaget's mountains revisited: Changes in the egocentric landscape. *Developmental Psychology, 11*, 240-243.

Case, R. (1978). Intellectual development from birth to adulthood. In R.S. Seigler (Ed.), *Children's thinking: What develops?* Hillsdale, NJ: Erlbaum.

Case, R. (1985). *Intellectual development: Birth to adulthood*. New York: Academic Press.

Cole, M., & Cole, S. (1989). *The development of children*. New York: Freeman.

Damon, W. (1983). *Social and personality development: Infancy through adolescence*. New York: Norton.

Damon, W., & Hart, D. (1982). The development of self-understanding from infancy through adolescence. *Child Development, 53*, 841-864.

Denkla, M.B. (1984). Developmental dyspraxia: The clumsy child. In M.D.

Levine & P. Satz (Eds.), *Middle childhood: Development and dysfunction.* Baltimore: University Park Press.

Flavell, J. (1985). *Cognitive development* (2nd. ed.). Englewood Cliffs, NJ: Prentice-Hall.

Ginsberg, D., Gottman, J., & Parker, J. (1986). The importance of friendship. In J. Gottman & J. Parker (Eds.), *Conversations of friends.* Cambridge: Cambridge University Press.

Harter, S. (1982). The perceived competence scale for children. *Child Development, 53,* 87-97.

Inhelder, B., & Piaget, J. (1958). *The growth of logical thinking from childhood to adolescence.* New York: Basic Books.

Kail, R. (1984). *The development of memory in children* (2nd ed.). New York: Freeman.

Kamii, C., & DeVries, R. (1980). *Group games in early education.* Washington, DC: The National Association for the Education of Young Children.

Lange, G. (1978). Organization-related process in children's recall. In P.A. Ornstein (Ed.), *Memory development in children.* Hillsdale, NJ: Erlbaum.

Miller, P. (1989). *Theories of developmental psychology* (2nd ed.). New York: Freeman.

Pascual-Leone, J. (1970). A mathematical model for the transition rule in Piaget's developmental stages. *Acta Psychologia, 32,* 301-345.

Piaget, J. (1926). *The language and thought of the child.* New York: Harcourt, Brace.

Piaget, J. (1951). *Play, dreams and imitation.* New York: Norton.

Piaget, J. (1952). *The origins of intelligence in children.* New York: International Universities Press.

Piaget, J. (1954). *The construction of reality in the child.* New York: Basic Books.

Piaget, J. (1965). *The moral judgment of the child.* London: Kegan Paul.

Piaget, J. (1969). *The child's conception of the world.* Totowa, NJ: Littlefield, Adams.

Piaget, J. (1972). Intellectual development from adolescence to adulthood. *Human Development, 15,* 1-12.

Piaget, J. (1976). Autobiography. In S.F. Campbell (Ed.), *Piaget sampler: An introduction to Jean Piaget through his own words.* New York: Wiley.

Piaget, J. (1980). *The equilibration of cognitive structures.* Chicago: University of Chicago Press.

Piaget, J. (1983). Piaget's theory. In P. Mussen, (Ed.), *Handbook of child psychology.* Vol. 1., History, theory, and methods, (Ed. Wm. Kessen). New York: Wiley.

Piaget, J. (1985). Correspondences and transformations. In F.B. Murray (Ed.), *The impact of Piagetian theory: On education, philosophy, psy-*

chiatry, and psychology. Baltimore: University Press.

Piaget, J., & Inhelder, B. (1956). *The child's conception of space*. London: Routledge and Kegan Paul.

Piaget, J., & Inhelder, B. (1969). *The psychology of the child*. New York: Basic Books.

Ratcliff, D. (1988). The cognitive development of preschoolers. In D. Ratcliff, (Ed.), *Handbook of preschool religious education*. Birmingham, AL: Religious Education Press.

Selman, R. (1976). Social-cognitive understanding: A guide to educational and clinical practice. In T. Lickona (Ed.), *Moral development and behavior: Theory, research, and social issues*. New York: Holt, Rinehart and Winston.

Selman, R. (1980). *The growth of interpersonal understanding: Developmental and clinical analyses*. New York: Academic Press.

Siegler, R.S., & Richards, D.D. (1982). The development of intelligence. In R.J. Sternberg (Ed.), *Handbook of human intelligence*. Cambridge: Cambridge University Press.

Sullivan, H.S. (1953). *The interpersonal theory of psychiatry*. New York: Norton.

Tanner, J.M. (1978). *Fetus into man: Physical growth from conception to maturity*. Cambridge, MA: Harvard University Press.

Teitz, C.C. (1982). Sports medicine concerns in dance and gymnastics. *Pediatric Clinics of North America, 29*, 1399-1421.

Weissberg, J.A., & Paris, S.G. (1986). Young children's remembering in different contexts: A reinterpretation of Istomina's study. *Child Development, 57*, 1123-1129.

Wellman, H.M., & Estes, D. (1986). Early understanding of mental entities: A reexamination of childhood realism. *Child Development, 59*, 386-396.

Whiting, B.B., & Whiting, J.W.M. (1975). *Children of six cultures: A psychocultural analysis*. Cambridge, MA: Harvard University Press.

Youniss, J. (1980). *Parents and peers in social development: A Sullivan-Piaget perspective*. Chicago: University of Chicago Press.

Chapter Two

Faith Development
and the Language of Faith

JEROME W. BERRYMAN

When a shadow falls across us in a strange place, we go on alert, ready to stand and fight or flee. Anxiety warns and prepares us for such action, even though the danger is not clear. The opposite of such anxiety is faith. There is a mysterious sense of God's presence that allows us to know that we are at home.

Religious anxiety and faith relate us to our existential limits such as death, aloneness, the need for meaning, and the threat of freedom. They are two polar extremes that help identify the quality of the relationship we have with God, self, others, and nature by which we cope or do not cope with our existential limits.

The Christian tradition has identified the qualities of hope and love in addition to faith as critical to our being at home in the world. The focus of this chapter, however, is primarily on faith.

Religious language, the language of existential faith, refers not to the world immediately around us but to our existential world, the outer limit to our being and knowing. There is a deep connection between the world we live in and the language we use. Edward Sapir (1949, p. 162) wrote: "The fact of the matter is that the 'real world' is to a large extent built up on the language habits of the group. No two languages are ever sufficiently similar to be considered as representing the same social reality. The worlds in which different societies live are distinct worlds, not merely the same world with different labels attached."

The Whorfian (or "Sapir-Whorf") hypothesis has a strong form which claims that language determines thought and experience. A weaker form of

21

the hypothesis claims that language influences perceptual experience. The weakest form says that language only affects the memory and expression of experiences. The last is the most favored interpretation today.

Language seems to have little effect on our perceptual experiences themselves, but it does affect our ability to codify percepts and thus to remember experiences, to communicate experiences to other people, and to relate experiences themselves to one another. This is an important issue when one wishes to center religious education around the experience of Christ as many Christians do.

One view is that the experience of God is self-authenticating. The opposite view is that religious experience is *nothing but* interpretation. This chapter moves between these two extremes. All perception requires some training. This training helps make the percepts more likely, directs one's attention to them, sharpens one's perceptual skills for them, and provides the concepts by which they can be tested and better understood (David, 1989).

Religious education is training to know God and to be at home in God's world. The means by which this knowing and being at home is fashioned in the Christian tradition is through a language of parables, sacred stories, and liturgical acts by which we can know God and our existential environment indirectly, as well as develop a respect for silence in God's presence.

Most of the time we do not want to think about our existential limits. We would rather assume that children are always happy than have to attend to their questions about death, aloneness, the threat of radical freedom, and the deep need for meaning. This prevents the awakening of our own anxiety about such matters and our lack of art for using religious language to make meaning and find direction in life and death. Some people become so defensive about their existential limits that they expend most of the energy they might otherwise use for growth to keep such questions in check and hidden. Sometimes they even call such denial religious education.

This brings us to the main questions of this chapter. How do we teach children the means of communication and invite them into a world where the quality of the relationships with God, self, others, and nature is one of faith? How does this relationship change over time? How can we do this in a way that does not arrest their growth?

Such questions cannot be answered very well by using the wealth of information we have about secular education. This is because the language of everyday life is vastly different from religious language. One way to understand that difference is to look carefully at the language of faith.

A DIFFERENT VIEW OF FAITH DEVELOPMENT

Faith development usually dominates today's discussions about the relation of faith to religious education. James Fowler's research and writing for the English-speaking world and Fritz Oser's work in Europe have been especially prominent. We shall return to Fowler and Oser in some detail but for now let us turn to Richard of St. Victor, who lived during the twelfth century in Paris at the Abbey of St. Victor. This will help put the faith development interests and language of our time into perspective.

The Victorines were a cloistered group under the Rule of St. Augustine. In addition to contemplation they also maintained a vigorous intellectual life open to the ferment of the schools of Paris. Richard was a master of mystical knowing, as well as one deeply involved in its analysis, and teaching. The emphasis of our century has been on the masterly use of science to explore the material and mental world, but Richard was a master of the experience of God.

My goal here is to present enough detail about Victor's analysis[1] to suggest that he and other great mystics are important for Christian educators to know something about. This is to complement our modern focus on secular teaching techniques and the view of faith development arrived at by using the scientific method.

Two of Richard's books, *The Twelve Patriarchs* and *The Mystical Ark* (Zinn, 1979), especially are useful for understanding his developmental scheme. He believes that knowing has three distinct levels. The first level involves the kind of meaning that is made by the *senses* about the material world. The second level is composed of meaning made by the *mind* using reason. The third level is that of the *spirit* where meaning is made by contemplation. The upper levels include the lower ones. The lower levels cannot control or understand the upper ones, but intuitions of the upper can sometimes inform the lower.

In *The Mystical Ark* Richard used a sophisticated network of images drawn from the description of the Ark of the Covenant in the twenty-fifth chapter of Exodus to elaborate what in those days was called *contemplation*, which refers to a state of awareness or beholding.

Richard's classic definition of this term followed that of Hugh of St. Victor, who died some ten or more years before Richard arrived in Paris. Here is Richard's famous definition: "Contemplation is the free, more penetrating gaze of a mind, suspended with wonder concerning manifestations of wisdom" (1:4). The penetrating gaze, the suspension with wonder, and the concern with the manifestation of God's wisdom are what distinguish contemplation from reason.

Richard's analysis of the objects of contemplation are beheld from a position within the level of the *spirit* where meaning is made by contemplation. Piaget's formal operations and the dichotomizing, dialectical, and synthetic versions of formal operations Fowler has identified, belong in Richard's second realm of the *mind*.

The spiritual standpoint from which Richard's analysis takes place is breathtaking. It is as remarkable to us in our time as our ability to use the scientific method would be to Richard in his day.

Richard summarized six objects of contemplation. The first two are the sensual kinds of knowing. The first object is what is perceived by the bodily senses. The second object of contemplation is knowing about the rational principles of physical things.

The third and fourth objects of contemplation are in the realm of the mind and are known by reason. The third kind of object for contemplation is the invisible reality created by means of similitudes drawn from the physical world. This is a kind of implicit interiorization. The fourth kind of object for contemplation is complete interiorization. Richard called it "in reason according to reason." Imagination was excluded from this process.

The final two kinds of objects are from the transcendent world of spiritual realities. The fifth object of contemplation is that which is consistent with and yet not able to be understood by reason. Such objects are given by God. This has to do with the divine substance and unity. The sixth object of contemplation is beyond reason and sometimes is even contrary to reason, such as the plurality and unity of the Trinity's Presence.

The first four kinds of contemplation are ordinarily experienced in nonecstatic ways while the last two are ecstatic (4:22). In addition to the six kinds of objects for contemplation there are three different modes of contemplation.

Contemplation differs not only according to the levels of objects but also to the way the contemplation is done. The three modes of contemplation are: 1) enlarging the mind (*dilatio mentis*); 2) raising up of the mind (*sublevatio mentis*); and 3) alienation of the mind (*alienatio mentis*) or ecstasy (*excessus mentis*)(5:2). When one moves into the realm of the spirit one can perform operations on objects in both the mental and the sensual realms.

The primary distinction among the three modes of contemplation has to do with the relationship of human effort and grace. Enlarging the mind is the result of human effort alone. Raising up of the mind comes from joining human effort with the divine grace of a "showing" (5:4). Alienation comes from greatness of devotion, greatness of wonder, and greatness of exultation.

Greatness of devotion comes from a loving desire for ecstasy. Greatness of wonder arises from the sudden shock of an unexpected vision from a divine showing. Greatness of exultation comes from what Richard described as "divinely infused inner joyfulness and sweetness" (5:14). Unaware of what is taking place in the worlds of sense or rational activity the quiet soul is open to a completely new level of experience.

When this complex differentiation is completed, it even goes beyond differentiation. Unity results. The last two kinds of contemplation are beyond rational consciousness. Some retain a memory of the experience but see it "as though in the middle of a cloud." This is a kind of "unknowing." Richard expanded on such language to say, "We lack the ability to comprehend or call to mind either the manner of seeing or the quality of the vision. And marvelously, in a way remembering, we do not remember, and not remembering, we remember (4:23).

The introduction of a theorist, researcher, and teacher like Richard of St. Victor raises the question of the difference between what his point of view can teach us compared to what we can learn from the scientific tradition of Piaget which Fowler and Oser use for their research. We need to ask ourselves if there has been a category mistake about the spiritual life that has led religious education astray.

A CATEGORY MISTAKE?

What is a category mistake? Bertrand Russell and Alfred North Whitehead (1910, 1912, 1913) introduced this philosophical problem in their *Principia Mathematica*.[2] They noticed that objects in a class (chairs 1,2,3, and 4) are of a different logical type from the class itself (the class of all chairs), and used this observation to solve some kinds of paradoxes.

Benjamin Whorf (1956) extended Russell and Whitehead's observation about logic to the area of communication. His *Language, Thought, and Reality* referred to the context for communication as metacommunication and argued that the context determines the meaning of the communication within that context. For example a simple greeting, "Good morning," has a different meaning within the context of a smile, a shrug of the shoulders, or a scowl.

Fowler, Oser, and others have written about religion from within the context of the language of science about the material world. The context out of which Richard wrote was the language domain of the Christian religion. The implications of this for religious education can be seen more clearly by the work of Gregory Bateson.

Bateson (1975, 1979) made the hierarchy of logical types one of his six criteria for the phenomenon of mind. His last book, *Mind and Nature: A Necessary Unity* described how a dolphin discovered a higher logical type. Usually she was rewarded with a fish for a repeated behavior such as a tail slap. A new situation was set up. She was given no reward for doing any *repeated* act when she swam into the tank. The result was that in the fifteenth session the dolphin performed eight new behaviors, four of which had never before been observed in this species of animal.

The dolphin had made the jump into the new context, a context of contexts. She stopped trying to repeat old performances, because she realized that what was being asked for now was a class of new behaviors. She shifted from the class of repeated behaviors to the higher type of behavior which was to create new behaviors.

If we approach the teaching of religion from a point of view that is the wrong logical type, the context for our teaching may teach something we don't mean to. Category mistakes also can lead to confusion about what kind of evidence is appropriate for determining the success of such teaching and the foundational research which undergirds it. Like the dolphin, perhaps, the goal of religious education is to get the children to leap into the spiritual level, a context of contexts, and a different logical type than the level of the mind by which we develop theories about the experience of faith development or the level of the senses by which we test them.

The mistake most likely to occur in the religious education of our time is the attempt to use the senses to verify or falsify a theory made by reason from the point of view of the second level's logical type. The powerful measurements that explain the natural world will not work for measuring and explaining the meaning of the world by the mind or spirit. The mind can generate experiments that can be verified or at least falsified by using the senses for measurement, but such experiments are related to reality by the mind and senses and not by the spirit. The problem is that while the mind can generate explanations about the natural world that can be tested by the senses, the resulting meaning made is inappropriate for the realm of the spirit.

A confusion of the three fundamental levels can bring about profound mistakes. The second level discipline of psychology for example often reduces the spiritual realm to pathology, because it is not normal. Religion is considered to be an illusion, a projection, or some other reduction of the spiritual into the realms of reasoning and the senses.

Physics, on the other hand, is used sometimes to elevate the sensorial to the spiritual, because matter is not considered to be as substantial today as once was thought. *The Tao of Physics* by Fritjof Capra (1975) and *The Dancing Wu Li Masters* by Gary Zukav (1979) are rather respectable reductions of the spiritual to the physical realm, but some New Age writers are better known for their enthusiasm than their scholarship.[3]

If religious education is to teach children the art of using religious language to enter into the spiritual realm then care must be taken to teach the art of using the language of faith in an appropriate way. The evaluation and foundational research for religious education must also use an appropriate measurement for testing the experience and analysis on which it is based.

The spiritual includes the mental and the mental includes the material. The spiritual can shape the mental as the mental shapes the world we sense to be there. The upper levels can be intuited implicitly by the senses and the mind, but the lower kind of knowing cannot explicitly and clearly understand the higher.

A religious education program to enter the spiritual level of meaning needs to be evaluated according to the criteria of the spiritual realm rather than the world of the body or the mind, since the spiritual is not fully intelligible to the body or mind. This leaves us with an interesting question for both the study of faith development and the practice of religious education. How can we know what development is like in the spiritual realm?

Evidence as well as knowing differ at the three levels, but the same sort of general plan for knowing applies equally in all three. This is equally true for the scientific method which appeals to the senses for validation, the canons of literary criticism or the logic of philosophy which appeal to reason in the middle realm, and contemplation such as that described by Richard of St. Victor and others. In the spiritual realm appeals are made to the experience of God's presence for validation.

This general plan for knowing, regardless of level, has three steps. The first step is to stipulate a method (to know X do Y). Second, a direct experience of the desired cognition takes place according to the method. Third, the knower checks with others who have done the first and second step in the same way to see what their awareness of the experience was like. This general method pertains whether the object of the knowing is the moon, the meaning of *Don Quixote*, or the experience of the presence of God.

The problem is that reasoning about God is like trying to picture the sun shining and not shining at the same time. God is present in the self, others, and nature but is also distinct and independent. The non-dual reality of the spiritual realm cannot be understood by making distinctions. When reason attempts to conceptualize the spiritual reality it generates contradictions such as God being "a coincidence of opposites" or a God-man. What is paradox to the mind can become unity only when one lives the paradox at the more comprehensive spiritual level.

Faith looked at from this three-level point of view becomes more clear and is closer to the biblical foundation for religious language than the definitions necessary for scientific investigation. Faith is what gives us the ability to keep on moving despite the ego's loss of meaning. It is not an expression of human fulfillment but a means to heal our brokenness. Faith is grounded in the transcendent realm of the spirit rather than in something automatically present as a human universal to supply structure to our awareness. Faith is everywhere accessible and effective, but it is not always received. Faith gives us a steady state out of which to grow, even when the meaning of the first two levels identified by Richard of St. Victor are overwhelmed.

If it is true that biblical faith is best known from within the spiritual realm, then the theological virtues of faith, hope, and love can influence us at the levels of thought and the senses, but they are truly theological virtues and cannot be described or measured most appropriately by those realms.

What are we to do then when we teach children (and others) faith and the language of faith? Using the secular transfer model for education can only teach the cultural artifacts of our religion such as history or its sociology. Teaching an ascent of the faith development ladder by talking about religion in the structures of one stage above the child's present faith stage might help move him or her into the next stage, but it will not help move children into the spiritual realm. Faith development views of the way we talk *about* religion do not invite the children *into* the language of faith to discover the presence of God. Where then should our central focus be in religious education?

THE CREATIVE PROCESS AND THE JOURNEY OF FAITH

How can religious education help move one toward the spiritual realm? Like the dolphin Gregory Bateson described, Christian education can set up a new context into which we ask the children "to leap" beyond ordinary sense experience and thought. In an obscure literary review Søren Kierkegaard (1864/1946, p. 264), the Danish existentialist theologian, wrote about the trap reason, and by inference the senses, can become:[4]

> Reflection is and remains the hardest creditor in existence; hitherto it has cunningly brought up all the possible views of life, but it cannot buy the essentially religious and eternal view of life; on the other hand, it can tempt people astray with its dazzling brilliance and dishearten them by reminding them of all the past. But, by leaping into the depths, one learns to help oneself, learns to love others as much as oneself, even though one is accused of arrogance and pride—-because one will not accept help—-or of selfishness, because one will not cunningly deceive people by helping them, i.e. by helping them to escape their highest destiny.

Religious education must be wary of getting distracted by the transfer of cultural data, theological abstractions, or providing children with second-hand, prefabricated answers. It must allow children to make their own journey of faith, and equip them with the skill to use language that can help them make meaning for their lives in the community of the Christian Way. The primary task of religious education is to help God shape the children to be creative within the larger environment of their existential limits, so they can enter the spiritual realm in a more complete way, and discover their identity in the image of the Creator.

To shape persons to be theologically creative does not determine what they will create.[5] We can only give them the appropriate language, teach them the art of how to use it, and trust religious language, the community, and God to see them through. This is because creativity is a higher type or category of language than the unique outcomes to which it refers. Children need to learn how to grow up within this identity if they are to more than occasionally visit the kingdom where the mystery of God is always present.

The creative process provides us with the pattern by which knowing at all three levels takes place. This process will be sketched here, but Loder's (1981) *The Transforming Moment* and the chapter, "The Imagination and Godly Play," in my book, *Godly Play* (Berryman, 1991), provide the background for this suggestion. *Godly Play* also applies this approach to religious education with an emphasis upon practice as well as theory.[6]

The creative process is opened by a break in one's circle of meaning. This might be a hard or soft break. A crisis causes a hard break while wonder expands present meaning to make a soft break. Next, scanning takes place until an insight is felt that incorporates the implications implicit in the break-up of the old meaning and is transformed into a new way of seeing and being in the world.

What is felt at the moment of transformation is a shift of energy. The energy that was invested in the scanning process becomes invested in the articulation of the new meaning. Shaping the new meaning with appropriate language continues until there is closure after appropriate testing. The new circle of meaning then awaits a crisis or wonder for the process to begin again. As you can now see, this process is the foundation for "the general plan for knowing" for all three realms mentioned above.

What does this have to do with faith? The concept of the creative process joins faith development with the classical theological virtues.[7] The purpose of a virtue, as it is used here, is to help achieve happiness. Happiness is related to our nature and is achieved by our natural capacities when they are well-used.

The four cardinal[8] virtues (justice, fortitude, temperance, and prudence) provide an important context in which the creative process and constructive actions flowing from it are best worked out, but we are drawn toward a higher kind of happiness by such action. It is here that St. Thomas attempted to join Aristotle and scripture. This Godly happiness cannot be acquired by our human capacities alone. Our efforts need divine assistance. The theological virtues of faith, hope, and love are infused in us by God and give the fullest range of power to the creative process.

The definitions of faith, hope, and love are determined by their opposites for the purpose of this chapter. These opposites can be known at any level. Faith is the opposite of anxiety. The experience of hope is contrasted with despair. Finally, the experience of love is the opposite of hate.

As mentioned at the beginning of this chapter, anxiety is considered to be a state of arousal that takes place when the presence of an unclear threat is perceived. One prepares to stand and fight or flee, but when no specific danger is apparent the state of preparation continues. In time anxiety can wear down the whole human system—biologically, psychologically, socially, and spiritually.

Faith is the opposite of anxiety. It is the state of not being anxious. One is stable, centered, alert, balanced, and prepared to deal with specific fears and the nonspecific dangers of daily life with equilibrium. It signals profound spiritual meaning beyond the limits of Richard's first two levels of knowing, as do hope and love.

Despair is a pervasive loss of expectation. Things are impossible. There is no way out, but there is no single thing that is the focus of despair, as one might find in sadness about a known loss. Despair is like "the pit" spoken of in many of the psalms. It is a pit without time and space. There is only doom.

Hope is the opposite of despair. It is open to the future. There is expectation. Eager anticipation blooms. Instead of an empty pit there is a pervading sense of the possibility of fulfillment. There is a way out. There is room to go on.

Hate destroys. It separates. It drives people apart. It moves people against each other. It takes advantage of people. It destroys creativeness in others.

Love is the opposite of hate. Love creates. It creates families and children. It creates relationships. Love moves people toward each other. It builds people up. It helps create creating in others.

The theological virtues are positive powers. One cannot refrain from the states of anxiety, despair, or hate by choice alone. It is not enough to refrain from acts stemming from such states. Movement toward the constructive aspect of these polar opposites is the only way to resist a life of destruction grounded in anxiety, despair, and/or hate.

Movement toward hate, despair, and anxiety is movement toward a closed mind. A closed mind leads us toward becoming a closed system, one that is winding down. Our potential becomes used up. One becomes empty. There is nothing left to create with or from.

Movement toward faith, hope, and love is movement toward the renewing of one's energy. It draws one by means of the imagination into an open system, so there is always new potentiality rather than the using up of a limited quantity of energy in a closed system.

Faith, hope, and love are very much involved with the imagination. Faith is the safe place in which one can create and take the risks of the imagination's discoveries. Hope is the open door, held open for the new to come in. Love is the movement toward the unknown as it comes to meet us, coming through an open doorway in the world created by our language.

Faith, hope, and love make a circle that reinforces itself. Particular strengths (the theological virtues) support different steps in the process. Hope is what helps us open the process with wonder, and prevents despair from overwhelming the possibility of the process moving toward completion. Love creates the image that is drawn out into language. Faith is what undergirds the whole process, and enables closure by an act of the will.

The central focus of religious education, therefore, should be to support the pattern of the creative process that undergirds the art of using religious language to make meaning and to find direction in the world of the everyday. This is centrally important, because it is this process that provides the way to grow toward experiencing the world of the everyday in a theological perspective. We turn now to an important curiosity about the religious language of the Christian tradition.

BEING IN AND TALKING ABOUT
THE LANGUAGE OF FAITH

One of the many interesting things about religious language is that it is both specific and yet open. This ambiguity allows people at the many different stages of faith development to use the same parables, sacred stories, liturgy, and silence together and yet find their own faith through them in a way appropriate to their developmental and theological needs. This is very important, because the religious life is both very private and very much involved in a kind of community that allows one to be aware of one's existential situation.

The paradox of ambiguity and specificity is one reason why people at different stages of faith development can be in religious language and worship together. There is a second reason. When we are in religious language the stage structures by which we usually think about our experiences seem to become useless before the presence of God. They are overwhelmed. It is only as one begins to draw back from such an experience that the structures begin to function again.

It is in the context of the silence or the stagelessness of being in religious language that Jesus' assertion about becoming like children to enter the kingdom makes a great deal of sense. Recognition of this phenomenon also allows us to respect the ability of children to enter religious language in a naive way while we adults often must enter by a conscious act as of will, to be described in a moment.

The recognition of the stagelessness or silence that pertains when one is in religious language is very important for religious education. Without respect for this phenomenon there is very little about the art of using religious language that can be taught to children by adults, since most of this teaching is by example, as in any art. Part of this teaching by example includes giving up one's control of meaning to approach God's presence and dwell for a time in the larger environment.

Let us use the symbol of the cross to explore the distinction between being in and talking about religious language. I will use my own experience to demonstrate what is meant here by "entering into" religious language, although one might draw on the growing body of research about religious experience such as at the Alister Hardy Research Centre in Oxford.[9] This is because I know my own experience best. To validate this I suggest that you actually try to do this yourself. It is then that a search of the literature on religious experience and the classics of the spiritual life will enrich one's judgment about such matters.

First, I relax and begin to be aware of the cross. It might be anywhere, but today I am in the Cathedral. The cross is above and behind the altar. My eyes move over the details of its surface. I then begin to focus on the image as a whole. After a while my eyes begin to lose their focus. The cross blurs. It disappears to my consciousness.

As I lose awareness of the image of the cross, I become involved in its meaning, and move my attention inward. The story from Nativity, to Easter, to Pentecost, floats in and out in juxtaposition. Episodes of the story and faces merge. The faces are charged with mystery. Sometimes I recognize bits of family and friends in them, but there are other shapes. Saints? Apostles?

I lose track of time. What I am doing becomes absorbed into the wonder and mystery of doing it. The distinction between subject and object fades. Relationship becomes everything. Anxiety fades and the sense of home emerges as being connected with the larger world of God, self, others, and nature.

After a while I become conscious of the cross again. Its image is there in front of me. I notice what is around it, and I run my eyes over its details. A memory of my father sitting in church and the stained glass window at the end of "our" row comes into view. Pictures of my mother and of three generations of my family now gather in that brown, wooden pew. They move in and out of my senses. Concentration then shifts to a kind of relaxed daydreaming. Soon I sense I am finished.

I cross myself, a sign of respect and value for what has happened, and I stand since my custom is to kneel, but one need not do this. As I take my leave, I feel refreshed.

Meaning and direction have been reshaped, grounded in the spiritual realm. Faith, hope, and love have been renewed. Being at home again in the larger world puts the world of everyday life into a different and more profound perspective. New and creative connections will be made between what I have experienced and the world about me as the day and night come and go.

Nothing special happened in the experience and yet it did. It is very hard to know what, since most of the meaning was not yet "in language" so that it might be studied. When the experience moved into the realm of language the totality and depth of the experience faded. Most of the experience could not be recalled, since it was outside of or had pierced the language world.

Certainly, there is more here than meets the eye (and other senses) or the mind. I have tried to describe a fairly uneventful entering into a single "piece" of religious language. Entering parables and sacred stories or silence itself are slightly different doorways. This is certainly much less than Richard of St. Victor and others would have noticed, but even my own ordinary spirituality can be very helpful both to me personally and as a teacher of children.

Now by way of contrast, I would like to construct a hypothetical description of talking *about* the cross. This will illustrate the power of what the theorists and researchers like Fowler and Oser have to teach us about teaching (we will return to their work in some detail).

This theoretical construction of how Christians might think about the image of the cross at various times in their lives is formed largely on the basis of Fowler's research and theory. It shows not only the distinction between being in religious language and talking about it, but also what a powerful tool for communication and mutual understanding Fowler's work has become.

First, the intersection of the cross is absorbed by babies while peering into the face of the mother, father, or other parenting people. They see the line made by the eyes crossing the line made by the nose and mouth. The child absorbs that image before language and associates it with the sensations surrounding those relationships. This is not to say that the final meaning and emotional connotation of the cross can be reduced to this, but it is to say that it is a fundamental image of life like water, bread, and wine.

As the baby grows the intersection of crossing lines might be pointed to by a parent in church or in other places. Perhaps, the sign of the cross is made over the child with the hand or on the forehead of the child with the thumb. Perhaps, the child learns how to make the sign of the cross himself or herself. By these means the symbol is identified, named, and valued for the child. It is a "cross," but it is not yet part of a larger and coherent system of religious language for the child.

A third step occurs when the image of the cross becomes associated with the denomination one belongs to. The question, "What is a Presbyterian?" or "What is a Roman Catholic?" is usually answered at this stage by talking about the building where one goes to church. The cross marks the place rather than an abstraction. The cross by this time also may signal some episodes from the story of Christ, such as the crucifixion, as well as being the mark of a blessing and other aspects of the Christian language system.

During the elementary school years the variety of shapes for the cross begin to be noticed. These shapes, such as the Jerusalem cross or the Greek cross, give added dimensions to the symbol. Variety is also noted in the contextual meaning of the crossed lines. Roads cross. A plus sign means addition. There is a red cross. Strange, bent variations of the cross suggest Hitler or evil. The cross often begins to symbolize the whole story of Christ now as a total narrative rather than an episode within it.

Talk about the cross begins to be more abstracted during middle school and high school. Awareness of different religions becomes more explicit. Their primary symbols and their history can be compared to the cross and its tradition. These distinctions also can begin to make the cross more and more a sign of one's identity in a more formal and explicit way than before.

The cross is not always felt to be a positive symbol. It also can become a symbol that one resists or rebels against. It may signal meaningless authority, irrelevant words and actions, guilt and shame, or other painful connotations. The cross can signal confusion as well.

The years of college and young adulthood pass. The valuing of persons and places where one first experienced the cross sink into a kind of tacit knowing. From time to time one might acknowledge the cross, as in a procession or on another formal occasion, but little is done to explore what the cross means for an adult at this stage of life.

If there is a tragedy one might become involved with the cross in a deeper way, but usually things go on with a lighter step. Careers get established. Children begin to arrive. Finally, the gap between the religion of one's childhood or adolescence and the current point in one's journey as parent and/or career person begins to be felt. Ultimate issues about the cross and its meaning begin to work their way back into the adult experience as questions and a vague yearning for a larger meaning than that provided by the everyday world.

During the period of young adulthood one may begin to use some of the intellectual skills acquired in college and elsewhere to analyze religion to attempt to find answers to the questions raised by this stage's experiences. Anthropology, psychology, sociology, and many other "ologies" are used to try to understand the cross.

This keeps the cross an object, held at a distance for study. When the cross is held at a distance it cannot be used personally to make meaning and find direction. To demythologize the cross may enable one to learn much about it, but it also cuts one off from the cross as a tool to open the door to the holy.

When one's experience of life and language begins to suggest that there is not as much control over events as one thought earlier, the cross can sometimes engage the creative process to open and move one toward constructing another stage where the cross is used again in an existential manner. This use is no longer naive, however, as when one was a child. Now one must consciously exclude the kinds of knowing available to think about the cross, so that it can be used as a tool for making existential meaning by entering into its power as language.

Finally, the oneness with Christ that is beyond words can become a customary way of life. At this final kind of stage Fowler might describe the cross and the self as transparent. There is a lived reality that only occasionally needs to be symbolized for one's self. Yet, there is a need for community. Community needs a language. For others and for the needs of community, one at this place in life often continues to speak and gesture his or her oneness with

God in Christ by making the sign of the cross and/or bowing to the cross (if that is your custom), and speaking of it. One also recognizes his or her responsibility to pass on the spoken and unspoken use of the cross to the young.

As an observer there is much to say about the stages of thinking about the cross, but there is no way to study what one knows when one is *in* the cross, meditating. One is not sure until afterwards what *has* happened, or even that something has happened. The presence of our existential home—God, self, others, and nature—engages the creative process in an existential way to discover new meaning, but this meaning is not able to be "languaged" as the process begins. When this experience enters language, it becomes greatly limited as compared to the source from which it came. It is this Source that we wish to invite the children to know, and the art of using religious language is one of the most important means to help them make that journey.

There is one final observation to make. My own experience of moving in and out of religious language seems to suggest that as one comes out of religious language there is a recapitulation of the stages from silence to one's ordinary faith development stage. Out of the silence comes sensorial images. They get combined by a juxtaposition logic and later by the logic of narrative. Meaning is then organized by concepts, and as one reflects on the experience over the following days or even years new meaning can emerge, even meaning about how the meaning was derived in the first place as we are doing now.

Our discussion continues now with a view of the phenomenon of faith and its language from the standpoint of the scientific method. We turn now in more detail to the important contributions to religious education by James Fowler and Fritz Oser.

THE STRUCTURAL DEVELOPMENTAL VIEW OF FAITH

To look at this approach to the study of faith and the language of faith we turn to three important researchers, theorists, and teachers. We will begin with Jane Loevinger whose work about ego development shows little interest in theological matters. We will then turn to James Fowler's work on the structures of faith development which incorporates a good bit of the ego's development to arrive at conclusions. Finally, we will look at Fritz Oser's work about the cognition of the relationship with the Ultimate (God).

Loevinger
Jane Loevinger did much of her work as a research associate at The Social Science Institute at Washington University in St. Louis, where she was also a professor of psychology. The reason she chose to measure ego development was that it is the "master trait," as she put it.

Loevinger did not build her research method on the structuralism of Piaget. Fowler and Oser have both relied primarily on Piaget, but Loevinger (1976, pp. 51-53) noted in *Ego Development* that Piaget's interests were drawn excessively to patterns of action such as ordering, dividing and grouping, and numbering to capture the personality. The ego cannot be reduced to points at the intersection of actions, or replaced by numbers or other abstract symbols. The development of personality, she said, is related to logical development, but cannot be reduced to it.

Loevinger used a kind of structuralism like that which "underlies the Gestalt approach to visual forms, Werner and Kaplan's approach to symbols, Erikson's analogical approach to zones and modes, the traditional study of myths, and other kinds of thematic analyses" (p.53).

"From my view, the organization or the synthetic function is not just another thing the ego does, it is what the ego is" (p.5). She said, "The ego is above all a process, not a thing. The ego is in a way like a gyroscope, whose upright position is maintained by its rotation" (p.58). For her the striving to master, to integrate, to make sense of experience is not one ego function among many but "the essence of the ego."

To measure the ego, Loevinger looked at four aspects. One focus is on impulse control and character development. A second aspect involves interpersonal style. Her third interest was in the subject's conscious preoccupations. Her final focus was on cognitive style.

The seven stages of ego development she identified were: Self-protective, Conformist, Conscientious-Conformist, Conscientious, Individualistic, Autonomous, and Integrated. She named the stages by the characteristics that usually prevail during each period of development, though nothing less than the total pattern defines a stage. These names leave an impression of each stage, even without further description, and in turn suggest Loevinger's view of the flow of ego development across the life span.

Loevinger did not give an age for each stage, so her descriptions could apply to a wide range of ages. Of course, the earliest stages are rare after childhood and the highest stages are impossible in childhood and rare in adolescence. She described what persons of each stage have in common, whatever their age.

Middle childhood might be associated with the Conformist Stage. At this stage impulse control and character are associated with conformity to external rules, shame, and guilt from breaking rules. The child identifies with authority: parents first, then later other adults, and then peers. The interpersonal style is one of belonging, and of a superficial niceness. The conscious preoccupations are appearance, material things, reputation, social acceptability, and belonging. The inner states perceived are simple ones such as feeling sad, happy, glad, angry, love, and understanding.

This is a period of great cognitive simplicity. There is a right way and a wrong way which is considered the same for everyone, all the time. It is also assumed to be the point of view of broad groups defined by ethnic and other demographic traits but most often by gender. Rules are affirmed because they are socially accepted. The style of thinking is one dominated not only by conceptual simplicity but by stereotypes and cliches. People at the conformist stage constitute either a majority or a large minority in almost any social group regardless of age, so this important set of characteristics is not limited to children.

Loevinger was not a clinician and attempted to provide her research subjects a paper-and-pencil medium for expression. Because of the pencil-and-paper nature of her work she was able to collect her data from a wide sweep of human nature—-women and men, boys and girls, normal people, delinquents, neurotics, and psychotics from many countries.

When we turn from Loevinger to the work of Fowler we move from an interest in the ego alone to an interest in faith. This is not to say that ego development ignores faith but only that Loevinger had neither a special interest in the ultimate environment nor an explicit interest in theology as Fowler does.

Fowler

Fowler's interest in the journey of faith began while listening to his father, also a Methodist minister, communicating in different forms with the different people he served. This interest in each "pilgrim's progress" became more explicit when Fowler worked with Carlyle Marney as associate director of Interpreter's House in 1968-69, helping people tell their own stories to clarify their identity and values.

My own interest in Fowler's work prompted me to visit him at Harvard in 1974, the same year his pivotal article, "Toward a Developmental Perspective on Faith" (Fowler, 1974) was published. I invited him and Sam Keen to participate in a conference on May 10, 1975, at the Institute of Religion in Houston's Texas Medical Center, where I was teaching and doing my own research with children in hospitals and churches. This resulted in the publication of *Life Maps: The Journey of Human Faith* (Fowler & Keen, 1978) which I edited. This book was a major resource for understanding Fowler's work until the publication of *Stages of Faith* (Fowler, 1981).[10]

One of the problems with Fowler's work has been his broad definition of faith. For example, James Loder (Fowler & Loder, 1982) suggested that the main title of Fowler's book, *Stages of Faith*, ought to be exchanged with its subtitle, *The Psychology of Human Development and the Quest for Meaning*. His point was that the ego's ability to structure meaning is potentially but not necessarily related to Christian faith in a biblical or theological sense. Additional critiques of Fowler's faith definition, such as those by

Craig Dykstra, J. Harry Fernhout, and John M. Broughton, are collected in *Faith Development and Fowler* (Dykstra & Parks, 1986).

The study of faith is ripe for misunderstanding, because many conflicting traditions and meanings lie latent in this ancient term. One of the best surveys of faith's multiple meanings is James Michael Lee's (1990) *Handbook of Faith*. Craig Dykstra (1986, p.45) suggested that the only way out of this ambiguity is to confine our discussion to "if-then statements," if faith means X then Y follows. This prevents getting discussions bogged down with definition problems so that Fowler's work is never critiqued in relation to its own terms.

Dykstra's advice is very good for general discussions about faith development research. Our situation is a bit different in this book. We are concerned with the religious education of particular traditions, such as the Christian one. The study of faith, therefore, must have some connection with how faith is defined within the context of a teacher's particular tradition.

Fowler defines faith as a human universal. It is the ability to make meaning and compose ultimate environments. His goal is to see if the faith structures he has identified are present in all human beings. This is a perfectly valid program for study, but the context of this definition places Fowler's work firmly within the scientific method and outside what Richard of St. Victor called the spiritual realm.

This issue is raised from a different but related perspective by Dykstra. How does Fowler's definition of faith relate to the biblical language of idolatry, unfaithfulness, and baptism? These terms give faith a definition that involves a relationship with God, an activity, and a kind of knowing. Fowler would agree, but the context of biblical or Christian religious language gives faith specific meanings Fowler cannot use if he is to show that faith is a universal phenomenon of humankind.

In biblical terms the relation to God is more important than the construing of what we take to be God. The Bible warns that we can make a mistake about the image we form our world coherence about. In that context it is critical that we worship the living God and not an idol. Fowler needs to avoid the question of truth in his definition. The meaning faith makes for Fowler's research needs to be true only for the person who is a subject of his empirical investigation. The interest of faith development investigators must be confined to the structures by which one worships and not what or whom one worships if faith as a human universal is to be tested.

The issue of truth is important for the atheist as well as for the believer. To the atheist God may be an illusion. His or her ethic is lived out with this fundamental view in mind. Both the Christian and the atheist, however, sense that there is more to faith than a generic composing of a reality. Neither knowing that God does not exist nor that God does exist is a human universal, but the structure of this knowing may be, and Fowler has set out to see if this is true.

Second, if one thinks biblically about the activity of faith ("faithing"), the part of the action that is important is responding to God and to God's action. We may or may not be engaged in this. Again, we can and often do make mistakes. Even when we think we know what God wants we sometimes turn against that knowledge. Rather than saying that this is a failure to compose an ultimate environment, it is more accurate in biblical terms to say we are unfaithful and disobedient. Serving God is even more rare than knowing or not knowing God, so this activity is even less a human universal.

Third, there is the kind of knowledge one needs to be faithful and avoid idolatry. We need to know who God is and what God is doing to respond to God adequately or well. This means that we need to be involved in a community and a tradition, such as the Christian tradition, to learn its skills, habits, language, and to be part of its supportive community and history.

One cannot know religion-in-general any more than one can know language-in-general, math-in-general, or music-in-general. Human beings must know specific languages to communicate, specific base systems to calculate, and specific music systems to sing together rather than make noise.

One can be ignorant, unskilled, and wrong about religion. There is no automatic, inherited ability to be a Christian or a true follower of any other tradition. There is always the potential to be a Christian, and God's grace is everywhere and powerful, but to be an authentic Christian is also more rare than it is a human universal. The same is true for the followers of other religions.

Let us return to Fowler's definition of faith and its relation to religious education. There are three major reasons why Fowler's view of faith is difficult to define for educational use. First, the theory has been growing and changing for around twenty years, so hunting for quotes from Fowler's writing to pin down the concept to a final collection of words is misleading. The general direction of the research is clear, however.

Second, Fowler often does his defining more like a poet than a scientist or a philosopher. Fowler has done this with full intention. In reference to a critic Fowler (1986a, p.281) once wrote, "He lacks musicality with the essentially metaphorical and evocative way in which I have written and spoken about faith."

Finally, there are some 10-12,000 pages of transcribed data which continue to inform Fowler's theory construction and testing as he interacts with his critics to discover new possibilities in the data. Fowler's main contribution to religious education may be his theory construction rather than any kind of successful or failed theory confirmation. He has taught us how to look for the right questions, and what he proposed as answers have been so incisive that the debate about his view of faith continues to inform us.

There is another way to cut through the jungle of definition questions that surround Fowler's view of faith. Our strategy will be to focus on what he and his associates actually do when they look for faith structures. The first filter they use is the set of questions that guides the interviews which provide them with their data. The second filter is the model by which they organize the data.

What is measured is that part of reality which is evoked by the interview questions. There are four kinds of questions used to gather data. The first and most important step is to encourage a rather open-ended telling of one's story, organizing it into critical "chapters," and including crises and existential concerns. This strategy makes the research vulnerable to many kinds of bias, but it also keeps the data close to the lives of people, at least as they understand their lives to have been lived.

The other three kinds of questions are in relation to one's story. The second group probes details and seeks clarification about important people and experiences that give one's life meaning. A third kind of questions asks the subject to reflect on his or her beliefs and values in neutral terms. The final set of questions used in the interview has to do with religion. It probes for one's thinking about religious experience, prayer, religious truth, the relation between religion and morality, and one's view of faith.

When we turn to the second filter, Fowler's model for organizing the data gained from the interviews, we can see more clearly what the issues are that Fowler thinks are important to reveal what faith is.

Fowler's interpretative grid involves two kinds of structuring activity. Fowler calls one type the "logic of rational certainty," and the other he calls the "logic of conviction." The logic of rational certainty comes from the research tradition of Piaget, and Fowler says that Piaget's cognitive stages are necessary but not sufficient to determine a faith stage. The logic of rational certainty structures our ways of thinking about nature, our perspective taking in social situations, and our moral reasoning. These kinds of thinking are three of the seven aspects in a faith stage. Fowler assigns them the letters A,B, and C.

The logic of conviction is quite different from the logic of rational certainty. It is made up of the remaining four aspects of a faith stage lettered D,E,F, and G. This is the kind of logic that changes the knower by what is known. These four aspects of a faith stage are a "more comprehensive mode of knowing." It "contextualizes," "qualifies," "transcends while including," and "anchors" the logic of rational certainty, but it does not negate it (Dykstra, 1986, p.23).

This does not mean that there is "a capitulation to unbridled fantasy or subjectivity, nor does it mean a relinquishing in faith of the critical role of rational reflection" (Fowler, 1986b, p. 25). Instead, Fowler is calling our attention to an interplay between the conceptualizing, questioning, and evaluating function of the logic of rational certainty and the "imaginal and generative knowing" in the logic of conviction. In Fowler's terms, the use of the two logics is an attempt to "grasp the inner dialectic of rational logic in the dynamics of a larger, more comprehensive logic of convictional orientation."

The logic of conviction helps generate the structures of faith out of a person's "attachments or commitments to centers of supraordinate value which have power to unify his or her experiences of the world" (Fowler, 1986b, p.25). The relation to these centers of value and power can be traced structurally by the aspects D (Bounds of Social Awareness) and E (Locus of Authority). The unity that comes from such images can be traced by aspect F (Form of World Coherence), and the way the language that evokes the centers of value and power functions is followed by aspect G (Role of Symbols). A faith stage is determined by the average level calculated from the seven individual structures.

We have already illustrated the six stages of Fowler's faith development at work by the discussion about the ways the cross might be understood at different times in one's life. Since this brief panorama has been given, there is no need to suggest the whole scheme now. Let us look instead at middle childhood to see what Fowler can tell us that Loevinger did not about the children we teach.[11]

Fowler has noted that world coherence is founded in tales of significant people and action. In his terms this is the time of Mythic-Literal Faith. Often by about the age of seven years children begin to give their own order to the world by the stable categories of causality, space, and time. These abilities are what give the child the competence to enter into the perspectives of others and to capture life meaning in stories. Fowler's interest in existential issues and theology has drawn this aspect of the child's world much more into the foreground than did Loevinger.

The structures of the logic of rational certainty give order to and a developing control over the images and feelings stimulated by stories, gestures, and symbols taken in during the Intuitive-Projective Faith of early childhood as well as later. Fact and fantasy are distinguished in middle childhood and fairness takes on an appreciation of the views and feelings of others. Goodness is thought to need reward and badness needs to be punished. Both Fowler and Loevinger agree on this.

The dominant faith development issues during the period of childhood include belonging and being cherished. Children are able to differentiate the self and one's own group from others in the society the child is familiar with. A learning of the lore, legends, and language of the child's religious group becomes important. Despite differences in method and issues addressed there is somewhat common agreement on this as well.

Fowler's work follows the issue of existence and control in a way that Loevinger does not. The development from silence, to the episodic use of language, to narrative, on to the master story, and then to the use of concepts gives the growing person more and more control over the way he or she coordinates actions in the world to give the world coherence. A sense of an apparent control of existence by language and thinking begins to take over the coordination of actions in which one is embedded. This can be shattered, however, by a break in health, the loss of a loved one, or by some other crisis during which one learns that he or she is not God. This theme has special importance for religious educators.

Sometimes the goal of religious education seems to be to give the child a sense of control in terms of answers to existential questions. This is helpful to the growing child unless the answers are provided to the child in a second-hand way and are forced on the child despite his or her resistance or misunderstanding. A child can memorize answers to questions, as in a catechism, and yet not be able to use such language to create meaning and find direction in life and death. Sometimes this kind of religious education is so laden with guilt and shame that children get stuck in the religion of their childhood and try to live as adults with a borrowed identity that is also inappropriate structurally for adult questions.

What is important is that religious language be given to children in a way that does not arrest their faith development and get them stuck in the religion of childhood while the rest of their cognitive abilities interacting with the secular world develop beyond that stage. When this happens the ability to have a discussion with one's self, much less others, about how one's religion relates to the everyday world becomes conflicted, uncomfortable, and confusing. Such pain means that thinking about the relevance of religion to one's life and death will be avoided or even repressed.

Fowler's theory not only gives us clues about religion avoidance but also about the function of the ego and religious education. The pre-language stage and the sixth stage have something in common. They are both very difficult to research. Neither stage involves an identity built around the ego. The early pre-stage is pre-ego, and the sixth stage of post-ego. It should be noted that one does not give up the abilities of earlier stages as one develops. Rather one loses interest in their structures, because more powerful, more comprehensive, and more differentiated ways of knowing develop.[12]

The sixth and last layer of language is one that is silent because it is overflowing with experience, much like the world of the pre-language children. While the infant's silence is wise and naive, the adult's silence is not. It is wise and profound. The value of being with God far exceeds the value of talking about God. This special interest in the upper and lower limits of the developmental model is also something that Fowler provides that Loevinger does not.

In his beginning and ending stages Fowler has identified some very important clues for understanding the function of religious language. At the other stages it is assumed that one can construe and control the world by logical structures that develop in a regular sequence. What differs is the kind of structure. It is quite clear, however, that prior to language acquisition such control is impossible. At the "end" of language this control by and in language is understood in a non-naive way to be impossible. One becomes too aware of the actual coordination of actions by which we live and relate to our ultimate environment.

People at Fowler's sixth stage begin to ask the question about why they should continue to try to control the world rather than letting go and letting be. The answer is that there is no answer. There is a relationship with a presence unlike what is present in the natural world, and it cannot be reduced to words. This is one reason why it is hard for Fowler and his associates to publish stage six interviews to show us what they are talking about. One of the few such published interviews is a four-page excerpt in *Life Maps* (Fowler & Keen, 1978, pp.91-95).

The faith stages describe the structures people use to give shape to their constructs of ultimate meaning. This form cannot be separated from what one has faith in except for purposes of analysis. The sequence of these stage constructs develops in a consistent way from person to person so one can make educated guesses about which particular faith stage is being used. This may be one of the most important uses of Fowler's program of study. Certainly, communication can be improved by keeping these stages in mind, so the speaker does not project his or her stage onto the other person but allows the other person or people to be who they truly are.

Tuning in the right stage "channel" for communication improves understanding and reduces frustration. When one begins to use religious language, however, something curious happens. People at all different stages seem to be able to participate in the same parable, sacred story, or liturgical act regardless of stage. Religious language is a kind of communication that can include multiple stage understandings in its symbols. The trouble begins when people begin to talk *about* what the language is saying. That is when the cross-stage static can interfere with the communication.

For religious education, Fowler's stages are useful to increase awareness of the variety of ways people put their worlds together. On the other hand, the power of this usefulness has turned our attention away from research to the spiritual aspect of theological cognition. As we have noted above, there is also a stageless and silent aspect of theological cognition which is open alike to children and adults.

In general we have seen that Loevinger was interested in how the ego relates to the world. She stressed impulse control and character development, interpersonal style, the subject's conscious preoccupations, and cognitive style. All of these issues are important for general classroom management and individual understanding of children.

Fowler's faith development model adds to what we can learn from ego development. The list includes the importance of story, the issue of control and existence, a way to understand arrested faith development, a way to explain religion-avoidance in adults, the importance of silence in religious language, and how to understand and sort out cross-stage static in communication about one's faith world.

Special note should be made of Fowler's contribution to understanding the function of religious language by his stress upon the four aspects of the logic of conviction. This gives us a powerful set of tools to understand the child's use of religious language in ways that Loevinger's theory does not.

Most of the same contributions can be counted among the benefits derived for religious education from the work of Fritz Oser. Loevinger did not use Piaget's research approach. Fowler used it for three-sevenths of the issues he has used to understand faith development. Oser is much more narrowly focused on using Piaget's structural developmental theory and method. He has been more clear about definitions, method, and research than Fowler because of this.

Fritz Oser

Fritz Oser is the Director of the Pedagogical Institute of the University of Fribourg in Switzerland. He has worked closely with Paul Gmünder, so this research is sometimes referred by both names, Oser and Gmünder (1984), together. In 1980 Oser's work was introduced to English-speaking people by his chapter in *Toward Moral and Religious Maturity*.

Fritz Oser's focus is on the relationship between persons and an Ultimate Being (God) to which the subject actually refers. The relationship is not defined by an assumption about an a priori definition of the Ultimate Being but rather is defined by looking at the relationship itself.

Of course, no one can step back and stand somewhere outside of God and humankind to observe the relationship between them. This is what makes the relationship unique and unlike relationships such as those we have with nature, with manufactured things, or social relationships. Since it is the human side of this relationship that is studied, the interest falls within the legitimate province of developmental psychology, Oser argues.

Actual events are observed to provide the data for the study. One kind of action observed is how people cope with existential contingencies. The experience of what is impermanent and perishable raises ultimate questions. Another kind of action observed is how one gives religious meaning to a situation. Making religious meaning out of one's life and death also raises ultimate issues. Third, observations of how people interpret religious messages are included in this program of study. Finally, the act of praying is observed.

A second way to gain access to reasoning structures used in religion is by dilemma stories that stimulate existential issues. The researcher probes and pushes the subject with a gentle firmness to the limit of his or her reflective abilities to uncover the developmental structures used to think about such experiences.

The Paul-dilemma is a now classic example of what a dilemma story is like. This story is about keeping a promise made to God in an extreme situation. Another dilemma is about bad things happening to good people. This leads to questions about whether, after all, the person should still try to believe in God. In addition to the "Paul-dilemma" and the "Theodicy-dilemma" there is the "Chance-dilemma." This third example stimulates questions about whether luck is a gift of God or should be ultimately understood by a probability calculation.

The effect of interventions by religious teaching and discussions using reasoning that is "higher" in stage than customary has also been studied. It was found that one-way transmission of religious content is an ineffective kind of stimulus. Either children do not understand and thus reject the commentary or they reinterpret the statements according to their usual religious judgment reasoning level (Oser, 1988a).[13]

Biographical interviews are also used. They are no substitute for longitudinal observations and questioning, but this retrospective research has yielded some interesting conclusions. First, every subject described a religious orientation which fit one of the five stages. Second, no one reconstructed a stage above their own current stage (Oser, 1988b, p.16).

The dimensions of the relationship with God gradually has become clear from the above kinds of studies. In 1980 the operations of religious thought and choice were thought to lie within the frame of reference characterized by nine elements: 1) meaning; 2) mastering the negative; 3) freedom; 4) causality; 5) transcendence; 6) personal sense of God's actuality; 7) institutionalization; 8) catharsis/change/conversion; and 9) cult, ritualization (Oser, 1980, pp.279-280).

By 1988 religious judgment was conceptualized by a series of seven polar dimensions. They are 1) transcendence vs. immanence; 2) freedom vs. dependency; 3) trust vs. fear; 4) holy vs. profane; 5) hope vs. absurdity; 6) eternity vs. ephemerality; and 7) functional transparency vs. opaqueness (Oser, in press, pp.4-5). The seven polarities describe the dynamic relationship between the human being and the Ultimate Being, but they are also used in the studies to stimulate religious thinking as well as to describe an empirical stage.

The changes in the way the relationship with God functions structurally have been identified as five stages, although Schweitzer's (1987, pp.131-132) description of the stages in *Lebensgeschichte und Religion* adds a hypothetical stage six. The five empirical stages have been given consistent identifying names and general descriptions.

1. *Deus ex machina* (the all-powerful God who surprises you) summarizes the first stage. God controls all and we must obey God or the relationship will be broken. God is active and interferes with the world in sometimes unex-

pected ways. The individual is reactive and feeling-directed. God causes all things from life to accidents.

2. *Do ut des* (I give so that you give) sums up the second stage. You can influence God by prayers, gifts, and following the rules. If you care about God and pass the tests God sends, you will experience God as a trusting and loving father and be happy and successful.

3. *Deism* (having created the finished universe, God looks at it from a distance) is what Oser and his colleagues call the third stage. The individual assumes responsibility for his/her life and for events in the world. Meaning is linked to one's own decisions. God is apart and different with a freedom, hope, and meaning of God's own. Transcendence and immanence are separated from one another. There is often a rejection of religious and other authorities involved. The formation of an ego-identity is related.

4. *Correlation* (reciprocally related) is the fourth stage. An indirect, mediated relationship with Ultimate Being comes into existence. The individual continues to assume responsibility, but he or she begins to see the relationship with God as a way to overcome a lack of meaning and hope. Transcendence is now understood as being within the individual, at least in part. God is the condition for the possibility of human freedom.

5. *Communication* (intersubjectivity and autonomy) is the fifth stage. God is present in every human commitment and yet transcends humankind at the same time. Transcendence and immanence interact completely. Total integration renders possible universal solidarity with all human beings. The "realm of God" becomes the symbol for peaceful and fully committed human potential which creates meaning that not only detaches one from the world but also involves one most deeply. The individual assumes a fully religious position and no longer needs to be supported by a plan of salvation provided by a religious community.

The brief tracing of the stages of religious judgment shows how the elements of autonomy and integration become more pronounced as one develops, according to Oser's research. This comes about through related changes in autonomy and connectedness, differentiation and integration, and universality and uniqueness of thought. As one becomes more autonomous and integrated the bond with God becomes deeper.

In terms of autonomy one might characterize the five stages as being: 1) dependence; 2) influence; 3) independence; 4) correlational (reciprocally related); and 5) complementarity (to coordinate different explanations for one problem or entity). Complementarity thinking in religion is the special province of Helmut Reich's work with Oser. His article, "The Chalcedonian Definition: An Example of the Difficulties and the Usefulness of Thinking in Terms of Complementarity?" (Reich, 1990) provides an excellent introduction to this theme in English.

Structural transformation seems to take place in a pattern of four steps.

First, there is cognitive contradiction. Issues that cannot be dealt with adequately anymore begin to challenge us and cause a defensive reaction. Second, there is a wavering between various beliefs, opinions, and approaches. Third, an integration of the new elements takes place, and the new structures are considered more valuable. Finally, the new structures are used to engage other issue areas in addition to the one that leads the way for this development.

A major goal of this research program, in addition to defining stages of religious judgment, is to uncover the mother structure of religious cognition. Mother structures are structures which cannot be reduced to more fundamental ones. The search for mother structures came from Piaget's research which discovered the mother structures for mathematics. In math for example all structures can be reduced to three: 1) algebraic structures; 2) ordering structures; and 3) topological structures.

The importance of mother structures is that the genesis of new structures must be considered more within the framework of the coordination of elements of mother structures than within their own frameworks. Four elements that appear to be present in religious mother structures are: 1) a universal desire and search for peace, happiness, and God; 2) the abandonment of everyday involvements to search for God outside the ordinary frame of life; 3) God approaches human beings and cannot be controlled so that human beings meet God and God meets human beings; 4) God is found in the immediate environment, the everyday. These four elements challenge any program of religious education to be included.

Additional themes have been examined as this group of researchers continues to elaborate their work, but this should be sufficient detail to suggest the importance of this research in Europe of an area known roughly in this country as faith development. As you can see, this research is more clearly defined and limited in its scope than Fowler's. The explicit theological interest in the relationship with the Ultimate, unmixed with a general ego development, is what makes this research very important for teachers.

Rather than making faith the broad category that Fowler does and risking confusion with ego development, Oser has defined faith as trust. It is included in one of the seven polarities, "trust versus fear," used to characterize the relationship between a person and God.

Oser has recently developed three major dimensions to religious development.[14] The first is religious judgment. We have been discussing this primarily up to this point. The two other dimensions of religious development are religious attachment (levels of involvement with God and/or the language of religion), and religious knowledge (learning about religious tradition). All three of these issues are important for teachers.

The stages of religious judgment give religious educators an indicator as to how we should talk about God with children. Fowler has also given us a powerful tool for this, but the other two dimensions go beyond Fowler, as least in clarity of their application.

The second issue for teachers is that attachment in terms of levels of concentration on the experience of God and the use of religious language could be measured and is significant in the classroom as well as in other arenas of life. Third, the involvement in religious knowledge itself is important as well as more familiar dimension for teachers. This is the content that is being taught while the other two dimensions are more about the way the content is taught.

Oser's three-pronged analysis of religious development gives the teacher a way to differentiate among the structures of religious judgment, the depth of concentration on the religious life and language, and the involvement with the tools of the tradition (religious language). The relative strength of these three aspects of religious development can then be weighed. This can give us a way to better understand each child and prescribe activities to strengthen his or her tendency toward development.

This model also gives teachers a way to diagnose why a child or an adult has gotten stuck in a stage that is appropriate for children but not for adults, or assess why an adult's religious development has become destructive rather than creative. For example, one might have learned a great deal of content and show deep concentration but still be at a stage that is appropriate for a child rather than an adult. This suggests the possibility of exposure to religion lacking an association with the creative process or that the teachers did not use or leave open the religious judgment structures above those customarily used by the child to stimulate such growth. Any religious education program would benefit by keeping an eye on all three of these dimensions to religious development.

As the work of Oser and his associates on the stages of religious development becomes more available in English, the interaction with Fowler's faith development will become richer. This can only benefit religious educators' knowledge of the children we teach and how we ought to teach so that faith may grow and the language of faith be used more appropriately.

CONCLUSION

Many matters of interest for the religious education of children have been suggested by this chapter. A few of these issues need to be underscored. This summary will be in the form of warnings rather than conclusions or findings, because much of what has been presented is foundational in nature rather than strictly about the act of teaching itself.

Beware the Category Mistake!

It is easy to become confused and make a category mistake in religious education. For example the knowing of the spirit, mind, and senses all use the same approach, but physics, literary criticism, and the knowledge of God are all different in kind. Each kind of knowing relies on a method, an experience, and the checking of the experience by those who are masters of the first two steps.

One can study faith development or religious development by the method of science, as Fowler and Oser have done, but when religious experiences are drawn into that language context their meanings change to fit the needs of knowing by the mind and senses. Since religious terms, such as faith, are being studied we sometimes think that conclusions about spiritual knowing result from such studies, so we appeal to them to set goals for religious education.

Studies such as those of Fowler and Oser can make us better teachers, but they are not what we are called to teach. We are called to be masters of spiritual knowing rather than masters of the scientific method. What often happens is that we turn out to be masters of neither. This is why the warning of the category mistake is so important.

Beware the Loss of Religious Language!

Religious language does not operate by the rules of everyday language. It is a tool not so much to describe or explain but to become involved in so that one can pierce the language of everyday life and enter into the larger environment of one's existential limits. This gives one a profoundly realistic view of everyday matters. Religious language works indirectly, however, because the existential limits are not what we want to think about. We would rather pretend to be God, and use our everyday language to paper over our lack of control with pictures of machines and other things we can control.

There is a special quality of religious language that appears to be both silent and stageless that needs to be guarded. It is a point where adults and children have different gifts. The child's ability to contemplate life in an undifferentiated way is natural and naive. Adults have important abilities that enable them to perform the scientific method, but these "advanced powers" work against them when they attempt to enter religious language to know God. If they cannot do that in their own lives how can they teach this art by example to children?

Beware the Runaway Stage Coach!

Fowler and Oser have given us tools to better understand each other. This is especially important for teachers of children, since many adults are one or more stages beyond the way that children put their worlds together. It is hard for us to enter their worlds and the way they use language. The result is that we often project our way of knowing onto what we do not know about them. This is especially true when we are under stress.

Teachers can sense the distress this causes children, so to correct this misunderstanding the stages of faith development or religious development are studied and children begin to be squeezed into a different kind of distortion. Children then are assumed to live in the religious or faith stage in which we then have caged them on the authority of Fowler or Oser, neither of whom would ever say that all children are at all times in any of their stages.

God can break through at any stage, just as can death, the loss of meaning, the threat of freedom, or the awareness of our fundamental aloneness. Children have private lives, too. We must be careful to respect and take time to get to know them. They are full of surprises!

Beware the Loss of Center!

Guilt, shame, fear, threat, or other emotions can distort the language for knowing the Creator. The central identity of Christian teachers is related to the image of the Creator. We do not create from nothing. We do not create Christians. We only help create creating with our tradition's religious language. That language and God create Christians. This may not be true for other traditions, but it certainly seems true for this tradition.

Beware Getting Lost in the "Spiritual"!

If the spiritual realm is the one that puts the mind and the senses into perspective, what puts it in perspective? We cannot get outside of the spiritual realm, so we need a point within our identity as creatures to ground us in that realm. The creative process is the center of religious education, because it is our core identity but also because it gives us a way to check on our spirituality.

To value the spiritual way of knowing is not to advocate irrationality. Richard of St. Victor was not a lunatic. He was very careful of his method, authentic about his experience of God and careful to evaluate his spirituality himself and with the help of others. He was also happy. When the creative process is at work amid the relationships of God, self, others, and nature our deepest needs are met, so we are happy.

The work of Fowler and Oser is also needed to ground our spirituality and teaching in the realms of the mind and senses. For example Fowler can help us with our communication and monitor our growth. Oser can help us balance the stages of religious judgment with content and attachment. In addition, the mother structures of religious thinking he is beginning to explore provide a very useful model for evaluating a religious education plan.

Conclusion

This chapter and its five warnings are intended to help re-center research and teaching in a larger perspective. It is with the masters of the spiritual life on one side and the masters of the scientific method on the other that we can advance as teachers to better serve the children.

NOTES

1. This approach was suggested to me by Ken Wilber's (1990) book *Eye to Eye: The Quest for the New Paradigm*. My interpretation of Richard is somewhat limited to the interpretation of Grover A. Zinn (1979) who translated and introduced *The Twelve Patriarchs*, *The Mystical Ark*, and *Book Three of the Trinity* in *Richard of St. Victor*. The larger historical situation was set for me especially by Francois Vandenbroucke's (1982) "The Schoolmen of the Twelfth Century," in *The Spirituality of the Middle Ages*.

2. The part I have referred to may be found at page 39 of Vol. I, 1910, and much of my interpretation of this difficult work is based on William Kneale and Martha Kneale (1964), *The Development of Logic*, cf. especially Chapter XI.

3. This is the problem of what Ken Wilber (1990) calls "the pre/trans fallacy." We begin by assuming that human beings do in fact have access to three general realms of being and knowing—the sensory, the mental, and the spiritual. The prerational and the transrational realms are both in their own ways nonrational, so they appear to be the same to the untutored eye. A confusion of "pre-" and "trans-" takes place, and the transrational gets reduced to prerational status or the prerational gets elevated to the transrational. Wilber considers this fallacy to be one of the primary obstacles to the development of a truly comprehensive worldview.

4. The many references to "the leap" in his *Concluding Unscientific Postscript* from the same period are passed over for quotation only because this passage is so concise [for Kierkegaard] and so to the point.

5. To shape a person to be creative does not shape what he or she will create because (logically) creativity is a higher type or category of language than the unique outcomes to which it refers.

6. The four functions of religious language for the purpose of this approach to religious education are parable, sacred story, liturgy, and overflowing silence. A book on each with education materials will follow. The concluding volume of this series will be about the theology of childhood. A book about the historical roots of this approach in the work of Maria Montessori, E. M. Standing, and Sofia Cavalletti is now underway.

7. The English word *virtue* comes from the Latin, *virtus*. This word signifies both strength and power (*vir*). When St. Thomas spoke of a virtue in the *Summa Theologiae*, for example, he implied the perfection of a power. A virtue was for him the activity of human power at its best. The virtuous person was not considered to be grim, stern, and overbearing, as is often inferred today as a result of the Puritan experience. For St. Thomas the truly virtuous person was someone who enjoyed acting virtuously.

8. The word "cardinal" comes from the Latin *"cardinalis"* which first meant "pertaining to a door-hinge." It implies something pivotal. It was

later extended in meaning to indicate "that on which something depends." St. Thomas' interpretation, of course, was influenced greatly by Aristotle.

9. The research taking place at the Alister Hardy Research Centre in Oxford was the resource for this survey. The Centre's many publications about their research were consulted, but if one were to read a single book about this research it should probably be David Hay's (1987) *Exploring Inner Space: Is God Still Possible in the Twentieth Century?*

10. In addition to Fowler's work there are related studies that keep theological issues in mind. At Iliff Seminary in Denver a research group has remained close to the data and kept a modest but clear goal in mind. The focus of their study is the structural development of the interpretation of scripture.

Many of this group's theoretical papers and empirical reports are unpublished. Students are pretested as they enter Iliff and are tested again after graduation. Subjects continue to be monitored at various points in their later life to see what structural change if any has taken place when they perform the task of hermeneutics. Follow-up studies are now underway, including the possibility of work with children.

Clarence Snelling is the leader of this interdisciplinary team which includes Ed Everding Jr. and Mary Wilcox. Professor Everding is a New Testament scholar who also has been trained in religious education. Mary Wilcox was trained as a geologist and then in theology. Her book, *Developmental Journey: A Guide to the Development of Logical and Moral Reasoning and Social Perspective* (Wilcox, 1979), is the major theoretical statement of the group to date. Clarence Snelling is not only the leader of this group but his unique contribution has been to personally carry on cross-cultural studies using their approach in Mexico, South America, and Africa.

11. There are two reasons that we introduced Loevinger's model for ego development earlier. One is to compare the issues she and Fowler think are important to evoke the human personality. The second reason is that Fowler attempts to use the method of Piaget to help graft together the interests of ego development and theology. Loevinger explicitly refused to use Piaget's research as the centerpiece for her ego development research, and she was not as interested in existential issues as Fowler is.

12. Fowler's interest in ego development has been present since the beginning of his theory construction. Loevinger's comprehensive book, *Ego Development*, appeared in 1976, while *Life Maps* was being edited. Rather than turning to the work of Loevinger, however, Fowler's work was in conversation primarily with Robert Kegan's view of ego development.

Robert Kegan's studies of Piaget prompted him to look past the stages to the movement that the stages mark. He argued that it is the *movement* of development that should be in the foreground while the stop-action descriptions of stages should be in the background of our interests. In Kegan's words "the constitutive activity rather than constitutions" should be what we are looking for. Kegan's later book expanded on these observations: *The Evolving Self: Problem and Process in Human Development.*

Kegan does not call the creating of meaning an act of ego. His view is that this is done by the "creative motion of life itself," and that this process is philosophically real, biologically real, psychologically real, socially real, religiously real. It is "the holy, the transcendent, and the oneness of all life." This kind of knowing takes into consideration that there is no knowing without feeling and no feeling without knowing as well as the changes that take place in the knower as he or she knows, *especially* in ultimate, existential matters. It was Kegan's work more than any other that showed Fowler the way to join the two kinds of knowing he incorporated in his theoretical model with feeling and thinking, so often separated from each other for purposes of research in the tradition of Piaget.

13. Please see p. 11 of "Towards a Logic of Religious Judgment: A Reply to My Critics" for the summary of the educational views. Also, please see Oser (1988b) for additional reports of educational studies in German.

14. Taken from a lecture given by Oser at the International Seminar on Religion and Values in Denmark during the summer of 1990 at which the author was present.

Please see *Wieviel Religion braucht der Mensch?*, and mention of this aspect in English by K. Helmut Reich (in press).

For the relationship between religious judgment, Kohlberg's moral judgment, and Fowler's interest in world coherence see: Fritz Oser and Helmut Reich (1990).

For the latest general view of religious development in English see: Oser (1991).

REFERENCES

Bateson, G. (1975). *Steps to an ecology of mind.* New York: Ballantine.

Bateson, G. (1979). *Mind and nature: A necessary unity.* New York: Dutton.

Berryman, J. (1991). *Godly play.* San Francisco: Harper & Row.

Capra, F. (1975). *The tao of physics.* Boulder: Shambhala.

David, C. (1989). *The evidential force of religious experience.* Oxford: Oxford University Press.

Dykstra, C. (1986). What is faith? An experiment in the hypothetical mode. In C. Dykstra & S. Parks (Eds.), *Faith development and Fowler.* Birmingham, AL: Religious Education Press.

Dykstra, C. & Parks, S. (1986). *Faith development and Fowler.* Birmingham, AL: Religious Education Press.

Fowler, J. (1974). Toward a developmental perspective on faith. *Religious Education, 69.*

Fowler, J. (1981). *Stages of faith: The psychology of human development and the quest for meaning.* San Francisco: Harper & Row.

Fowler, J., & Keen, S. (1978). *Life maps: Conversations on the journey of faith.* J. Berryman (Ed). Waco, TX: Word.

Fowler, J., & Loder, J. (1982). Conversations on Fowler's Stages of faith and Loder's The transforming moment. *Religious Education, 77* (March-April), 2, 133-139.

Fowler, J. (1986a). Dialogue toward a future in faith development studies. In C. Dykstra & S. Parks (Eds.), *Faith development and Fowler.* Birmingham, AL: Religious Education Press.

Fowler, J. (1986b). Faith and the structuring of meaning. In C. Dykstra & S. Parks (Eds.), *Faith development and Fowler.* Birmingham, AL: Religious Education Press.

Hay, D. (1987). *Exploring inner space: Is God still possible in the twentieth century?* London: Mowbray.

Kegan, R. (1980). There the dance is: Religious dimensions of a developmental framework. In J. Fowler & A. Vergote (Eds.) *Toward moral and religious maturity.* Morristown, NJ: Silver Burdett.

Kegan, R. (1982). *The evolving self: Problem and process in human development.* Cambridge, MA: Harvard University Press.

Kierkegaard, S. (1864/1946). The present age: A literary review. In R. Bretall (Ed.), *A Kierkegaard anthology.* Princeton: Princeton University Press.

Kneale, W., & Kneale, M. (1964). *The development of logic.* Oxford: Clarendon Press.

Lee, J. (1990). *Handbook of faith.* Birmingham, AL: Religious Education Press.

Loder, J. (1981). *The transforming moment.* San Francisco: Harper & Row.

Loevinger, J. (with A. Blasi) (1976). *Ego development.* San Francisco: Jossey-Bass.

Oser, F. (1980). Stages of religious judgment. In J. Fowler & A. Vergote (Eds.), *Toward moral and religious maturity.* Morristown, NJ: Silver Burdett Company.

Oser, F. (1988a). Toward a logic of religious judgment: A reply to my critics. In K. Nipkow, F. Schweitzer, & J. Fowler (Eds.), *Glaubensentwicklung und Erziehung.* Gutersloh: Mohn. (Translated with revisions and published as *Stages of faith and religious development,* J. Fowler, K. Nipkow, & F. Schweitzer [Eds.], New York: Crossroad, 1991.)

Oser, F. (1988b). *Wieviel religion braucht der mensch? Erziehung und entwicklung zur religiosen autonomie.* Gutersloh, Germany: Gerd Mohn GTB.

Oser, F. (1991). The development of religious judgment. In F. Oser and W. Scarlett (Eds.), *Religious development in childhood and adolescence.* New Directions for Child Development Series (W. Damon, series Ed.). San Francisco: Jossey-Bass.

Oser, F., & Gmünder, P. (1984). *Der mensch-stufen seiner religiousen entwicklung: Ein struckturgenetischer ansatz.* Zurich: Benziger. (Reprinted in 1988 in Gutersloh, Germany, by G. Mohn. Translated with minor revisions and published as *Religious judgement*, Birmingham, AL: Religious Education Press.)

Oser, F., & Reich, K. (1990). Moral judgment, religious judgment, world view, and logical thought: A review of their relationship [part one and part two]. *British Journal of Religious Education, 12*, 94-101, 172-181.

Reich, K. (1990). The chalcedonian definition: An example of the difficulties and the usefulness of thinking in terms of complementarity. *Journal of Psychology and Theology, 18*, 148-157.

Reich, K. (in press). Religious development across the life span. In *Life span development and behavior*, vol. 12. Hillsdale, NJ: Erlbaum.

Russell, B., and North, A. (1910, 1912, 1913). *Principia mathematica*, vols. 1, 2, 3. (Second editions released in 1925, 1927, and 1927 respectively). Cambridge: Cambridge University Press.

Sapir, E. (1949). *Selected writings in language, culture, and personality.* [D. Mandelbaum, Ed.] Berkeley: University of California Press.

Schweitzer, F. (1987). *Lebensgeschichte und religion: Religiose entwicklung und erziehung im kindes-und jugendalter.* Munich, Germany: Kaiser.

Vandenbroucke, F. (1982). The schoolmen of the twelfth century. In J. Leclercq, F. Vandenbroucke, & L. Bouey (Eds.) *The spirituality of the Middle Ages*, Vol. 2, New York: Seabury.

Whorf, B. (1956). *Language, thought and reality.* [J. Carroll, Ed.] Cambridge, MA: MIT Press.

Wilber, K. (1990). *Eye to eye: The quest for the new paradigm.* Boston: Shambhala Publications.

Wilcox, M. (1979). *Developmental journey: A guide to the development of logical and moral reasoning and social perspective.* Nashville, TN: Abingdon.

Zinn, G. (1979) (trans.). *Richard of St. Victor.* [Includes *The twelve patriarchs, The mystical ark*, and *Book three of the trinity* by Richard of St. Victor]. New York: Paulist.

Zukav, G. (1979). *The dancing wu li masters: An overview of the new physics.* New York: Morrow.

Chapter Three

The Religious Concepts of Children

RENZO VIANELLO, KALEVI TAMMINEN, AND DONALD RATCLIFF

Acquiring religious concepts is a central task of religious education. While it is not the only task with which we should be concerned, the average person probably sees religious education as learning concepts about God, the Bible, the church, and so on. Since faith can be understood in terms of structure apart from religion (Fowler, 1981), cognitive content is essential to making children's faith genuinely religious in nature.

The study of religious concepts is one of the older areas within the social sciences, yet it continues to provoke contemporary interest. Initial studies were conducted in the last century (Brown, 1892; Barnes, 1892), while the present decade has already brought three major works on the topic (Hyde, 1990; Coles, 1990; Tamminen, 1991).

The predominant theorist in child development for the last several decades, Jean Piaget, has powerfully affected much of the research of religious concepts. This is explicitly stated in the landmark study by Goldman (1964), as well as the work of Bassett (Bassett et al., 1990) but Piagetian constructs and assumptions are latent in many other research studies. While in recent years there has been increased questioning of certain aspects of Piaget's stage theory, the Piagetian paradigm continues to be a central reference in child development.

The present chapter summarizes the research of children's religious concepts conducted by the two primary authors, which often made use of several Piagetian constructs and assumptions (although the results are not always consistent with his stage theory). The present chapter is a survey of a num-

56

ber of studies related to children's concepts, emphasizing the research studies of the primary authors.

Vianello documents dozens of research studies of more than 10,000 Italian children which describe several religious concepts of youngsters between three and fourteen years of age. Nearly all of those studied received instruction in the Roman Catholic faith. This work is more fully documented in Vianello (1980) and Vianello and Marin (1985). Tamminen concentrates upon his major 1974 study, a 1986 replication, and follow-up studies in 1976 and 1980, but also includes results from smaller complementary projects. These studies of about 3000 Finnish youngsters, ages seven to twenty, analyze children's religious development using a wide variety of research instruments. Nearly all of the children came from a Lutheran background and received Lutheran religious education in school. The topic of religious concepts is but one aspect of his multifaceted work on religious development (Tamminen, 1991).

Several key issues will be considered. First, what religious concepts are easily accessible to children and which are rejected or confused because they require thought processes not typical of childhood? To what extent do the tendencies suggested by Piaget (such as egocentrism, artificialism, and magical thinking) interfere with the acquisition of religious concepts? Are religious beliefs of children compartmentalized from daily life? How do religious concepts change with age?

CONCEPTS OF GOD (VIANELLO)

The understanding of God is influenced by the child's cognitive abilities. The child forms a mental schema of God in much the same way he or she comes to understand any concept, thus the structural assets and limitations of the intellect can be expected to impinge upon the concept of the God.

God as Superman

Anthropomorphisms significantly influence the God concept (Terstenjak, 1955; Bovet, 1961; Elkind, 1971a & 1978; Mailhiot, 1964; Horbert, 1967; Haavisto, 1969; Vaataienen, 1974; Nye & Carlson, 1984; Keskitalo, 1987; Kjellgren, 1987). Anthropomorphism, the attributing of human characteristics to divinity, is not always inappropriate, indeed even the Bible describes God in this manner. However, the child's anthropomorphisms overextend the concept of the divine; God becomes a man who is bigger and more powerful than other humans, but not fundamentally more than human.

Why do anthropomorphisms occur? Several researchers (Arago-Mitjans, 1965; Vergote, 1966; Sarti, 1970) suggest that they are the result of immature intellectual ability (lack of formal reasoning).

Clavier (1926) noted that up to the age of eight children's understandings of God are permeated by simple anthropomorphism, in which God is regarded as a man like any other human. From eight to twelve years *mitigated* anthropomorphism prevails, in which God is considered human but different from all other men.

Our studies (Vianello, 1980) indicate that when children are six or seven, God is considered a giant, a magician, or an invisible man. From eight years of age there is an increasing understanding of God's spirituality, seen in comments such as "(he) is sort of transparent," "you can't see him, but he is present in many places," and "he is enormous...when he is here he may also be at school." Ten- and eleven-year-olds make fewer anthropomorphic descriptions of God, affirming that God is invisible, he is in us or in our souls, or he is always near us. Barbey (1947) and Thun (1959) note that some children ten years and older try to avoid anthropomorphisms, yet are unable to comprehend God as spirit, so they refuse to provide any description.

Table 1. Percentages of subjects with some anthropomorphic concepts of God (Vianello, 1980)

Age:	4	5	6	7	8	9	10	11
God as man	100	100	96	64	12	8	4	-
God as special man	-	-	4	36	78	42	14	4
Approaching God as spirit	-	-	-	-	10	46	62	47
God as spirit	-	-	-	-	-	4	20	49

Further evidence of the abandonment of anthropomorphism with age is a developmental progression in comprehending the attributes of God. Our work (Vianello, 1980) indicates that the omniscience of God surfaces first at about age six to seven, second, the omnipotence of God is affirmed by age eight, and finally the omnipresence of God and his fundamental spirit nature are described by eleven to twelve years.

Table 2. Percentages of subjects who affirm God as omniscient, omnipotent, omnipresent, and spirit (Vianello, 1980)

Age:	4	5	6	7	8	9	10	11
Omniscience	8	33	79	95	100	100	94	84
Omnipotence	-	17	31	56	81	83	81	64
Omnipresence	-	-	-	-	-	17	33	79
Spirit	-	-	-	-	-	4	20	49

The degree to which children overcome their anthropomorphism is also seen in the study of ideas related to Easter. Young children see Easter and other holidays in terms of subjective interests (candy, activities, and so on), whereas by middle childhood more objective and factual information is added to their understanding (Elkind, 1971b). Nine- to eleven-year-old children describe Easter in relation to Jesus, not God, and emphasize that the "God-man" brought about the resurrection simply by thinking. Children state, "He thought about going away and he went," "He thought about going up to heaven and the next thing he knew he was there."

Children eleven to thirteen years of age are often at a transition point, thus they demonstrate pseudo-anthropomorphisms (Sarti, 1970). For example they state: "I feel he is an eye, in front of me...but these are only images because I think that God exists everywhere" (girl, 12.4 years), "I imagine him as an old man with a long beard and long white clothes. But I know that God is a spirit and so he wouldn't have clothes" (girl, 9.4 years). Another states, "I think of God as a person like us, but he is a spirit" (girl, 11.0 years).

Our research strongly indicates an implicit egocentrism in children's conceptualizations of God (Vianello, 1980). Likewise Godin and van Roey (1959) found that children articulate God's omnipotence and protection in a self-centered manner; prayer is important because that is how God serves people. Deconchy (1964) cites children describing God as obliging, devoted, kind, loyal, and sincere. Braido and Sarti (1967) note finalistic perspectives even among thirteen- and fourteen-year-olds ("God is in heaven and walks up and down waiting for good people").

Godin and van Roey (1959) distinguish affective and imaginative anthropomorphism. The affective variety refers to the tendency of children to project their affective relationship with the family upon God, while imaginative anthropomorphism refers to portraying God with human features.

While the individual child's description of God may vary, the general developmental trend is away from a humanized God and toward an understanding of God as spirit, but the majority do not fully comprehend the latter until adolescence. This is probably due to the arrival of formal operational thinking at that time.

God as Creator

In early childhood youngsters affirm the creation of the universe by God. Yet, because God is considered to be only a superman, this implies that creation is a human feat. This fits well with Piaget's (1926) concept of artificialism which holds that natural events, such as rain, clouds, and even mountains and rivers, exist due to human actions. Piaget held that human and divine artificialism are one and the same, since God is considered a glorified man and adults are perceived as having divine characteristics.

Our research confirms that young children, including the majority of those six to seven years old, understand God to be creator. However, creation in this sense does not mean creation out of nothing, but rather creation in the sense of building or making something out of available materials.

Yet there is a strong indication that this concept of creator is not as clearly understood as it will be later in childhood. The evidence for this is that when children respond to questions such as "Was it God who created the stars?" or "Who created the world?" the vast majority state that God was the creator. Likewise in stories that imply a creator, children readily affirm God as creator. Yet when the theme of nature predominates in a story, without a suggestion of creator, God was mentioned in only a handful of cases. This confirms Piaget's statement, "We have been struck by the fact that the majority of children turn to God [to explain phenomena] when there is no one else to turn to" (Piaget, 1926, p.358). Likewise Castiglioni (1928) noted that it is very rare when overwhelming natural events evoke the idea of God in children up to eight years of age.

In contrast, nine- to eleven-year-old children mention God even in situations when there is no prompt. Braido and Sarti (1967) and Sarti (1968, 1970), studying both Catholic and Muslim children, found that at this age the most common attribute associated with God is being creator. Deconchy (1964), in his study of eight- to ten-year-olds, also found this to be the case. The linkage between God as creator and natural phenomena is stronger with nine- to eleven-year-olds, and by ten or eleven years origins are understood as being creation from nothing rather than merely constructing or building.

God as Magician

Sociology makes a fundamental distinction between religion and magic. Essentially the difference is that magic attempts to provide human control over specific events via ritual, whereas religion involves appeals to the divine without attempts to manipulate (van den Berghe, 1975). Magic is a means to an end, while religion is an end in itself (Tischler, 1990, p.382). Piaget (1926) understood children to have magical thinking in which internal thoughts produce external results, thus thinking certain thoughts results in outward consequences. This is due to egocentrism, Piaget suggested, and thus they see events as the result of someone's private thinking rather than natural causes. For example, a parent's death may be due to a transient wish by the child that the parent was dead.

While a number of researchers have documented this magical component in children's religion (Arago-Mitjans, 1965; Gruehn, 1956; Tersteniak, 1955; Vergote, 1966), our research (Vianello & Marin-Zanovello, 1980) indicates that the magical God is not only due to egocentrism and precausal thinking but also because of latent cultural influences. Religious instruction that includes an atmosphere of mystery tends to reinforce the magical component in the concept of God (Vergote, 1983). In other words, adults often encourage immature thinking in this regard rather than helping children overcome the tendency. It should be noted, however, that this magical component also exists to a lesser extent in relation to human beings as well as God.

While magical thinking is most likely in the preschool years, six- to eight-year-olds are more able to distinguish magical and non-magical thinking, and they resort to the former only when they want to explain or understand something mysterious. Since God acts in such a mysterious manner, he is conceptualized to be a normal human being who has magical powers, an understanding that disappears with the gradual abandonment of anthropomorphism and acceptance of God as spirit. For example one seven-year-old, when asked if God could bring a drowned child back to life, replied: "Yes, God can bring him back to life."

Researcher: "And how does he do it?'

Child: "He does a bit of magic, he says 'abra cadabra abra cadabra'; and the child comes back to life, because God is powerful."

The sacraments, other rituals, prayers, and dogma particularly are likely to be infused with magical components by children. Godin and Marthe (1960) note that most children eight years old and younger consider the sacraments to be effective regardless of the attitudes of the person receiving them, because sacraments are considered to be magical. These researchers found that this perspective tends to disappear between eight and eleven years, but some fourteen-year-olds continue to have remnants of this magical perspective. Vergote (1966) and Dumoulin and Jaspard (1973) note that magical qualities are found in children's understanding of rituals and dogma, particularly if these are difficult to understand. Likewise prayers, when understood as rigid and unalterable verbal formulas, include a magical component for children.

God as Parent

Long ago Freud stated that the view a person has of God is very similar to the concept held of one's father, while Jung believed it was similar to the mother. Later researchers (Strunk, 1959; Siegmann, 1961; Godin & Hallez, 1974; Vergote, Bonami, Custers, & Pittijn, 1967; Vergote et al., 1969; Vergote & Aubert, 1972) conducted research with adults attempting to establish some relationship between the concept of God and the image of one or both parents.

While there may be merit in studying adults in this respect, adult understandings and recollections of childhood are often quite different from the actual experience of children. Thus we undertook a broad study of 437 children, ages six to fourteen, to consider the relationship between the God concept and perceptions of parents, making use of three different kinds of measures adapted for children and comparing them with the Piagetian interview approach. With the Semantic Differential Technique, the image of God is more like the father than the mother for both boys and girls. The God-father linkage is also stronger than God and friend. The father-God correlation is highest for nine- and ten-year-olds. This peak is difficult to explain, but may be due to the intensity of religious instruction for children this age in Italy.

While the father-God association is predominant, the correlation between the mother and God concepts is higher for girls than boys. This is opposite the finding with adults recorded by Nelson and Jones (1957) who found the God-mother correlation to be highest with men.

A Q technique found that the concept of God is quite positive for children, who emphasize God as protector to a greater extent than God as judge. This relationship is strongest with older children. From six to ten years the view of God strongly incorporates ideas of forgiveness and rewards for obedience, although protection predominates. From eleven years on the protection by God is understood not to be manifested by direct intervention or miracles (although God is understood to be capable of miracles), thus people are expected to deal with difficulties on their own. These children regard God not so much as one who punishes, but rather as one who is good, forgiving, concerned about humanity, and protecting individuals through nature.

Another study using the Semantic Differential Technique (Vianello, Carrajo, & Lis, 1978) compared children living with their parents with institutionalized youngsters. Those in special care facilities had a less positive image of the father, the mother, their teacher, and God. This suggests that the concept of God is directly affected, positively or negatively, by parents, and contradicts the "compensation" hypothesis that states that children idealize the image of God to make up for deficiencies in their parents.

THE CONCEPT OF GOD (TAMMINEN)

The concept of *anthropomorphism* is central to Goldman's (1964) presentation of the concept of God in childhood. He found that a child's God concept is anthropomorphic up to the age of ten or eleven. An intermediary stage develops sometime between ten and twelve, followed by the development of a symbolic concept of God. Vianello (1980) also emphasizes a turning point at about ten or eleven.

Our studies of the God concept (Tamminen, 1991) made use of three separate instruments, including a sentence completion task ("When I think about God..." or "In my opinion God is..."), an essay on the topic "What my God is like," and eight projective photographs. One of the photographs portrayed a contemplative girl, accompanied by the description, "This girl is Karin. She is sitting and thinking about God and Jesus. She is thinking..." [An equivalent picture of a boy and corresponding text were substituted with male subjects.] Several measurement procedures were used to evaluate responses, including a semantic differential test.

Only a few Finnish children gave coarsely anthropomorphic, physical descriptions of God in response to the open-ended questions. Even more surprising, children in the lower grades gave no more anthropomorphic responses than youngsters in the upper grades, but those responses were evenly distributed across grade levels.

Anthropomorphic concepts of God may have different meanings at different ages. For example, an adolescent who uses very physical descriptions of God may have a God concept that has remained undeveloped since early childhood or has even retrogressed to a less-developed state. These youths often express a slighting attitude toward God or religion. In contrast, children who believe in God and who describe an experience of God's closeness clearly gave less anthropomorphic responses than those who found God to be more distant or did not believe in him.

At about age nine or ten children begin to speak of God as spirit, our research indicates. Such statements are most common at the age of ten to thirteen. After that age there is a decline in the number of positive expressions about God, partly because of increasing alienation from religion. Young elementary-aged children are the most likely to describe God as real and near, while such descriptions become less frequent with age. This change is most pronounced during the preadolescent period, between eleven and fourteen.

As Vianello stated, anthropomorphism is a complex issue; we cannot speak of God without using expressions that in some way are linked to human life. What is most important, from the perspective of religious education, is that anthropomorphic traits not be an impediment of religious thinking and that the God concept develops in correspondence with other thinking.

An adequate definition of anthropomorphism is crucial. If we include human traits such as loving, helping, trustworthiness, and power in the definition, then a large number of Finnish children and teenagers have anthropomorphic characteristics. These psychological attributes are the primary traits used to describe God at all grade levels but particularly in the early years (ages seven to ten).

As in Vianello's research, Finnish children also see God as primarily gentle, secure, and loving, while only a few see God as stern, frightening, or punishing. Figure 1 illustrates the vivid contrast in the number of children seeing God as stern as opposed to loving. As can be seen, the number of children who described a loving God decreases between sixth (twelve- and thirteen-year-olds) and eighth grades (fourteen- and fifteen-year-olds), but increases thereafter.

Descriptions of God as being close, real, caring, and forgiving are related to a close, positive relationship with parents. The correlation between these is strongest at the lowest grade levels.

In addition, many children speak of God as *creator*, but that is not the

Figure 1. Descriptions of God as loving or stern

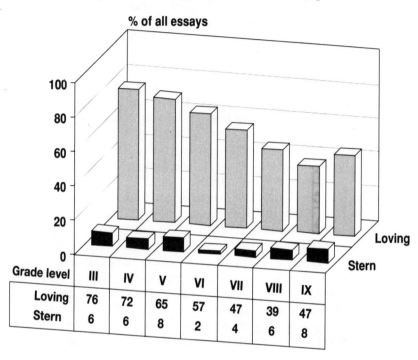

Grade level	III	IV	V	VI	VII	VIII	IX
Loving	76	72	65	57	47	39	47
Stern	6	6	8	2	4	6	8

dominant trait at any age. Nearly one-fourth of the nine- and ten-year-olds describe God in this manner, as do many of the older students. Uncertainty and doubt regarding the existence of God increase with age.

God's Influence

How do children perceive God's influence? Vianello found that from eleven years on children do not believe God directly intervenes or uses miracles to provide protection. Other studies also indicate that older children come to believe God works indirectly through circumstances and people.

In our research this issue was investigated by telling a story about a girl's grandmother who was seriously ill. The girl prayed for her grandmother, who later recovered. When the girl discussed the experience at school, her peers offered four opinions: God answered the prayer and cured the grandmother (direct intervention); God cured the grandmother through the medication (indirect intervention); the grandmother recovered only because of the medical treatment (denial of God's influence); and uncertainty as to why the grandmother recovered. In response to the story, children were to choose the alternative with which they agreed, answer the question, "Do you think prayer had anything to do with the grandmother's recovery?" and provide reasons for their opinions.

About half of the seven- to ten-year-olds chose the direct intervention alternative, while one-fourth chose the indirect influence option. After age ten the number of children who affirmed direct intervention decreased sharply while the number that chose the indirect alternative increased. At thirteen to sixteen, almost half of the students denied or were unsure about any influence by God. A similar trend toward skepticism in relating prayer to the grand-mother's recovery can be seen in Figure 2 (prayer will be considered in more detail later in this chapter).

Figure 2. The effect of prayer
Mary's grandmother's recovery; opinions about the effect of prayer (N=967)

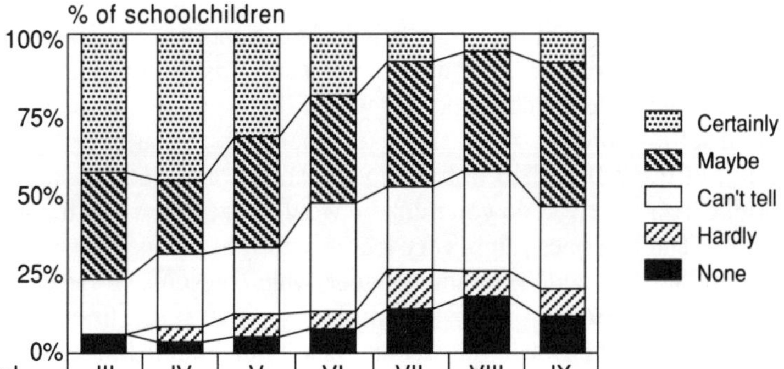

Grade level	III	IV	V	VI	VII	VIII	IX
Certainly	44	47	32	19	8	6	8
Maybe	33	23	35	33	39	36	45
Can't tell	18	23	22	34	26	31	26
Hardly	0	5	7	6	13	8	9
None	5	3	5	7	14	18	11

IMMANENT JUSTICE (VIANELLO)

Piaget (1932) noted that children generally believe in immanent justice, that punishment naturally results from misdeeds even if the parents do not punish. Others have verified Piaget's concept through their studies (Caruso, 1943; Havighurst & Neugarten, 1955; Loves, 1957; Godin, 1959, and Jahoda, 1964).

Piaget (1932) told six- to twelve-year-old children a story about two chil-dren who stole some apples. While one child was caught, the other escaped but fell into a river on the way home. The children were then asked if they thought the second child would have fallen into the water if he had not stolen the apples. The percentage of children attributing the fall to the stolen apples decreased by age, from 86 percent of six-year-olds to 34 percent of eleven-and twelve-year-olds. Piaget believed this year-by-year decline indicated a gradual decrease in belief in immanent justice.

More than fifty years after Piaget's original research, the writer and his colleagues (Vianello, 1980; Vianello & Marin, 1989a) conducted several studies that produced very different results. In three out of the four studies we found 14-17 percent of six-year-olds believed in immanent justice (the other study recorded 55 percent, still much less than Piaget's 86 percent). Seven- and eight-year-olds believed in immanent justice 19-58 percent of the time, in contrast with Piaget's finding of 73 percent. Less extreme differences were found for nine- and ten-year-olds, but 50-64 percent of eleven- and twelve-year-olds believed in immanent justice, compared with 34 percent in Piaget's studies. The neat developmental progression Piaget reported was entirely missing!

The failure to confirm Piaget's findings requires some explanation. Perhaps the discrepant results were due to a research instrument that failed to adequately measure the construct for which it was intended. In his story of the child falling into the river, the researcher asks the subject, "What do you think of that? If he had not stolen the apples and had crossed the unsafe bridge over the river, do you think he would have fallen into the water in any case?" The last question is very leading, as it assumes immanent justice; it puts the stealing and the falling together, which presumes some causative linkage. The question calls for the simple logic that if stealing results in punishment (the given), will nonstealing result in nonpunishment (the query). A correct response by the subject not only requires a full understanding of the logic of the question but also correcting the story's (and researcher's) implicit but faulty assumption of immanent justice. It may be that sixty years ago young children were more hesitant to correct a mistaken adult than they are today. The "developmental progression" away from immanent justice in Piaget's data may in fact only show that older children were more likely to challenge an adult openly at that time, whereas today's young children are bolder in this respect.

How, then, are we to explain the slight *increase* in immanent justice with age found in our research? In another series of studies, Vianello and Marin (1989a) considered not only a posteriori justice (a negative *consequence* described in the story due to the misdeed) but also a priori justice (anticipating punishment for a misdeed *prior to* the description of the consequence). To contrast with both of these *punitive* forms of justice, *compensatory* justice was also evaluated (would children be positively compensated for doing good deeds). A priori versions of the story did not imply immanent justice. For example the a priori punitive justice story read, "One day two children stole some apples from a tree. Suddenly a farmer arrived and the two children ran away. One was caught. The other . . . How would you finish the story?"

More than 1400 Italian children, ages four to fourteen, were evaluated. At every age range children were more likely to believe in compensatory justice than punitive justice. This difference was particularly strong at ages six to nine and eleven to fourteen. When told Piaget's story without the negative consequence for the second child, most children did not finish it with a punishing conclusion. None of them finished it with a punishment from nature, as in the original story. Essentially the same results were found with the compensatory justice stories (both a priori and a posteriori versions), although there was a greater tendency for the main character to be rewarded.

Causal reasoning is apparent as early as four or five and is well developed by age six, as indicated by children's denial of any relationship between the theft and the fall. They do not believe bad actions are always punished and are only slightly more likely to believe good actions will always be rewarded. Regardless of age, they also realize that if they are caught punishment is not inevitable (for example, they may be forgiven). They also realize that people who do good receive approval or reward only part of the time. Children realize that those who do good deeds may feel inner satisfaction as a result of their good deeds, or even be punished if the good deeds require disobedience to parents.

Perhaps the most perplexing of the results is the apparent *increase* in immanent justice with age, directly opposite Piaget's findings. How is this to be explained? Perhaps children learn that God will guarantee justice from religious instruction (for example, from certain Bible stories). Vianello, Marin, and Bozzolo (1979) documented the effects of religious instruction upon the expectation of justice. As seen in Table 3, the number of years of religious instruction proved to be a significant influence, while gender, father's profession, and other variables were found to be insignificant.

Table 3. Percent believing in justice (Vianello, Marin, & Bozzolo, 1979)

	Age: 4-5	6-7	8-10
Amount of Religious instruction:			
Below average	25%	29%	33%
Average	34%	38%	45%
Above average	44%	50%	54%

It is apparent that Piaget underestimated the environmental influences upon belief in immanent justice, including the kind and amount of religious education given, and overestimated the importance of the innate component of cognitive development. This was in part due to the use of an inadequate and overly demanding research intervention, as noted before.

PRAYER AND IMMANENT JUSTICE (TAMMINEN)

The principle of immanent justice is very much related to children's concepts of prayer, as children may think that through prayers impending punishment may be avoided. Studies of immanent justice have been rare in the last few decades. Loves (1957) and Jahoda (1958) found that belief in justice as inherent within events clearly decreased with age but belief in justice resulting from God's intervention increased. These studies complement Vianello's interesting results and consistently call into question Piaget's conclusions.

Godin and van Roey (1959) documented how six- to fourteen-year-olds understood the effects of prayer. Like Piaget, they found that immanent justice in the form of "punitive animism" decreased with age, but that "protective animism," in which danger is avoided by asking for God's protection, increases up to the age of twelve and decreases thereafter. These researchers believed that the increase in protecting animism was the result of religious education, which emphasizes turning to God in difficult situations.

In my research of immanent justice, a story was used to elicit responses from children:

Andy wanted to go rowing with his brother in the family's new boat. Father told them not to go because the weather forecast predicted a storm. Nevertheless the boys went. All of a sudden, when they were far from home, they were caught in a thunderstorm. In his anguish, Andy prayed that God would protect them. But the waves threw their boat against a rock and the boat was badly damaged. The boys narrowly escaped by swimming to a nearby shore.

The children studied were asked to choose from several possible options: "The accident was a natural consequence of the boys' disobedience" (immanent justice); "God did not answer Andy's prayer because Andy had been disobedient" (punishing animism); and "If Andy had not prayed, something worse would have happened" (protecting animism). (The first option might be seen as implying punitive animism, although this would have been more likely had the word "punishment" been used instead of "consequence." It might also be noted that the third option is quite close to magical thinking.) Three other options were included as well.

Agreement with the option representing immanent justice decreased sharply from the age of seven and eight (70% agreed) to eleven and twelve (45% agreed) and continued to decline after fifteen and sixteen (46% to

28%). Likewise the number who agreed with the punishing animism option also decreased from 57 percent at ages seven and eight to 34 percent at fifteen and sixteen. In the 1974 study there was a sharp decline in protecting animism, from 70 percent at age seven and eight to 18 percent at fifteen to sixteen. Curiously the 1986 replication found an increase in protecting animism between grades three and four (children nine to eleven years old), consistent with Godin and van Roey's study, but after that the decline was clear. These results tend to confirm Piaget's view of immanent justice declining with age. However, since the instruments were different, they may not have been measuring absolutely the same thing. In sum, Finnish children generally believe in the effects of prayer during the early school years, but belief decreases significantly in adolescence.

Many scholars describe *magical* components in the prayers of children, which relate to immanent justice. For example, Goldman (1964) distinguishes three phases in the fulfillment of prayer: the magical phase, up to about age nine, the *semimagical* phase between nine and twelve, and the *nonmagical/religious* phase after twelve. The concept of "magical" is defined quite broadly by Goldman, so that the polarities "magical" and "non-magical" generally correspond with the polarities "irrational" and "rational."

Clearly the issue of whether children's prayers are magical or not depends upon how "magical" is to be understood. I contend that petitionary prayer and/or belief in the effects of unseen forces do not necessarily reflect magical thinking. Rather, magical thinking is reflected by belief in immediate causal results of prayer. From my study of children's responses to the grandmother's recovery story (described earlier), from children's definitions of prayer and from their descriptions of personal answers to prayer, magical thinking (defined as belief in immediate causal effects of prayer) is rare at the age of nine or ten and afterward. On the other hand, evening prayers that make use of rigid verbal formulas, may include more magical traits.

THE CONCEPT OF THE BIBLE (TAMMINEN)

Goldman (1964) diagramed children's conceptualizations of the Bible as developing through various phases. In response to the question, "How did the Bible come to be written?" children up to age nine stated that it had a magical origin (God or some powerful or religious person wrote it). At about fourteen and a half the Bible is seen as multiple-authored from oral tradition or eyewitnesses, but specifics on how the Bible developed are unclear. After this phase young people tend to see the Bible as "inspired," which is considered of greater importance than factual accuracy. A somewhat similar progression is seen in response to queries regarding whether the Bible is true. Until about ten and a half children believe the Bible to be entirely literally true. Between ten and a half and twelve and a half the truth of the

Bible is affirmed on the basis of God's authority as the source, though not the writer, of the text. After about twelve and a half youngsters begin to question portions of the biblical account, judging the truth of Bible contents by other sources of information, inner experience, or belief that it is based upon eyewitness accounts.

In our study of Finnish children we found a number of divergencies from Goldman's research. Again, we must qualify this conclusion with the understanding that the methods and measures were not quite the same. We used Peatling's (1973) literalism scale from his *Thinking About the Bible* and our own *Veracity of the Bible*. Peatling's test provided three biblical stories (Moses and the Burning Bush, Crossing the Red Sea, and The Temptations in the Wilderness), the stories used by Goldman, each followed by the question, "Do you really think this happened?" The second instrument identified belief statements concerning the meaning of the Bible (Tamminen, 1991).

We found that about half of nine- and ten-year-olds understand biblical stories literally or nearly so, and the developmental progression is away from literal understanding. This continues in a linear manner until about fifteen to sixteen at which point only a few students interpret the Bible literally. These results roughly correspond with Peatling's (1973) research of North American, Episcopalian children.

Children's concepts of the Bible were also studied using a projective measure with photographs. In one of the pictures a girl is looking at the Bible with her younger sister. An open-ended story accompanies the photograph: "Helen was looking at the big family Bible. Her little sister asked 'What sort of book is it?' Helen said it was the Bible and continued, 'The Bible is...'" In another picture either a girl or boy is looking at the Bible. Accompanying this photograph is a story: "This is Mary (or Mark). She (he) is reading the Bible and wondering about something that has been on her (his) mind before. She (he) is thinking..."

In response to the projective photographs, younger children describe separate biblical events while older youngsters deal with whether the Bible is true or significant. Finnish children, from nine to ten years onward, do not attribute magical traits to the Bible (for example, believing it is a book "dropped from heaven"). This contrasts markedly with Goldman's findings with British children of the same age. This difference may, in part, be due to differences in religious instruction, as children in Finland study the nature of the Bible from various perspectives beginning in first grade.

DEATH AND AFTERLIFE (VIANELLO)

The question of how children understand death and life after death has intrigued researchers for many decades. Helpful surveys of the literature on the topic include Koocher (1973), White, Elsom, and Prawat (1978), Speece and Brent (1984), Friberg (1985), Ratcliff (1985), Stillion and Wass (1988), and Tamminen (1991).

The bellwether study in the area was that of Nagy (1948). Her study of Hungarian children shortly after World War II uncovered three stages in children's understanding of death. From three to five years youngsters have some realization of death being different from life, but generally they describe death as being like sleep. It is not until five or six years that death is seen as final and irreversible. Nagy found that children between five and eight personified death (an unusual anomaly in the research which has not been found in replications, probably a cultural artifact of the World War II era — see Friberg, 1985; Stillion & Wass, 1988). By age nine youngsters understand death to be universal and inescapable even for themselves. While more recent researchers have not always agreed with the timing and specific characteristics of Nagy's stages, some kind of developmental progression is generally proposed.

Ten years of research by the primary author, summarized in Vianello and Marin (1985 & 1989b) indicate that the understanding of death by children is more accelerated than normally suggested by other researchers. Even by the age of two or three, youngsters have some awareness of death, although with time that conceptualization becomes more organized. Surprise and pity are often expressed in response to the death of an animal or insect prior to age three. Our research indicates that they are able to differentiate death from sickness or sleep, describe death as being the opposite of life, recognize causes such as guns, knives, and accidents, and specify consequences such as the cessation of movement. They speak not only of animals dying but also adults and children.

By four or five most young children display an organized understanding of death that implies universality and irreversibility. After age five almost all see death as universal and irreversible, and they imply that vital functions cease. However their responses suggest that clever people may possibly avoid death. Death is understood to produce negative feelings in relatives and friends at this point.

Parents generally believe their children's concepts of death are less developed than what we found. Eighty percent state that no child less than five ever thinks about death and 50 percent say that their offspring have a very limited understanding of death until nine or ten years. The result of this misperception is that many parents fail to seriously consider the questions their youngsters ask and too often give undesirable responses.

Oddly enough parents and teachers who are not religious generally give children religious explanations for their questions about death. Adults who are religious often feel ill at ease with the topic of death and may give religious responses merely to postpone or avoid dealing with the issue. Children are left to ponder religious questions such as, "How can one be in heaven and the cemetery at the same time?" and "By what method does a person get to heaven?" without adequate explanations.

The belief that we go to heaven when we die probably allows children to face the issue of death with less anxiety, although religious instruction along this line may conflict with other understandings about death. For example, children may accept that the dead are placed into caskets and buried, but they also go to heaven. Likewise, although death is irreversible, the deceased are living again in heaven. In spite of the fact that death involves the cessation of vital functions, the deceased are believed to play games in heaven. The theological concept of "soul" may help resolve these contradictions, but at the age of five or six the idea of soul is likely to be concretized as being a material substance, a misconception that will require correction eventually. Many young children do not resolve the conflicting beliefs and simply accept them as one more mystery in an incomprehensible faith. This may produce a "fracture between the world and God," in which religion becomes compartmentalized from life. Yet children are strongly motivated to resolve this "fracture," as seen in the fact that belief in God guaranteeing immortality is the most frequent religious statement made spontaneously without being asked about anything religious.

Pagnin and Vianello (summarized in Vianello, 1980) surveyed 180 Italian children ages six to eleven about life after death. In general the children spontaneously spoke more about heaven than hell. When asked to complete a story about the death of a dishonest man, they still mentioned heaven more often than hell. From eight to nine years onward some children deny the existence of hell. Religious instruction affirming hell is disputed by some children, as God is perceived as a judge who rewards and forgives rather than one who punishes.

As seen in these studies, the problem of death is important to the assimilation of religious ideas by children. The understanding of death, and the emotions associated with death, affect religious conceptualizations in at least three ways: 1) God is increasingly dichotomized from the real world, 2) belief in heaven and God guaranteeing immortality are readily accepted by children, and 3) from the age of eight or nine children begin to doubt the existence of hell, which may be one of the first steps from a conformist religion to a more personal religious outlook.

DEATH AND LIFE AFTER DEATH (TAMMINEN)

Life questions of Finnish children and teenagers were considered as part of the eight projective photographs measure, described earlier. Only a part of the measure was used with seven- and eight-year-olds, while the entire measure was used with older children. Responses indicated that about 10-20 percent of youngsters at least once mentioned death or life after death. The number making such comments increases slightly by the time they reach eleven to fourteen. The topic of death interests younger children, but is of even greater interest to adolescents probably because it is related to identity (Tamminen, 1988).

The kinds of statements made about death varied considerably. These were researched in greater detail through the use of a photograph in which two children, a girl and a boy, were visiting a cemetery. With the picture was this text: "Elizabeth and Henry came to see the grave in which someone was buried the day before." The reactions of seven- and eight-year-olds emphasized concrete situations and events, while older children increasingly thought about death with less and less concrete conceptualizations. Reflection upon death in general and mortality increased with age.

Vianello states that his Italian children spontaneously speak more about heaven than hell. This was also found in our studies; only one-half of one percent speak about hell or the contrast between everlasting life and damnation. Apparently hell and damnation are not relevant to Finnish children, whereas many of the children spontaneously mention heaven at all grade levels. In the early school years children emphasize everlasting life, reflections upon what heaven will be like, and how one gets there. After eleven or twelve years questioning and doubts about heaven surface increasingly, although this change is quite gradual.

The concept of heaven was specifically surveyed through the open-ended statement, "I think that in heaven..." Responses tended to be very concrete, with most describing it as a good place, either with external descriptors such as "beautiful," "clean," "full of light" or more internal, feeling oriented terms such as "safe" or "no sorrow." In childhood particularly, but also extending into adolescence for many, heaven is placed somewhere up in the clouds or in outer space. Concrete, localized descriptions of heaven are quite common until the high school years. Such a concrete view of heaven makes it difficult for young people, and to some extent even children, to accommodate the concept of heaven to their view of the world.

EMERGENCE OF PERSONAL RELIGION (VIANELLO)

In late childhood the child begins to move away from a conformist religion and begins to doubt, as is seen in the questioning of hell's existence. The raising of doubts about religion is a predecessor to the development of "interiorization" between twelve and seventeen years of age (Deconchy, 1967). Research studies by McDowell (1952), Graebner (1960), and Goldman (1964) underscore the importance of a transition phase between twelve to fourteen when conformist assimilating of belief gives way to symbolic understanding and autonomous personalizing of religion. Vianello (1980), consistent with Castiglioni (1928), suggests that this transition is in part due to a "fracture" between the world of everyday experience and religion; they are considered two different realities.

The author and his associates (Vianello & Netti, 1984) undertook a study of this conformity/personalization transition in late childhood (or preadolescence) to determine how general personality traits at this age relate to the child's religion. We were particularly interested in how these help resolve the "fracture" between the everyday world and God.

Ninety-six Italian Catholics between twelve and fourteen years were given a Rorschach projective test and a Piagetian interview regarding several aspects of religiosity. Personality traits were chosen and scored according to techniques used by Dreger (1952, 1958), Klopfer (1968), Wurston (1970), and many others. Ten experts in developmental psychology rated the youngsters' responses about religious beliefs, with each protocol being evaluated by at least four judges. Personality traits and religious belief scores were then correlated (p <.01).

Among twelve-year-olds the personality trait "search for security" was significantly related to a number of religious components. These included magical thinking (r=.76), belief that religion improves human relationships (.64), affirming God as protector (.60) and judge (.57), belief that God helps resolve moral conflicts (.54), and a search for a personalized relationship with God (.49).

By age thirteen, young people are less likely to affirm magical thinking. A predominant personality trait linked with religion is "conformity." This trait correlates highly with accepting God as judge (.73), stating that God helps to resolve human conflicts (.60), and reporting a personalized relationship with God (.53). Interestingly, conformity is inversely related to the belief that religion enhances human relationships (-.52).

With fourteen-year-olds a critical attitude toward religion correlates with all five intellectual indexes considered. This suggests that they make use of increased intellectual reasoning abilities by being more critical of religion. This criticism of religion is also related to self-direction (.66), a close relationship with parents (.56), and social integration (.49). In other words, their criticism is not only the result of their own personal reflection but is also related to relationships with parents and society, as well as a sense of autonomy.

This research clearly indicates that late childhood is a period of transition in respect to religion. Religiosity reassures twelve-year-olds, indicated by the many positive correlations between religious beliefs and the search for security. By age fourteen, however, the understanding of religious concepts was more related to intellectual and affective autonomy; the critical attitude toward religion was related to both intellectual and social factors, while several aspects of intellectual development related strongly to the belief that religion enhances human relationships. Twelve-year-olds assimilate religious elements passively, not critically, while fourteen-year-olds are beginning to consider religion in a personalized, critical, and self-directed manner.

METHODOLOGICAL CONSIDERATIONS

A wide variety of research methods have been used in the study of children's religious concepts. The earliest studies involved adult recollections of childhood, but these are no longer considered to contribute to the serious study of child development because adults often reinterpret their early years in light of subsequent experiences.

As has been seen in this chapter, many other approaches have been used by researchers. These include pure observation, questionnaires, projective techniques, drawing pictures or responding to drawings, attitudinal scales, analysis of children's prayer, the Q-technique, Osgood's Semantic Differential Technique, the Piagetian interview, as well as essays and stories with completion and/or interpretation.

Piaget (1926) noted that it is important to distinguish several kinds of answers by children:

1. "Any old answer" — here the child is not genuinely interested in what is being asked and thus just gives any response that comes to him or her. The child is not trying to be imaginative or humorous but gives an answer at random or deliberately fabricates.

2. Fabulation — the child makes up a story or fable. This would include more imaginative responses, perhaps given out of boredom or desire to entertain, rather than reflection.

3. Prompted belief — the youngster attempts to answer a question but because the question is leading or because he or she is trying to satisfy the researcher the response reflects more what is expected than the child's own thinking.

4. Induced belief — the question is new for the child and he or she weighs the answer replying from genuine reflection and not from external prompting.

5. Spontaneous belief — the child does not need to reflect upon the question, probably because he or she has thought of the matter previously and thus has a ready response or can easily formulate one.

The first three should generally be ignored in serious research. They may have value in describing the creativity of the child, conducting a personality analysis, or analyzing unconscious influences, but even then a high degree of interpretation is required by the researcher, thus faulty conclusions are likely. Prompted beliefs are the most difficult of the three to identify. Piaget notes, "It requires long experience to be able to recognize and avoid the countless possible kinds of prompts. There are two forms which are particularly hazardous: prompts by means of words and prompts caused by persistence" (Piaget, 1926, p.17).

Induced beliefs can be very revealing, but the answer might have been different had the child considered the question on his or her own in a less structured situation. It is likely that children, like adults, come to better conclusions after they have thought on the matter for a while. Yet induced beliefs are likely to indicate the "cutting edge" of children's initial acquisitions of concepts in a given area.

Spontaneous beliefs are helpful but have the disadvantage that they may be verbalizations, rote recitations of what they have learned previously. Some children are quite adept at rephrasing and paraphrasing what they have heard so that they appear to understand a concept, yet with detailed probing they may be found to have not really comprehended the underlying idea.

Another issue we have considered earlier in this chapter is the possibility of dichotomizing conceptualizations. Religious thoughts need to be organically linked with ideas (and practices) in other domains, yet too often religion is assimilated apart from everyday life. If a concept is relegated to an obscure area (such as only thinking about religion in church on Sunday morning) and not infused within the rest of life and the rest of one's thinking, its importance is minimal. One measure of organicity and interrelatedness would be spontaneous religion in response to natural events (for example, thinking of God when seeing a beautiful landscape).

CONCLUSION AND APPLICATIONS

It should be noted that this chapter has considered only the highlights of detailed studies of religious concepts. A more complete analysis is possible by reading the authors' book-length reports. To date only one is available in English (Tamminen, 1991). This chapter has emphasized the research of leading researchers from two specific countries, but one must be careful not to quickly overgeneralize from one cultural, denominational, or church context to another. There is considerable continuity in how children's religious concepts develop from one context to another, but several distinctives have also been noted. As a result, the conclusions and applications offered are tentative rather than definitive.

The child's concepts of religion are an important clue to what should and should not be included in religious education at this age. Concepts that are likely to be distorted and misapprehended should, if possible, be withheld from the religious education curriculum until a more appropriate age. Quality religious education should aim for teaching concepts that will not have to be corrected at a later time, making use of a developmentally sensitive pedagogy applied at the optimum teachable moment.

For example Vianello's research would suggest that the concept of God as spirit is likely to be misunderstood by school-aged children. However it might be possible to teach precursors to that concept (see Torrance & Torrance, 1988). The Bible is an adult book and not all of it is appropriate for children. One might also question the use of excessively violent or sexually explicit content, overly complex or obscure material, or certain culturally bound material that is likely to overwhelm or confuse children.

To replace notions of immanent justice, the religious educator might consider teaching "autonomous justice." The latter affirms the possibility of achieving justice in an unjust world, underscoring the personal responsibility implicit in autonomy. Children need to learn that justice is not inherent but the result of conscious efforts through one's lifestyle and sacrificial response to needs. Religious educators can help accomplish this goal by encouraging children's involvement in social action. Children learn by doing, and mature concepts of justice are more likely when they *do* justice.

How can religious educators foster more mature concepts of prayer and death? Self-centered prayers require a nudging toward more advanced levels. Parents and teachers can do this by modeling others-centered praying and encouraging imitation. Likewise, more advanced understandings of death involve a recognition of the child's level of thinking and encouraging more mature understandings. Again, one must make the most of the teachable moment (such as discussing the topic of death after a television program that portrays death graphically).

The more passive receptivity of children twelve and under would suggest that this may be a time beneficial for substantive (though not formal and abstract) teaching. In contrast, the more critical nature of fourteen-year-olds would seem to call for more reflective and dialogical religious education during the teen years. Finally, the strong linkage between understandings of parents' and children's religious concepts underscores the weighty responsibility of parental example and the importance of high quality, family-based religious education.

This chapter has focused almost entirely on the intellectual comprehension of religious concepts. This is only one side of children's religion. It is also important that children enter (via imagination and feeling) into stories (see chapter two), as narrative theology and method emphasize.

REFERENCES

Arago-Mitjans, J. M. (1965). *Psicologia religiosa del nin.* Barcelona: Herder.

Barbey, L. (1947). *La notion de Dieu chez l'enfant.* Bruxelles: Lumen Vitae.

Barnes, E. (1892). Theological life of a California child. *Pedagogical Seminary, 2,* 442-448.

Basset, R. L., Miller, S., Anstey, K., Crafts, K., Harmon, J., Lee, Y., Parks, J., Robinson, M., Smid, H., Sternes, W., Stephens, C., Wheeler, B., &

Stevenson, D. (1990). Picturing God. *Journal of Psychology and Christianity, 9*, 73-81.

Bovet, P., 1961). *Le sentiment religieux et la psychologie de l'enfant.* Neuchatel-Paris: Delachaux et Niestle.

Braido, P., & Sarti, S. (1967). L'idea di Dio presso ragazzi Italiani della scuola dell'obbligo. *Orientamenti Pedagogici, 5*, 1128-1157.

Brown, A. W. (1892). Some records of the thoughts and reasonings of children. *Pedagogical Seminary, 2*, 358-396.

Caruso, I. (1943). *La notion de responsabilite et de justice immanente chez l'enfant.* Neuchatel: Delachaux et Niestle.

Castiglioni, (1928). Ricerche ed osservazioni sull'idea di Dio nel fanciullo. *Contribute del Laboratorio di Psicologia dell'Universita, III.* Milano, Vita e pensiero.

Clavier, H. (1926). *L'idee de Dieu chez l'enfant.* Paris: Fischbacher.

Coles, R. (1990). *The spiritual life of children.* Boston: Houghton Mifflin.

Deconchy, J. P. (1964). L'idee de Dieu entre 7 et 17 ans; base semantique et resonance psychologique. *Lumen Vitae, 19*, 277-290.

Deconchy, J. P. (1967). *Structure genetique de l'idee de Dieu chez des Catholiques Francais, garcons et filles, de 8 a 16 ans.* Bruxelles: Lumen Vitae.

Dreger, R. M. (1952). Some personality correlates of religious attitudes as determined by projective techniques. *Psychological Monographs, 3*, 1-18.

Dreger, R. M. (1958). Expressed attitudes and needs of religious persons compared with those determined by projective techniques. *Journal of General Psychology, 58*, 217-224.

Dumoulin, A., & Jaspard, J. M. (1973). *Les mediations religieuses dans l'univers de l'enfant.* Bruxelles: Lumen Vitae.

Elkind, D. (1971a). The development of religious understanding in children and adolescents. In M. Strommen (Ed.), *Research on religious development: A comprehensive handbook.* New York: Hawthorn.

Elkind, D. (1971b). What do you think? [Film]. ACI Productions, Geneva Press (United Presbyterian Church).

Elkind, D. (1978). *The child's reality: Three developmental themes.* New York: Erlbaum.

Fowler, J. (1981). *Stages of faith.* San Francisco: Harper & Row.

Friberg, N.C. (1985). A developmental approach to understanding death attitudes. In M. R. Leming & G. E. Dickinson (Eds.), *Understanding dying, death and bereavement.* New York: Holt, Rinehart and Winston.

Godin, A., & Hallez, M. (1974). Images parentales et paternite divine. *Lumen Vitae, 19*, 323-340.

Godin, A., & van Roey, B. (1959). Justice immanente et protection divine. *Lumen Vitae, 14*, 133-152.

Godin, A., & Marthe, S. (1960). Mentalite magique et vie sacramentelle chez des enfants de 8 a 14 ans. *Lumen Vitae, 15*, 268-288.

Goldman, R. (1964). *Religious thinking from childhood to adolescence.* New York: Seabury.

Graebner, O. E. (1960). *Child's concept of God.* River Forest, IL: Lutheran Education Association.

Gruehn, W. (1956). *Die Frommigkeit der Gegenwart.* Munster: Axendorf.

Haavisto, L. (1969). Lasten uskonnolliset kasitykset. *Tampereen yliopiston psykologian laitoksen tutkimuksia, 20/1969.* Institute of Psychology of the University of Tampere.

Havighurst, R., & Neugarten, B. (1955). *American Indian and white children.* Chicago: University of Chicago Press.

Horberg, U. (1967). *Barn och religion.* Unpublished manuscript, Institute of Psychology of the University of Uppsala.

Hyde, K. (1990). *Religion in childhood and adolescence.* Birmingham, AL: Religious Education Press.

Jahoda, G. (1958). Immanent justice among West African children. *Journal of Social Psychology, 47,* 241-248.

Jahoda, G. (1964). Magie, sorcellerie et developpement cultural (Ghana). *Lumen Vitae,* 19, 334-344.

Keskitalo, M. (1987). 4-6 vuotiaided uskonnollinen ajattelu ja jumalakuva. Unpublished Master of Theology thesis in Religious Education. The Library of the Faculty of Theology, Institute of Practical Theology, University of Helsinki.

Kjellgren, M. (1987). Om brans gudsbild. Unpublished manuscript, Institutionene for socalt arbete. Socialhogskolan. University of Stockholm.

Klopfer, W. G. (1968). The theoretical foundations of projective methods. *Rorschachiana, 9,* 20-25.

Koocher, G. (1973). Childhood, death and cognitive development. *Developmental Psychology, 9,* 369-375.

Loves, H. (1957). Ancestal beliefs and Christian catechesis. *Lumen Vitae, 12.*

Mailhiot, B. (1964). E Dio si fece fanciullo. Italian translation of A. Godin, (Ed.). *Adulte et enfant devant Dieu.* Bruxelles: Lumen Vitae.

McDowell, J. B. (1952). *The development of the idea of God in the Catholic child.* Washington, DC: The Catholic University of America Press.

Nagy, M. (1988). The child's view of death. *Journal of Genetic Psychology, 73,* 3-27.

Nelson, M. O., & Jones, E. M. (1957). An application of the Q-technique to the study of religious concepts. *Psychological Reports, 3,* 293-297.

Nye, C. W., & Carlson, J. S. (1984). The development of the concept of God in children. *The Journal of Genetic Psychology, 14,* 137-142.

Peatling, J. (1973). *The incidence of concrete and abstract religious thinking in the interpretation of three Bible stories.* Ph.D. dissertation, School of Education, New York University. Ann Arbor, MI: University Microfilms.

Piaget, J. (1926). *La representation du monde chez l'enfant.* Paris: Alcan.

Piaget, J. (1932). *Le judgement moral chez l'enfant.* Paris: Alcan.

Ratcliff, D. (1985). The development of children's religious concepts. *Journal of Psychology and Christianity, 4,* 35-43.

Sarti, S. (1968). L'idea di Dio presso ragazzi eritrei. *Orientamenti Pedagogici, 6,* 1305-1334.

Sarti, S. (1970). Modo di descrivere Dio da parte di ragazzi di diversa confessione religiosa. *Orientamenti Pedagogici, 1,* 102-119.

Siegmann, N. W. (1961). La notion de Dieuet l'image du pere. *Lumen Vitae, 16,* 289-292.

Speece, M. S., & Brent, S. B. (1984). Children's understanding of death. *Child Development, 55,* 1671-1686.

Stillion, J., & Wass, H. (1988). Children and death. In L. A. Platt & R. G. Branch (Eds.), *Resources for ministry in death and dying.* Nashville, TN: Broadman.

Strunk, O. (1959). Perceived relationship between parental and Deity concepts. *Psychological Newsletter, 10,* 222-226.

Tamminen, K. (1988). *Existential questions in early youth and adolescence.* Research Reports on Religious Education C5/1988. Institute of Practical Theology, University of Helsinki.

Tamminen, K. (1991). *Religious development in childhood and youth.* Helsinki: Finnish Academy of Science.

Terstenjak, A. (1955). *Psicologia e pedagogia nell'insegnamento religioso.* Milano: Vita e Pensiero.

Thun, T. (1959). *Die religion des Kindes.* Stuttgart: Verlag.

Tischler, H. (1990). *Introduction to sociology* (3d ed.). Fort Worth: Holt, Rinehart and Winston.

Torrance, E., & Torrance, J. (1988). Creativity and teaching concepts of God. In D. Ratcliff (Ed.), *Handbook of preschool religious education.* Birmingham, AL: Religious Education Press.

Vaatainen, R. L. (1974). 7 ja 8 vuotiaiden uskonnolliset kasitykset. *Uskonnonpedasgogiikan julkaisuja A, 10/1974.* Institute of Practical Theology, University of Helsinki.

van den Berghe, P. L. (1975). *Man in society.* New York: Elsevier.

Vergote, A. (1966). *Psychologie religieuse.* Bruxelles: Dessart.

Vergote, A. (1983). *Religion, fei, incroyance.* Bruxelles: Mardaga.

Vergote, A., & Aubert, C. (1972). Parental images and representations of God. *Social Compass, 19,* 431-444.

Vergote, A., Bonami, M., Custers, A., & Pittijn, M. R. (1967). Le simbole paternel et sa signification religieuse. *Archiv fur Religionspsychologie, 9,* 118-140.

Vergote, A., et al. [Tomajo, Pasquali, L., Bonami, M., Pittijn, M. R., & Custers, A.] (1969). The parental images and the concept of God. *Journal* for the Scientific Study of Religion, 8, 79-87.

Vianello, R., (1980). Ricerche psicologiche sulla religiosita infantile. Firenze: Giunti.

Vianello, R., Carraro, G. C., & Lis, A. (1978). L'immagine della divinita e l'assimilazione della nozioni religiose in bambini istituzionalizzati. Orientamenti Pedagogici, 4, 630-643.

Vianello, R., & Marin, M. L. (1985). La comprensione della morte nel bambino. Firenze: Giunti.

Vianello, R., & Marin, M. (1989a). Belief in a kind of justice immanent in things: A revision of the Piagetian hypothesis. Early Child Development and Care, 46, 57-61.

Vianello, R., & Marin, M. (1989b). Children's understanding of death. Early Child Development and Care, 46, 97-104.

Vianello, R., & Marin-Zanovello, M. L. (1980). Ricerca di sondaggio sull'atteggiamento magico infantile. Eta Evolutiva, 7, 24-39.

Vianello, R., Marin, M., & Bozzolo, L. (1979). La natura si allea ai genitori nel punire? Psicologia Contemporanea, 36.

Vianello, R., & Netti, L. (1984). Religious beliefs and traits of personality in the first adolescence. Paper presented at the 23rd International Congress of Psychology, Acapulco, Mexico, September 2-7, 1984, Abstract Vol. 192.

White, E., Elsom, B., & R. Prawat. (1978). Children's conceptions of death. Child Development, 49, 307-310.

Wurston, H. (1970). The relationship between Piaget's developmental theory and the Rorschach method. In B. Klopfer (Ed.), Developments in the Rorschach method. New York: Harcourt Brace Jovanovich.

Chapter Four

Moral and Affective
Dimensions of Childhood

JERRY ALDRIDGE AND JEAN BOX

How do children distinguish right from wrong and what influences their ability to make right choices? Children's religious education must provide support for children as they develop moral values, attitudes, and feelings. How children develop morally, affectively, and aesthetically will be the focus of this chapter. Individuals who work with elementary-level students in religious settings should be able to identify various developmental theories of moral development and examine how children acquire feelings, emotions, attitudes, and aesthetics.

THEORIES OF MORAL DEVELOPMENT

Moral development theories provide a description of how individuals learn right and wrong as well as what governs children's reasoning or decision making regarding moral questions. Five moral development models, including the cognitive-developmental theory, behavioral theory, cognitive learning theory, psychoanalytic theory, and humanistic theory, have impacted religious education. Each theory describes a particular model of how children develop into moral adults. Basic theoretical concepts, empirical support, strengths and weaknesses, and applications to religious education of children will be described for each theory.

Cognitive-Developmental Theory

Cognitive-developmental theories of moral development have been proposed by Piaget, Kohlberg, and Damon (Vander Zanden, 1989). These theories have two distinct features. First, they indicate that moral development takes place in stages with clear, distinct differences and changes between stages. A child's moral reasoning at one stage will be qualitatively different from his reasoning at a higher stage. A second feature is the emphasis on reasoning or thinking rather than on behavior. A child's behavior is not as indicative of moral level as the motive behind the behavior.

Piaget's Theory. Jean Piaget developed a two-stage theory of moral development based on children's responses to both stories with moral issues and reactions to rules used in playing games such as marbles (Massey, 1988). His stages are known as "heteronomous morality" in which the children depend on adults for rules, and "autonomous morality" where children develop mutual respect among peers. Table 1 shows the difference between heteronomous and autonomous morality.

Table 1
Piaget's Stages of Moral Development

HETERONOMOUS STAGE	AUTONOMOUS STAGE
Approximate Ages - Preschool through age 8	Approximate Ages - Eight years and up
Characteristics	Characteristics
1. Absolutism - Rules are unquestionable.	1. Relativism - The same rules may not always apply all of the time in all places.
2. Consequences of behavior are more important than intent.	2. Consequences are looked at more in terms of intent.
3. Rules cannot be changed.	3. Rules can be changed if everyone agrees.
4. Immanent justice prevails. Wrong-doers will be punished by God.	4. The beginnings of the idea that justice is not always equally administered to trangressors.

Kohlberg's Theory. Lawrence Kohlberg developed a cognitive-developmental theory of moral development by extending and refining Piaget's basic theory (Kohlberg, 1963, 1969, 1981, 1984). Kohlberg designed his theory by asking subjects questions about hypothetical dilemmas. Through analysis of responses, Kohlberg designed a three-level theory with two stages per level. Table 2 summarizes Kohlberg's levels and stages of moral development. Stages 1, 2, and 3 are most indicative of elementary school children's moral development. As children approach middle school, some reach the moral reasoning abilities of Stage 4.

Damon's Theory. William Damon (1977) took a different approach to posing moral questions. He believed that Kohlberg's moral dilemmas were too removed from the child's day-to-day experiences. Damon investigated children's moral decisions as they related to what he called distributive justice. Distributive justice refers to how children go about sharing things which

Table 2
Kohlberg's Stages of Moral Development*

LEVEL AND STAGE	CHARACTERISTICS
LEVEL I - Preconventional Morality	
Stage 1 - Fear of punishment orientation	Children are moral for fear of being punished.
Stage 2 - "What's in it for me?" orientation	Children are moral to get something
LEVEL II - Conventional Morality	
Stage 3 - Nice person orientation	Children are moral to get approval from others
Stage 4 - Rules orientation	Children blindly follow the rules
LEVEL III - Postconventional Morality	
Stage 5 - Human rights orientation	Individuals believe that sometimes laws must be broken to serve mankind
Stage 6 - Universal regard for mankind orientation	Individuals follow internal principles or standards. Respect for individuals is more important than set rules

*Most elementary children are in stages 1, 2, and 3

are scarce (Damon, 1983). He found an orderly sequence of levels in the development of this phenomenon. Damon's levels are shown in Table 3. By the time children reach elementary school, many are in Stage 3. As they approach middle childhood, they progress through Stages 4, 5, and 6.

Table 3
Damon's Progression of Distributive Justice

LEVEL	CHARACTERISTICS
1	Children state their choices in favor of themselves without an explanation.
2	Children state their choices in favor of themselves with the rationale "I would get more because I am bigger (or older, or smarter, etc.)."
3	Children state their choices based on fairness.
4	Children state their choices in terms of merit, such as "The ones who work harder should get more."
5	Children state their choices based on moral relativity. There is more of a benevolent outlook.
6	Children state their choices based on both equality and equity.

Much research has been completed on the cognitive-developmental theory of moral development, both by advocates and opponents. Clouse (1985) reports:

> Advocates, having accepted the basic assumptions of cognitivism, opt for methodological changes or call for a more careful analysis of how a person moves from one stage of moral judgment to the next. Opponents, questioning the very foundation of a morality based on reasoning, prefer a behavioral or affective approach to a study of morality, or they object to the nonrelative stance of the cognitive theorist that says that higher stages are more moral than lower stages (p.119).

Carol Gilligan (1982) has been highly critical of Kohlberg's stages because much of his research was composed of male samples. Her research suggests that males and females have a different orientation to morality. Males are apparently more socialized toward justice while females experience a morality of care.

Some analyses of cognitive-developmental theory are concerned with reasoning versus behavior. Proponents of the theory teach that thinking is directly related to moral judgment; cognitive and moral development have a strong positive correlation. The reasoning behind the actions is seen in how children construct morality. Yet critics suggest that behavior is a valuable part of moral judgment, and those opposed to developmental theory may see behavior as the determinant of morality (Skinner, 1978).

Cognitive-developmental theory can be applied to the religious education of children through "teaching of children in the church school or Sunday school" (Clouse, 1985, p.147), and through appropriate interactions of adults with children when children spontaneously face moral situations (Kamii, 1984). Bible stories can provide an important source for moral issues. Teachers can present the lesson in such a way that children can interact and discuss what they would have done in the situation. Using this approach the teacher would accept each child's opinion and ask questions which pose modern-day application of the story. However, it is very important that the concepts and discussion be at an appropriate level. Children construct values from within; morals cannot be poured into children's heads by well-meaning teachers.

Appropriate interactions between adults and children are important in cognitive-developmental theory. Interactions should be based on mutual respect, not rewards and punishments. This is a most important consideration in helping children develop into morally autonomous adults. Kamii (1984) reports: "Adults reinforce children's natural heteronomy when they give rewards and punishments, and they stimulate the development of autonomy when they evaluate points of view with children" (p.411). When adults use punishment, three results might occur. First, the child might calculate the risk of getting caught again. Second, the child might revolt or lash back. Finally, the child might blindly conform and not question the rules. All of these tend to result in heteronomous morality.

How, then, do children develop autonomous morality if not through rewards and punishment? Cognitive-developmental theorists make a distinction between punishment and sanctions by reciprocity. Adults help children develop autonomously by using sanctions by reciprocity. Piaget described six sanctions, four of which relate primarily to elementary school children. These four may be used in religious education settings to encourage moral autonomy.

1) *Restitution.* When a child makes an error, he must make good his mistake. For instance, if a child spills paint, restitution is achieved by the child cleaning up the spill. However, some moral problems cannot be solved through restitution and another form of reciprocity must be applied.

2) *Calling the child's attention to the consequences of his behavior.* During the early development of autonomous morality, this strategy is often effective. For example, if a child is destroying crayons, the teacher might say, "When you have damaged all of the colors, we will have no more to use."

3) *Depriving the child of what he has misused.* If a child continues to destroy the crayons, then this sanction can be applied. The child is simply not allowed to use something he has abused.

4) *Exclusion from the group.* This sanction can be administered when a child is intentionally disturbing the group. He is asked to leave the group and return whenever he believes he can participate.

Sanctions by reciprocity differ from punishment in that the consequences are directly related to the decisions the child is currently making. Further, the child is an active participant in making right what he has wronged. Piaget found that children develop autonomous morality when attention is directed at actions and consequences and when the child actively participates in reciprocity (Ginsberg & Opper, 1979).

Behavioral Theory

Learning theorists or behaviorists see morality as being synonymous with moral actions (Llewellyn, 1973). The environment plays the major role in the development of children's morality. Children are born neither good nor bad according to this theory; it is the environment that makes the difference. "Morality and immorality are learned behaviors" (Clouse, 1985, p. 24). Some learning theorists believe that morality can be learned through operant conditioning in which reinforcers and punishment are often effective (Skinner, 1938).

Limited research has been conducted on behavioral theory and moral development (Bufford, 1978; Captain, 1975; Edgerton, 1975; Eysenck,

1960). Much of the research has focused on other issues such as positive reinforcement to increase church attendance, Bible reading, or bus ministries (Clouse, 1985). Empirical support for moral development is limited to measurable and observable behavior.

There are certain strengths and weaknesses inherent in behavioral theory when applied to children's ministries. Learning theory can be effective in increasing church attendance, in learning Bible verses, and increasing many desired types of behavior through the use of a reinforcement system. As with cognitive-developmental theory, the strengths of the theory may also be the weaknesses. Reinforcers often have little relationship with what is being taught in church. If we provide children with rewards for learning Bible verses we may be diminishing intrinsic reward and motivation for learning. Extreme critics of behaviorism see rewards as bribery and believe behavioral techniques actually deter children from developing the morality desired.

Behavioral theory can be applied to children's ministry through two important techniques. These include behavior modification and programed learning (Hergenhahn, 1982). In its simplest form, behavior modification involves systematically rewarding those behaviors we want children to acquire. For example, children exhibit more sharing and cooperative behaviors when they are positively reinforced for such actions. Programed learning is useful in helping children remember facts. This type of learning involves presenting children a stimulus through small frames in workbooks or computer formats. Children select a response and receive immediate feedback on whether they selected the correct answer. Programed learning has greater application in teaching children religious facts while behavior modification may be more applicable to moral issues.

Cognitive Learning Theory

Some children acquire moral values through observational learning or imitation (Bandura, 1965). While cognitive learning theory is an outgrowth of behaviorism, it differs from traditional learning theories by emphasizing the importance of social learning. Some behaviors are learned through observing others rather than as a direct result of rewards or punishment (Vander Zanden, 1989). The basic tenet of this theory is that children learn moral behavior by watching others and copying their actions.

Walters, Leat, and Mezei (1963) studied social learning in which one group of boys watched a movie of a child who was punished by his mother for playing with toys which were off limits. A second group watched a boy being rewarded for playing with forbidden toys, and a third group (the control group) did not see a movie. After the movie, each boy was taken to another room and told not to play with the toys in the room. The boys who had watched the child being rewarded were more likely to play with the toys. Other studies reveal that dishonest models have a bigger impact on children than honest ones (Ross, 1971; Stein, 1967).

Strengths and weaknesses of this model involve the availability and influence of good Christian models. As children move from ages six through twelve, adult models become less and less important and the effect of peers becomes more critical in observational learning. Children who learn by cognitive learning theory principles will do best with the example of strong moral adults and as they reach middle school by positive peer example. This may, of course, be a weakness if poor adult and peer models are imitated.

The immediate implications for children's religious education are the presence of moral adult models, particularly during the early elementary years. What adults do in moral dilemmas as well as in everyday situations speaks louder than what adults say. If children are told that reading the Bible every day is important but adults do not read the Bible daily, the model provided is what is copied rather than what is said (Aldridge, 1989). Children are most likely to model people they like or admire. For this reason, the models children are provided in religious settings are of utmost importance.

Psychoanalytic Theory

The psychoanalytic theory of Freud was the first psychological theory of moral development (Vander Zanden, 1989). Unlike cognitive-developmental, behavioral, and cognitive learning approaches, the psychoanalytic model takes a negative view of humankind. Children develop moral behavior out of a fear of losing parental love and internalize their parents' standards in order to deal with anxiety and guilt. The optimal time for this development occurs between the ages of two and six and moral development is based on a context of defense and conflict (Clouse, 1985). During this time, aggressive impulses are turned inward and guilt results. Thus, Freud believed that moral development was basically determined before the elementary school years.

Moral development is related to defense mechanisms. Defense mechanisms are used by everyone to deal with reality when it becomes too painful. These mechanisms are not pathological in and of themselves, but they become a problem if an individual uses them to distort reality. Repression, regression, sublimation, projection, and introjection are all examples of defense mechanisms. Children often use defense mechanisms when confronted with moral dilemmas.

There is little empirical evidence for the psychoanalytic theory of moral development. Most of Freud's research was conducted on adults in therapy, not children. Further, Freud based his theory on the importance of the unconscious. The unconscious is very difficult to research and many conclusions about the unconscious are considered speculative. Most of the ideas of psychoanalytic theory are not applicable to moral development, but the fact that children internalize their parents' standards is still an important focus for current research (Hall, 1979).

Strengths of the psychoanalytic viewpoint include the concept of defense mechanisms. For instance, projection can be used by children to attribute to others those areas which are not liked about the self. A child who is obese might choose to call attention to children who are more obese than himself or herself. An understanding of defense mechanisms can help religious educators be aware of defensiveness in their children. Another strength of this approach lies in the importance of the parents; Freud underscored the importance of adults in early moral development.

Weaknesses of this approach involve research problems and an overemphasis on emotions in moral development. Psychoanalytic thought is the most difficult of the theories mentioned to support through research. The experimental method is not an acceptable tool for use with psychoanalysis based on Freud's thought. Another weakness of the model is the pessimism generated by an emphasis on emotions without much focus on cognition. According to Freud, children are driven by emotions and drives and, unlike the cognitive-developmental theory, he does not attribute great value to a child's thinking in the acquisition of morals. The result is a theory with a fatalistic viewpoint (Clouse, 1985).

Moral development based on the psychoanalytic framework is difficult to apply in children's ministry. While children's workers must deal with many issues and problems, they are not usually trained in psychotherapy. Many of Freud's methods are reserved for individual therapy with a psychoanalyst interpreting dreams and probing the unconscious. Such methods are inappropriate for traditional children's religious education. Further, some of Freud's ideas are in conflict with the church. Freud made it known that he was not a Christian and "saw religious worship as a compulsive act engaged in to relieve one's feelings of guilt" (Clouse, 1985, p.280).

Humanistic Theory

Humanistic psychologists support the idea that humans are born with the potential to develop into moral beings and the environment may enhance or impede moral development. Humanism is based on the premise that individuals are basically good and capable of determining their own development (Rogers, 1964). Maslow (1970) believed that there is a hierarchy of needs and the adult's role is to meet the basic needs of children so that they can become all they can be.

Much of the research conducted on humanism has been done in counseling with adults and is anecdotal or testimonial in nature with little empirical research evidence (Morain, 1980). Humanistic studies are also difficult to identify in the literature because there are at least three separate meanings for humanism. The term has been used to mean a liberal arts curriculum at universities, a type of psychotherapy, and the integration and development of the whole person (Clouse, 1985). Not only is humanism defined in several ways but as a theory of moral development it also has a limited research base.

One obvious strength of humanism is a belief in the potential of individuals. Since the orientation is that people are good, it follows that they are capable of developing moral choices. Humanism and children's religious education, however, are difficult to combine because morality is not relative and individual in the Christian perspective. Another weakness in applying humanistic moral education to elementary students is the negative connotation humanism has received. The issue of what some religious groups refer to as "secular humanism" is as heated as such topics as abortion and evolution (although a strong case can be made for "Christian humanism" — see Hitchcock, 1982).

Humanists believe that children need to explore their own individual talents and the church is an appropriate place for children to discover their God-given abilities and learn to make wise choices concerning them. This may require a somewhat less structured approach than would be recommended by behavioral theory. Children need opportunities to explore and share their development, which should be a key concern in religious education endeavors.

General Implications of Moral Theories

The five theories of moral development are different, each with strengths and weaknesses and applications to the religious education of children. No one theory of development can suffice in religious education to help children develop into moral beings. Complete acceptance of all theoretical concepts would also be inappropriate since views of one theory are opposed to views from another. However, ten guidelines can be distilled for the religious education of children based on theoretical perspectives, empirical research, and the Christian perspective.

1) *Teach moral values based on biblical principles.* While a common adage, "Morals are caught and not taught" may have merit, the direct teaching of moral values based on the Bible is necessary (Boyer, 1989; Christenson, 1981; Dirks, 1989; Joy, 1983). Dirks (1989) found that parental teaching through induction is an effective approach for teaching moral values. This approach can be used in church and other religious education settings as well. The method

> involves discussion of behavior expectations which have their roots in scripture, explaining reasons for standards, discussing how these relate to God's commandments, talking about internal dimensions such as attitudes related to the conduct standards, and asking questions of the child which encourage reflective thinking (p.85).

2) *Model Christian values and morals.* Teaching moral values has a minimal effect unless Christian values are lived. The contribution of cognitive learning theory to religious education has already been discussed. Children imitate those they admire. Teachers, parents, ministers, and children's workers impact moral values through their moral examples. Children are less likely to model those who are unimportant to them and unfortunately poor models are often imitated more than positive examples (Bandura, 1965).

3) *Pose moral issues based on both real life experiences and biblical examples.* Religious educators can pose dilemmas which actually happen to children as problem-solving situations. The sharing of various viewpoints helps children reflect on their own moral reasoning and decision making. Church school or Sunday school is the appropriate place to pose moral questions based on the Bible as are more informal religious education settings. Moses, Noah, Daniel, Zaccheus, Paul, Timothy, and numerous other biblical characters and events contain moral problems for children to discuss.

4) *Use rewards sparingly, if at all.* If rewards are used, make the rewards directly related to the situation. Some theorists believe rewards actually hinder moral autonomy (Kamii, 1984) while others find them necessary for moral development (Skinner, 1938). An acceptable recommendation is to make rewards relevant. For instance, if rewards are given for daily Bible reading, a Bible or devotional booklet could be the reward. Reinforcements such as stars, candy, or other unrelated rewards can give the message that Bible reading is a chore so it must be rewarded. Use rewards as a feedback device, not as a means of control (Bolt & Myers, 1984).

5) *Help children with restitution.* Occasional transgressions are inevitable even in religious settings. Supportive help in making amends is necessary to help children develop moral autonomy (Ginsberg & Opper, 1979).

6) *Accept children as they are and avoid making value judgments about them.* When children respond inappropriately, teachers can accept the students and then focus on the action. This is often accomplished by asking a child, "What did you do?" rather than "Why did you do that?" The first question focuses on the act. The second question implies there is something wrong with the child. Children can reflect on their own actions without feeling threatened when adults ask questions related to actions rather than motives (Aldridge, 1989).

7) *Balance acceptance with expectations.* Children who are accepted without any expectations are not challenged to examine moral issues. Conveying, "I expect much but I accept you as God does—just as you are" helps promote moral development (Clouse, 1985).

8) *Avoid inappropriate comparative and competitive practices.* Because children may be on different moral levels, comparison may be harmful. This is particularly true of comparing siblings or males with females. As Gilligan (1982) has pointed out, boys and girls may have a different moral orientation.

Similarly, strong competition can discourage those on lower moral levels from developing prosocial behavior (Canfield & Wells, 1976).

9) *Give reasonable responsibility.* Moral dilemmas often arise based on responsibilities. Providing children with chores or duties provides a natural environment for moral issues to develop (Aldridge, 1989).

10) *Examine current classroom practices.* Manning and Manning (1981) report that schools are now assaulting children through certain classroom practices such as excessive drill, worksheets, long periods of sitting and listening, and fragmentation. The shift in emphasis to constructive interactions can change this by focusing on moral problems through induction and discussion rather than some of the mindless activities now employed.

AFFECTIVE DEVELOPMENT

Affective development has two broad meanings. First, affective development refers to prosocial and altruistic behaviors as well as emotions, feelings, and attitudes. This side of affective development focuses on who children are. The other side of affective development is the aesthetic side developed through art, music, dance, or other creative media. This side refers to ways children develop their affect.

Affective Development—Who Children Are
Prosocial Development. Closely related to moral development is the acquisition of prosocial behaviors and altruism. Prosocial behavior is defined as the way children respond to others through helpful, comforting, sympathetic, and giving qualities. Prosocial and helping acts are different from altruism which refers to helping others without any expectation of reciprocity or reward.

Researchers using cognitive-developmental and psychoanalytic views report that children's understanding of another person's viewpoint and becoming altruistic do not usually develop significantly before the age of six. The elementary years are extremely important and critical in the development of both prosocial and altruistic behaviors (Vander Zanden, 1989).

Studies on prosocial behavior are quite extensive. Midlarsky and Hannah (1985) found that children are not likely to help others if they fear disapproval of others for such actions. Elementary children are equally likely to give help when others are around and when they are alone. This is in direct contrast to younger children who help more when others are around and adults who offer assistance more often when they are alone (Staub, 1970).

The relationship between adult and child has a significant influence on prosocial behavior. Bryan and Crockenberg (1980) report that children who come from loving and affectionate environments are more likely to help others.

Children learn prosocial behaviors in some of the same ways they develop morally. Some studies show that reinforcing prosocial behavior is important (Rushton, 1976; Staub, 1978), while other studies indicate that modeling plays a significant role in caring (Midlarsky, Bryan, & Brickman, 1973).

Altruism and prosocial development are also related to the child's general role-taking abilities (Damon, 1983). Selman (1976) developed a stage theory of role-taking levels from children's responses to stories. Between the ages of six and twelve, children pass through three stages of role taking. Early elementary students are usually in Stage 1 (ages 6 to 8) which is social-informational role taking. At this level, children know that others have a viewpoint different from their own, but they are not capable of coordinating several different views at once. By eight to ten years of age, children reach the self-reflective role-taking level (Stage 2) in which they can coordinate several perspectives but cannot "abstract from this process to the level of simultaneous mutuality" (Damon, 1983, p.125). Upper elementary children (ages 10 to 12) often reach Stage 3 which is mutual role taking. Children can now see a situation from a third person's perspective.

Religious educators can benefit from understanding that there are different levels of role-taking. Younger elementary children cannot be expected to see all sides of an issue while upper elementary students usually can. How we present Bible stories, moral dilemmas, and recreational activities should, therefore, reflect this difference between early childhood and upper-elementary pupils.

Emotions. Emotions are an important part of affective development. Emotions consist of feelings "accompanied by internal body reactions in the brain, nervous system, and internal organs—and observable expressions, especially those of the face" (McGee & Wilson, 1984, p.221). Emotions are often affected by temperament, age, sex, events, and status. Many different types of emotions exist. Watson (1931) believed that children are born with rage, love, and fear, but others insist that children are only born with the emotion of excitement (McClinton & Meier, 1978).

The development of fear provides a good example of how emotions are influenced by temperament, age, sex, events, and status. The development of fear is related to temperament, as introverts tend to be more fearful than extroverts (Keirsey & Bates, 1984). Some fears are also developmental or age-related. As children grow, their fears change. Kindergarten students are more likely to be afraid of animals, monsters, ghosts, and how someone looks than older elementary children (Bauer, 1976). However, second graders are more likely to be afraid of frightening dreams while sixth graders are more afraid of bodily injury. As children get older they are more afraid of what someone can do to them instead of how people look (Papalia & Olds, 1982).

Some fears are sex-related. Girls are socialized to be more dependent and are often more fearful than boys during middle childhood (Croake, 1973).

Some fears are event-related. Children who have lived through a tornado or hurricane are more likely to fear such events than those who have not. Children are also more likely to fear what their parents fear. This is especially true concerning fears of animals, insects, and weather (Hagman, 1932).

Finally, fears are status-related. Children from lower socio-economic homes report more fearfulness than children from more comfortable circumstances (Jersild & Holmes, 1935; Papalia & Olds, 1982). Poorer children often live in neighborhoods where more frightening events are likely to occur.

Religious educators sometimes have to deal with children's fears. Unfortunately, fears are sometimes caused by church-related events such as sermons that are misinterpreted by children or poorly represented by the minister (Dobbins, 1975). When this occurs, there are several ways in which fears can be addressed, some of which are not very helpful. Rationalizing and appealing to the children's intellect are rarely effective, while supportive listening, problem solving, and modeling are more likely to help (Papalia & Olds, 1982).

Attitudes. An attitude is defined as a predisposition to feel, think, and act in a particular way (McGee & Wilson, 1984; Oskamp, 1977). Attitudes have three major components. These include 1) emotions or feelings, 2) thoughts, and 3) behavior (McGee & Wilson, 1984). Usually a child's emotions and thoughts correspond to behavior, but not always. Sometimes when an attitude is weak, there is a discrepancy between feelings and behavior. Attitudes are more difficult to change than knowledge. Attitudes are learned through classical conditioning (Staats, 1968), operant conditioning (Insko & Melson, 1969), modeling (Baron & Byrne, 1981), and persuasion (Maddux & Rogers, 1980).

Children develop attitudes through classical conditioning by associating negative words with certain concepts. For example, while children are originally neutral about race, parents may make racist statements about a group of people. The child begins to associate the negative words with a minority group over time. Approval of friends may serve as a social reward for certain attitudes which are learned through operant conditioning. Many attitudes are learned by observing others or modeling.

Children often learn attitudes through persuasion. The effectiveness of persuasion is dependent upon the source, the message, and the audience (McGee & Wilson, 1984). Children are more likely to be persuaded when the source is credible to them. For example, children are more likely to believe the influence of drugs is disastrous from someone who has been a drug abuser and reports negative effects than from parents or teachers. The message is also important in persuasion. Children are more likely to believe a one-sided message when they already favor the opinion presented. If children have a negative attitude toward the opinion desired, a two-sided approach is better (Baron & Byrne, 1982). The audience is also important in attitudinal change. As children get older they are more influenced by their peers. This means that attitudinal change of an elementary-age audience is more likely if peer group leaders change first.

Attitudes toward Sunday school have been researched by Cook (1989). Using a semantic differential test, he developed an instrument to measure children's attitudes toward Sunday school. His findings indicate that "children in grades 3-6 have an idea that Sunday school is important. However, their evaluation of their experience in Sunday school is well below the ideal" (p.112). Children apparently do not receive all they expect in Sunday school. Might this also be true of more informal religious education as well?

Affect and Cognition. Prosocial behavior, altruism, emotions, attitudes, and affect do not develop in a vacuum. There is a strong relationship between affect and cognition (Piaget, 1981). Piaget believed that affect was the fuel that fed cognition. While affect was the source of energy, it was still the function of cognition to selectively attend to affective contents. The development of affect, then, is partially a function of cognition and intelligence.

Cognitive abilities influence affective expression. Gardner (1983) proposed a theory of multiple intelligences. Some intelligences are affective in nature, he suggested. Types of intelligence include linguistic, logical-mathematical, spatial, musical, kinesthetic, interpersonal, and intrapersonal.

What do cognition and theories of intelligence have to do with affective development in children's religious education? Each child has a specific gift or talent which needs some type of expression. Religious educators can help children find their gift(s) and then assist children in finding ways of using their talents in the religious education context (see Myers & Jeeves, 1988).

AFFECTIVE DEVELOPMENT—HOW CHILDREN EXPRESS IT

The church is an important place for children's affective development to be expressed through the performing and creative arts. Schickendanz, York, Stewart, and White (1983) have identified several valuable aspects of aesthetic education. These include enjoyment of the performing arts, reduction of tension, providing a means of self-expression, and developing an appreciation of one's cultural or religious heritage.

Aesthetic development is two-way—both receptive and expressive. Religious educators can provide opportunities for both. The following suggestions are made for enhancing aesthetic development of elementary children in church and other religious education settings.

1) *Help children develop an appreciation for sacred music.* This can be

accomplished through attending music concerts or through researching the background of hymns. Several sources exist which provide the history of hymns, including who wrote them and why they were written. An appreciation for diversity in style might be included.

2) *Look for individual musical talents and circumstances in which to express them.* Traditionally, children's music is accompanied by the piano in many denominations. There are other instrumental talents which can be used for accompaniment or solo performance. Having children present their musical talents not only increases aesthetic appreciation but also enhances self-esteem (Aldridge, 1988).

3) *Introduce examples of religious art forms.* Much of the Bible has been expressed through art. Some of the examples can be introduced while studying the Bible. Art serves to increase awareness of biblical concepts portrayed and encourages self-expression of Christian values. The variety of art forms through the ages may be used to teach various perspectives dominant in the church in different eras.

4) *Provide multiple media for children to express their own artistic talents.* Croft (1990) identified many materials needed for activity oriented expression. She suggested that children be encouraged to use art, music, drama, movement, and other modalities to express themselves aesthetically. Many of these media can be obtained at minimal cost for craft activities or free expression.

5) *Look for nontraditional aesthetic abilities.* Talents exist in the performing and creative arts but also in other areas of affective development. Dance, puppetry, gymnastics, and woodworking can all be used for self-expression (Croft, 1990) and can be readily adapted in religious education.

6) *Help children experience biblical content which illustrates various feelings.* One of the first picture book awards was given for *Animals of the Bible* by Dorothy Lathrop (Cullinan, 1989), which portrayed animals as they appeared in Bible stories. In addition, poetry, children stories, and novels have been produced that underscore the affect within a religious context (e.g., the *Chronicles of Narnia* by C. S. Lewis)

7) *Allow children to make their own written contributions.* Writing is often a source of aesthetic experience. All children profit from the experience of writing down their feelings and thoughts (Aldridge & Cowles, 1990), including those about religion.

Every child has something to write. "Whole language" activities encourage students to express themselves affectively through their writing (Aldridge & Rust, 1987). Two whole language activities which develop self-expression include "key words" and "the writing process." Key words can be adapted in religious settings for younger elementary children while the writing process may be used with older pupils.

The Key Words Approach. The key vocabulary approach to writing is made up of children's own words instead of a predetermined set of curriculum words. Children come to the religious education setting with rich experiences and vocabularies, and using their own words gives them an affective outlet. With this approach, the teacher has students individually name a word. As a child says his or her word, the teacher writes it on an index card. The child reads the word as the teacher writes it down. Then, the child is sent to do something with his word. He may want to write it on a chalkboard or draw a picture about his word (Veatch, Sawicki, Elliott, Barnett, & Blakey, 1979).

This approach can be adapted for religious education by having children select their own words about feelings, stories, or themes which are currently being studied. This creates a sense of significance because the child learns that he has something to say and that his ideas are respected by the teacher. The Bible might then become a resource from which to find similar ideas and feelings (Goldman, 1965).

The Writing Process. Older children can express themselves through the writing process (Graves, 1983). This method relies on a five-step procedure which includes rehearsing (brainstorming), drafting, revising, editing, and publishing. This technique helps children find and express their true thoughts and feelings. Calkins (1990) found that teachers can better reach children if they ask questions about the children's writing and then dwell on what is significant for each child.

The Importance of Moral and Affective Development

Children develop morality through observing others and through constructing values from within. The importance of adult models cannot be overemphasized. Parents and teachers are initial models for younger children while peers take their place to some extent with older children. Adults can provide a safe, positive environment in which children are free to explore and question ideas. Sometimes sanctions are needed to enhance moral development. These sanctions should be directly related to the children's transgressions.

Prosocial behaviors, emotions, and attitudes develop over time. In the process children need aesthetic examples and opportunities to bring forth their own affective potentialities. Religious education curriculum should provide a balance between cognitive learning and affective opportunities. Children's ministers and teachers have an important challenge to seek out the individuality of every child and then help find ways that abilities and affective talents can be expressed.

REFERENCES

Aldridge, J. (1988). How to build self-esteem in children. *Exploring for Leaders, 18,* 4-5.

Aldridge, J. (1989). Helping children build self-esteem. *Day Care and Early Education, 17*, 4-7.

Aldridge, J., & Cowles, M. (1990). The development of significance in students through the acceptance of personality, cognitive, and language differences. *Education, 110*, 323-325.

Aldridge, J., & Rust, D. (1987). Young children teach themselves to read and write. *Day Care and Early Education, 15*, 29-31.

Bandura, A. (1965). Influence of model's reinforcement contingencies on the acquisition of imitative responses. *Journal of Personality and Social Psychology, 1*, 589-595.

Baron, R., & Byrne, D. (1981). *Social psychology: Understanding human interaction* (3rd ed.). Boston: Allyn and Bacon.

Bauer, D. (1976). An exploratory study of developmental changes in children's fears. *Journal of Child Psychology and Psychiatry, 17*, 69-74.

Bolt, M., & Myers, D. (1984). *The human connection.* Downers Grove, IL: Intervarsity.

Boyer, E. (1989). The third wave of school reform. *Christianity Today*, (September 22), 16-19.

Bryant, B., & Crockenberg, S. (1980). Correlates and dimensions of prosocial behavior: A study of female siblings with their mothers. *Child Development, 51*, 529-544.

Bufford, R. (1978). God and behavior mod II: Some reflections on Vos' response. *Journal of Psychology and Theology, 6*, 215-218.

Calkins, L. (1990, August). *These are tough times for children and teachers.* Paper presented at the Virginia Horns-Marsh Lecture, Birmingham, AL.

Canfield, J., & Wells, H. (1976). *100 ways to enhance self-concept in the classroom.* Englewood Cliffs, NJ: Prentice-Hall.

Captain, P. (1975). The effect of positive reinforcement on comprehension, attitudes, and rate of Bible reading in adolescents. *Journal of Psychology and Theology, 3*, 49-55.

Christenson, R. (1981). Clarifying 'values clarification' for the innocent. *Christianity Today*, (April 10), 36-39.

Clouse, B. (1985). *Moral development: Perspectives in psychology and Christian belief.* Grand Rapids, MI: Baker Books.

Cook, S. (1989). An instrument to measure attitude toward Sunday school. *Christian Education Journal, 10*, 105-113.

Croake, J. (1973). The changing nature of children's fears. *Child Study Journal, 3*, 91-105.

Croft, D. (1990). *An activities handbook for teachers of young children.* Boston: Houghton Mifflin.

Cullinan, B. (1989). *Literature and the child.* San Diego: Harcourt Brace Jovanovich.

Damon, W. (1977). *The social world of the child.* San Francisco: Jossey-Bass.

Damon, W. (1983). *Social and personality development.* New York: Norton.

Dirks, D. (1989). Moral maturity and Christian parenting. *Christian Education Journal, 9,* 83-93.

Dobbins, R. (1976). Too much too soon? *Christianity Today,* (October 24) 99-100.

Edgerton, M. (1975). Sunday school uses bus fleet and candy to win kids' souls. *The Wall Street Journal,* (November 3) 1, 24.

Eysenck, H. (1960). The development of moral values in children: The contribution of learning theory. *British Journal of Educational Psychology, 30,* 11-21.

Gardner, H. (1983). *Frames of mind: The theory of multiple intelligences.* New York: Basic Books.

Gilligan, C. (1982). Why should a woman be more like a man? *Psychology Today, 16,* 68-77.

Ginsburg, H., & Opper, S. (1979). *Piaget's theory of intellectual development.* Englewood Cliffs, NJ: Prentice-Hall.

Goldman, R. (1965). *Readiness for religion.* New York: Seabury.

Graves, D. (1983). *Writing: Teachers and children at work.* Portsmouth, NH: Heinemann Educational Books.

Hagman, R. (1932). A study of fears of children of preschool age. *Journal of Experimental Education, 1,* 110-130.

Hall, C. (1979). *A primer of Freudian psychology.* New York: Penguin Books.

Hergenhahn, B. (1982). *An introduction to theories of learning.* Englewood Cliffs, NJ: Prentice-Hall.

Hitchcock, J. (1982). *What is secular humanism?* Ann Arbor, MI: Servant.

Insko, C., & Melson, W. (1969). Verbal reinforcement of attitude in laboratory and nonlaboratory contexts. *Journal of Personality, 37,* 25-40.

Jersild, A., & Holmes, F. (1935). Children's fears. *Child Development Monographs, 6,* 20.

Joy, D. (1983). Kohlberg revisited: A supra-naturalist speaks his mind. In D. M. Joy (Ed.), *Moral development foundations.* Nashville, TN: Abingdon.

Kamii, C. (1984). Autonomy: The aim of education envisioned by Piaget. *Phi Delta Kappan,* (February), 410-415.

Keirsey, D., & Bates, M. (1984). *Please understand me: Character and temperament types.* Del Mar, CA: Prometheus Nemesis.

Kohlberg, L. (1963). The development of children's orientations toward a moral order. I: Sequence in the development of human thought. *Vita Humana, 6,* 11-33.

Kohlberg, L. (1969). Stage and sequence: The cognitive-developmental approach to socialization. In D. A. Goslin (Ed.). *Handbook of socialization theory and research.* Chicago: Rand McNally.

Kohlberg, L. (1981). *Essays on moral development: Vol. 1, The philosophy of moral development.* San Francisco: Harper & Row.

Kohlberg, L. (1984). *Essays on moral development: Vol. 2, The psychology of moral development.* San Francisco: Harper & Row.

Llewellyn, R. (1973). A second look at B. F. Skinner. *Journal of Psychology and Theology, 1,* 3-7.

Maddux, J., & Rogers, R. (1980). Effects of source expertness, physical attractiveness, and supporting arguments on persuasion: A case of brains over beauty. *Journal of Personality and Social Psychology, 89,* 235-244.

Manning, M., & Manning, G. (1981). The school's assault on childhood. *Childhood Education, 57,* 84-87.

Maslow, A. (1970). *Motivation and personality.* New York: Harper & Row.

Massey, C. (1988). Preschool moral development. In D. Ratcliff (Ed.), *Handbook of preschool religious education.* Birmingham, AL: Religious Education Press.

McClinton, B., & Meier, B. (1978). *Beginnings: Psychology of early childhood.* St. Louis: Mosby.

McGee, M., & Wilson, D. (1984). *Psychology: Science and application.* St. Paul, MN: West Publishing.

Midlarsky, E., Bryan, J., & Brickman, P. (1973). Aversive approval: Interactive effects of modeling and reinforcement on altruistic behavior. *Child Development, 44,* 321-328.

Midlarsky, E., & Hannah, M. (1985). Competence, reticence, and helping by children and adolescents. *Developmental Psychology, 21,* 534-541.

Morain, L. (1980). Humanist manifesto II: A time for reconsideration? *The Humanist, 40,* 4-10.

Myers, D., & Jeeves, M. (1988). *Psychology through eyes of faith.* San Francisco: Harper & Row.

Oskamp, S. (1977). *Attitudes and opinions.* Englewood Cliffs, NJ: Prentice-Hall.

Papalia, D., & Olds, S. (1982). *A child's world: Infancy through adolescence.* New York: McGraw-Hill.

Piaget, J. (1981). *Intelligence and affectivity: Their relationship during child development.* Palo Alto, CA: Annual Reviews Inc.

Rogers, C. (1964). Toward a modern approach to value: The valuing process in the mature person. *Journal of Abnormal and Social Psychology, 68,* 160-167.

Ross, S. (1971). A test of the generality of the effects of deviant preschool models. *Developmental Psychology, 4,* 262-267.

Rushton, J. (1976). Socialization and the altruistic behavior of children. *Psychological Bulletin, 83,* 898-913.

Schickendanz, J., York, M., Stewart, I., & White, D. (1983). *Strategies for teaching young children.* Englewood Cliffs, NJ: Prentice-Hall.

Selman, R. (1976). Social-cognitive understanding. In T. Lickona (Ed.),

Moral development and behavior: Theory, research, and social issues.
New York: Holt, Rinehart and Winston.

Skinner, B. (1938). *The behavior of organisms: An experimental analysis.*
New York: Appleton-Century-Crofts.

Skinner, B. (1978). *Reflections on behaviorism and society.* Englewood-
Cliffs, NJ: Prentice-Hall.

Staats, A. (1968). Social behaviorism and human motivation: Principles of
the attitude-reinforcer-discriminative system. In A. G. Greenwald, T. C.
Brock, & T. M. Ostrom (Eds.). *Psychological foundations of attitudes.* New
York: Academic Press.

Staub, E. (1970). A child in distress: The influences of age and number of wit-
nesses on children's attempts to help. *Journal of Personality and Social
Psychology, 14,* 130-140.

Staub, E. (1978). *Positive social behavior and morality: Social and personal influences* (Vol. 1). New York: Academic Press.

Stein, A. (1967). Imitation of resistance to temptation. *Child Development,
38,* 157-169.

Vander Zanden, J. (1989). *Human development.* New York: Random House.

Veatch, J., Sawicki, F., Elliott, G., Barnette, E., & Blakey, J. (1979). *Key
words to reading: The language experience approach begins.* Columbus,
OH: Merrill.

Walters, R., Leat, M., & Mezei, L. (1963). Inhibition and disinhibition of
responses through empathetic learning. *Canadian Journal of Psychology,
17,* 235-243.

Watson, J. (1931). *Behaviorism.* London: Routledge and Kegan Paul.

Chapter Five

Lifestyle Content and the Family

BLAKE J. NEFF AND JUDITH W. SEAVER

Responding to parental frustration at the antics of a seven-year-old, a friend advised, "Do you know what is wrong with that child? He's disgustingly normal." Often parents are not satisfied with the normal developmental level of children. We really do not know what to expect in response to our plea to "act your age." "To rear children properly we must have a clear concept of the nature of childhood. We must know how our children see their world. We must recognize their wants, their goals, their needs, and their fears" (Narramore, 1972).

Who are the children in middle childhood? What are the demographic characteristics of their families? How do children ages six to twelve spend their time? Several trends in middle childhood bear careful examination.

DEMOGRAPHIC TRENDS

Recent national surveys and census data provide a basis for constructing a working profile of children ages six to twelve years (U.S. Government, 1989). For example, the United States is an aging society. The percentage of individuals under eighteen years has dropped from 36 percent in 1960 to a projected 26 percent in 1990. While there were 64.3 million children in the United States in 1990, the six- to eleven-year-old age group represents only 9 percent of the total population. Yet this age group constitutes one-third of all children.

Zill and Rogers (1988), examining the relative ratios of children to adults, report a "youth dependency ratio" per 100 persons of 60.6 in 1970 which

102

dropped to 42.6 in 1986. Fewer children means more adults are available for positive child-adult interactions and children potentially being considered more precious. Conversely, it may mean less attention, or even a benign inattention, as adults are otherwise focused on their own age-specific needs and not directly involved in child rearing tasks.

Health. While children are a relatively small segment of the total population, their health status has generally improved. Several national indicators point to progress in this area, with the middle childhood years being the healthiest age range overall. For those born in 1985, the average life expectancy is 74.7 years. Life expectancy has continued to increase steadily since the 1970s.

During the twenty-six year period from 1960 to 1986, death rates for children ages five to fourteen plummeted by an astounding 44 percent. Accidents, including those involving motor vehicles continue to account for about half of the deaths in this age group.

Minorities. Projections are that the proportion of minority children in the total child population will continue to grow in the next two decades. One out of three children will likely be from a racial or ethnic minority by the year 2010. These figures are even more significant to the ministry of the church when it is recognized that black and Hispanic children are two to three times more likely to live in poverty than white children.

The Family Structure. The number of households in the United States containing children under eighteen years of age has dropped. In 1987, 65 percent of the households were not directly involved with children on a daily basis.

Family sizes and number of siblings have changed greatly in the last three decades as well. Since 1960 the number of families with one or two children has increased from 36 percent to 40 percent, while families with three or more children have dropped from 21 percent to 10 percent. Today about 46 percent of children under eighteen live in metropolitan suburbs, 30 percent live in central cities, and 23 percent live in rural areas.

Parents. Parental characteristics and related family socio-economic variables add a significant dimension to the lives of children. Several trends in parent and family data have captured widespread attention and aroused considerable concern. These statistics highlight the trends (Zill & Rogers, 1988; U. S. Government, 1989; Schickedanz, Hansen, & Forsyth, 1990):

80 percent of elementary school children have parents who completed at least twelve years of schooling.

73 percent of all children live in two parent households; about 25 percent live in single parent families.

80 percent of the children ages six to fourteen years have mothers in the work force.

80 percent of all children born in 1980 are projected to experience a period of disruption by divorce, death, or other means in their family.

Particularly noteworthy is the statistic related to employment of mothers outside the home. While the 80 percent includes part-time and seasonally employed mothers, changes in maternal employment statistics have none the less prompted extensive research on the impact upon children's lives brought about by the absence of mothers from the home. Some researchers hold that changes in family situations due to maternal work will result in reductions in family-child relationships. Zill and Peterson (1981) point out that this position cannot account for interactive, synergistic adjustments to maternal employment. Other researchers who have considered only quantitative data with regard to maternal employment, find varying results (see Hoffman & Nye, 1974; Hayes & Kamerman, 1983).

The rising divorce rate also has implications for the middle childhood years. Approximately 2 percent of all children each year experience the divorce of parents. Hofferth (1985) projects that 70 percent of white and 94 percent of black children born in 1980 will spend some time before they reach eighteen in families with only one parent. Of these, white children spend 25 percent and black children 44 percent of their entire childhood years with one parent. A historical perspective cautions against an automatic conclusion of family pathology from such statistics (Aries, 1962; deMause, 1974).

All of this data indicates that there remain a great number of complex causal issues to unravel (Maccoby, 1984). "What the trend data seem to show is that the family is changing" (Zill & Rogers, 1988, p.99).

School. School provides children with the opportunity to acquire skills and knowledge. School also serves a variety of social functions which are less obvious. For example it 1) provides care while parents work or pursue their own interests, 2) delays entrance into the work force, 3) fosters social competencies, and 4) maintains or hinders social role-selection processes (Goodland, 1973).

While virtually all children ages six to twelve are in school, a growing number are receiving their education at home. "The home-spun school has become the fastest developing educational movement in America—now perhaps exceeding a quarter of a million students" (Moore & Moore, 1982, p. 9).

The National Assessment of Educational Progress samples of children nine, thirteen, and seventeen years old indicate modest gains in basic skill achievement for math and reading through 1984. However, declines have been detected for higher level skills (Zill & Rogers, 1988).

In analysis of children's school-related behaviors, Zill and Peterson (1982) report an increase in teachers' and parents' reporting of disruptive behaviors and discipline problems. Further, they state that parents' rank ordering of the important characteristics for children have changed from an emphasis on achievement to an emphasis on relationships:

1963 Ranking		1976 Ranking
1	obedient, minds well	6
2	helpful, cooperative	1
3	good student	15
11	affectionate, loving	2
8	considerate, thoughtful	3

"The segregation of children ages six to twelve in elementary schools provides a distinctive basis for the social definition of children and a social structure that constrains and channels development during this period" (Collins, 1984, p.2). Beyond academic measures we have little knowledge of the social impact of school and the varying response patterns of children from different socio-economic backgrounds (Epps & Smith, 1984).

Life Outside School. Maccoby (1984) hypothesizes a movement from parental regulation to co-regulation (shared between parent and child) to self-regulation by the child. Before or after-school day care for children reveals this transition. Six- to ten-year-old children are more likely to be supervised, while those who are eleven to twelve years old are more likely to be co-regulated or self-regulated.

The term "latchkey children" was coined to describe children leaving from or returning to empty houses after school. Census data from 1984 denote 2.4 percent of six-year-olds and 11.1 percent of twelve-year-olds as latchkey children. Since the validity of such parental self reports seems suspect, it is significant that the School Age Child Care Project (1982) reported a figure of 28 percent being latchkey school-age children.

The Children's Time Study (Medrich et al., 1982) was designed to explore the activities, social interactions, and time use patterns of children's lives outside school hours. The sample was drawn on the basis of geographic elementary school districts in California and included 764 sixth graders and their parents. Of the children in the sample 79 percent participated in some form of organized activity outside school at some time during the week. These activities included lessons, sports, fine arts, music, and church. About 21 percent of the children reported participation in a church activity which was not a regular church service (Rubin, 1983). There appeared to be no significant differences in children's participation rates by gender, family income level, or degree of mother's occupational involvement.

Zill and Peterson (1981) collected average parental estimates of time spent on a usual weekday for selected activities. Included in their results were the following:

Activity	Minutes
Watching television	126
Playing with friends	93
Talking or doing things with parents	69
Doing homework for school	46
Reading books, comics, or magazines	37
Playing alone	35
Working or doing chores	30

Zill and Peterson note that other studies have reported a much higher figure for television viewing time for this age group (see Comstock et al., 1978; Medrich et al., 1982). One possible explanation suggested for the discrepancy could be the difference between total time television is on in the home and the actual viewing time for children.

Collins (1984) describes time use findings for children's activities outside school from the 1981 data of the Panel Study of Time Use in American Households, conducted by the Institute for Social Research. Children spent about 60 percent of their time in necessary daily activities, leaving about sixty-seven hours per week for discretionary activities. Television viewing and time spent alone or with peers dominated these hours.

Electronic Media. For several decades, of all the activities of middle childhood, television viewing probably has prompted the most attention among concerned adults. Numerous studies have explored and detailed the potential impact of television watching on children's well-being. Time spent watching television is time not spent on other activities. This "opportunity cost" may be the least researched aspect of television (Zill & Peterson, 1981).

Other studies which investigate the impact of television on children include Hayes and Kamerman (1983) who discovered no correlation between the absence of the mother from the home and television viewing time for children.

Neither has it been conclusively found that television viewing creates poor students. Television viewing has not been found to be consistently related to any achievement indices or school variables. Several studies indicate that no reliable evidence suggests that television viewing interferes with reading capabilities (Epps & Smith, 1984; Messaris & Hornik, 1983). Other studies seem to point toward an inverse correlation between television viewing time and academic accomplishment (Neuman & Prowda, 1981).

There are, however, indications that television is associated with aggression, particularly with boys (Stein & Friedrich, 1975). Roberts (1985) concluded that the increased aggression may be a result of television fostering misconceptions about social reality. This is further substantiated by the fact that, with age, viewing preferences shift from children's programs to action oriented adventure dramas (Collins, 1984). O'Brien (1987) studied one aspect of the influence of television on perception of social reality. He discovered that television usually depicts Christians as women who are around fifty years of age, who generally are minor characters in the plot.

Warren (1988) observes that stories fashion the affections of children. The traditions of many religious groups are embodied and perpetuated in stories from the history and memories of the community. Postman (1987) traces the changes in religious storytelling. Children once learned their community's stories through oral discourse, but with the proliferation of print media, children needed language skills to participate in the group's written story traditions. Children had to go to school in order to become literate and acquire the necessary symbol systems to participate in the story life of their communities. Electronic media have again drastically altered cultural communication mechanisms. Now, as in the days of oral tradition, no special training period is required to have full access to the stories of the culture. Television's visual images and sound capacities allow all ages immediate and simultaneous access to stories. Who decides which stories will be told? Who decides or controls the social "realities" presented in these electronic stories? As Warren (1988, p.371) states, "The importance of who is telling the stories cannot be overstated." The electronic communication culture threatens to overwhelm schools and religious groups. Competition for access and selection of story content are critical issues.

The basic interests of the media are commercial. Newcomb (1990) states that, "spending on and by kids four to twelve years old jumped an estimated 25 percent last year, to $60 billion. This year the kiddie market is expected to hit $75 billion, approaching 2 percent of the entire U.S. economy" (Newcomb, 1990, p.126). Advertisers, media companies, toy manufacturers, and publishers have gotten the message. The results are:

Saturday morning television advertising is expected to top $50 million annually.

Many top movies are child oriented, such as "Batman" and "Indiana Jones and the Last Crusade."

Television's big hit is "The Simpson's," with Bart Simpson, a licensor's dream for commercial product tie-ins.

Music companies are promoting a rash of new performers, such as "Raffi" and "New Kids On The Block," with special appeal for the middle childhood age group.

Nintendo games capture the largest portion of the recreation dollar for children under twelve.

Barbie dolls and accessory sales continue to surge for girls ages nine to twelve.

There are now designer lines of clothing for the four- to twelve-year-old market.

Fast food chains target children in advertising because often they make the decision about where to eat.

Publishers report that book sales for children's books are booming.

Greeting cards are now available to help parents maintain "contact" with their children.

Statistics and studies on television and its impact on children have largely ignored the growing presence in homes and the culture of other types of electronic media. The findings of television research appears almost time-warped, as the range of electronic media has grown to include VCR's playing movie and music videos, public video arcades, video games such as Nintendo, and personal computers with computer games and other programs. Nielson estimates that over two-thirds of all television households have a VCR. In short, the term "television" no longer captures the range of electronic media available to children.

A summary of the demographic data and lifestyle of middle childhood casts serious doubt on the assumption that parents are the primary transmitters of socio-cultural influences (Maccoby, 1984; Zill & Rogers, 1988). Yet, in spite of these changes the family retains responsibility for the dissemination of its religious faith to the next generation. The key to success lies not in a return of socio-cultural factors to a day gone by (Balswick & Balswick, 1989), but in the retention of the principle known as lifestyle content.

LIFESTYLE CONTENT

From a Nazi prison Dietrich Bonhoeffer wrote a sermon for his niece's upcoming wedding. In the sermon he declares, "Marriage is more than your love for each other. It has a higher dignity and power, for it is God's holy ordinance, through which he wills to perpetuate the human race till the end of time. In your love you see only your two selves in the world, but in marriage you are a link in the chain of the generations, which God causes to come and to pass away to his glory, and calls into his kingdom. In your love you see only the heaven of your happiness, but in marriage you are placed at a post of responsibility toward the world and mankind" (Bonhoeffer, 1967, p.27).

Obviously Bonhoeffer intended to communicate to his niece that the family system exists for a purpose far larger than the simple preservation of itself. The system has impact on the generations and upon the whole world. Such a concept appears at the root of several scriptural commands concerning the home and family. Among them:

> And these words which I command thee this day, shall be in thy heart. And thou shalt teach them diligently to thy children, and shall talk of them when thou sittest in thine house, and when thou walkest by the way, and when thou liest down, and when thou risest up (Deuteronomy 6:6).

> Gather the people together, men, and women, and children, and the stranger that is within thy gates, that they may hear, and that they may learn, and fear the Lord your God, and observe to do all the words of this law. And that their children which have not known anything, may hear, and learn to fear the Lord your God, as long as ye live in the land whither ye go over Jordon to possess it (Deuteronomy 31:12).

> Give ear, O my people, to my law. Incline your ears to the words of my mouth. I will open my mouth in a parable. I will utter dark sayings of old, which we have heard and known, and our fathers have told us. We will not hide them from their children shewing to the generation to come the praises of the Lord, and his strength, and his wonderful works which he hath done. For he established a testimony in Jacob and appointed a law in Israel, which he commanded our fathers that they should make them known to their children, that the generation to come might know them, even the children which should be born; who should arise and declare them to their children that they might set their hope in God, and not forget the works of God, but keep his commandments (Psalm 78:1).

The importance of the family in the perpetuation of the Judeo-Christian faith may be summarized by the term "lifestyle content." James Michael Lee in *The Content of Religious Instruction* identifies lifestyle content as simply, "the overall pattern of a person's activities" (Lee, 1985, p.608). He declares that, "lifestyle is what a person really is" (p.629). Arguably, what one really is becomes transmitted to the next generation through the systemic family structure.

Lifestyle content is a holistic, integrated concept that transcends the parameters of any particular or single descriptive variable (Lee, 1985). Lifestyle content is an amalgam of the strands of theoretical and conceptual work in the social sciences. Data for analysis of lifestyle content is most likely to come from the ecological and demographic research traditions. Yet there is other support for the concept of the lifestyle of the family being significant in the religious education of the next generation. Lee (1982) notes that non-Christian religions also regard the lifestyle as important and utilize the lifestyle of the family in the perpetuation of faith. He notes, "Indeed, lifestyle is probably the most ecumenical feature of religion since each and every universal religion, regardless of its beliefs, places lifestyle at the center of its system" (Lee, 1985, p.631).

The practice of Jesus seems to support the lifestyle content approach to teaching the concepts of the faith. Repeatedly, Jesus walked with his disciples and used day-to-day, real-life examples to point out the principles he wished to incorporate into their system of thinking.

While there appears to be no experimental research directly related to lifestyle content, theoretical constructs in the social sciences, supported by experimental research, contribute to our understanding of lifestyle content. These theoretical foundations of lifestyle content fall into four general categories.

Attribution Theory. Attribution theory maintains that people need to explain what happens to them by attributing events to causes. Those experiences which challenge the system of meaning previously held are most likely to require a cause. Recent research has sought to combine the study of religion with attribution (Kelly & Michela, 1980; Spilka, Hood, & Gorsuch, 1985).

Some studies indicate that the tendency to attribute certain phenomena to God may be a result of previous religious training. For example, Slocumb (1981) discovered that students who were more religious in their orientation were more likely to attribute causality to the supernatural. Less religious students, on the other hand, sought physical explanations for the same events. Similarly, Gorsuch and Smith (1983) demonstrated that evangelical undergraduate students attributed events to God, rather than chance, more frequently than those with other belief systems. God is seen as responsible for sanctioning events, such students indicate (Smith & Gorsuch, 1989). Likewise, those with health problems have been shown to attribute causality to God in different ways. Some see God as punishing sin, others perceive God as responding in anger, and still others as charitable in the midst of the circumstances (Pargament & Hahn, 1986).

All of these studies and others similar to them suggest that lifestyle has a tremendous impact on religious belief through the process of attribution. One implication that can be drawn is that children are developing an attribution lexicon throughout the developmental years as a result of participation in the family system.

Cognitive Dissonance. A forerunner of attribution theory is cognitive dissonance theory. Originally developed by Leon Festinger (1957), the theory has been expanded and reviewed by a number of scholars (Brehm & Cohen, 1962; Zajonc, 1960; Brown, 1962).

The theory suggests that a cognitive element such as an attitude or opinion will have one of three relationships with other cognitive elements. They may be irrelevant, having little or nothing to do with one another. They may be consonant, which implies that there is a degree of consistency between them. Finally, the pair might be dissonant, meaning that there is inconsistency.

The theory argues that an individual's psychological system attempts to reduce tension or stress by eliminating dissonance. The greater the dissonance, the greater the need to eliminate the cognitive elements which are incompatible.

For example a child who is taught in Sunday school that Christians do not steal but then recognizes that Daddy brings home employer-purchased office supplies is likely to experience dissonance. Since he or she cannot accommodate both the elements in a personal belief system without dissonance, one or the other must be rejected; either stealing is acceptable, or Daddy is not a Christian.

Lifestyle content becomes even more important in light of recent studies which suggest that the child in this example will likely adopt the home environment example rather than formal and abstract teaching in Sunday school. This conclusion stems from more than just the assumption of love for Daddy. People tend to accept the nonverbal example rather than the verbal message. That is, "actions speak louder than words."

Mehrabian (1981) reported that when the verbal and nonverbal messages did not agree, respondents chose to believe the nonverbal message 93 percent of the time, and relied on the spoken word only 7 percent. Birdwhistell (1979) and Thompson (1972) found slightly different percentages but agree that the message delivered nonverbally will find far more receptive audiences than the verbal messages. Intuitively, one might argue that when children's greater receptivity is considered the findings of these scholars becomes even more dramatic.

Environmental Settings Theories. The concept of lifestyle content is rooted in the fundamental debate over the relative contributions of heredity and environment to intelligence. The question of environmental importance requires a definition of environment as well as quantitative analysis. Exactly what is it that constitutes environment? Is it the physical characteristics of settings, the dimensional aspects of relationships, the idiosyncrasies of individual perception, or the blending of these into a systemic whole?

Early work by Barker and Wright (1954) introduced an innovative ecological study of children's behavior within the context of setting. Wright (1967) defined behavior settings as those settings which 1) were a stable part of the physical and social milieu of a community, and 2) had an attached standing pattern of human behavior.

Barker's (1968) description of the methodology of recording streams of behavior within their environmental contexts confirms the idea of standing patterns of behavior being associated with settings. It also establishes a systematic basis for understanding the unique aspects of an individual's behavior within the setting. Bronfenbrenner's (1979) work on the ecology of human development helps delineate the connecting links between children's behavior and their environmental contexts.

The "ecocultural niche," an extension of the notion of environmental setting, was derived from cross-cultural comparative research. Weisner (1984) lists three dimensions as powerful ecocultural determinants: 1) family composition and personnel, 2) goals and tasks which give reason and meaning to children's behavior, and 3) plans, schema, and cultural scripts which give intentional cues and purposes for behavior. "The ecocultural niche describes the socio-cultural environment surrounding the child and his family.... Its most important elements are the relationships between participants in organized behavior settings or activity units" (p.336).

General Systems Theory. General systems theory was first articulated in the 1920s by Ludwig von Bertalanffy who explained it this way, "It seems legitimate to ask for a theory, not of systems of a more or less special kind, but of universal principles applying to systems in general" (Bertalanffy, 1968, p.32). Hence the term "general" systems theory, and the opportunity to apply the theory to the lifestyle content of the family.

While Bertalanffy's purpose included integrating across disciplines, the theory is defined in a slightly different way today. A system is said to be "an organized set of interrelated and interacting parts that attempts to maintain its own balance amid the influences from its surrounding environment" (Tubbs, 1988, p.13).

Seiler, attempting to apply the theory to organizational structure, notes that this theory provides a way to describe the complex interrelationship of forces (Seiler, 1967). The same might be said of the theory as applied to the family.

While little has been written which applies the theory directly to the family, a growing body of primary literature does indeed explore the field of human communication in general from the systemic viewpoint (Thayer, 1968; Watzlawick, Beavin, & Jackson, 1967; Ruben & Kim, 1975; Tubbs, 1988).

One of the very important qualities of systems is that of hierarchy. Every system consists of a number of subsystems. As a result, the system is a series of ever increasing complexities. A simple diagram serves to demonstrate (Kreps, 1990, p.97):

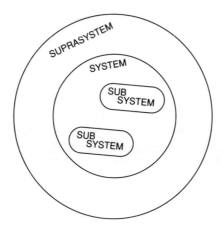

The fact that only three levels appear on the diagram does not mean that only three exist in a particular system. In fact, "Any of the system levels can be viewed as either subsystem, system, or suprasystem building macroscopically to larger and larger levels of organization or dissecting microscopically to smaller and smaller units of organization" (Kreps, 1990, p.97).

For example, the subsystem that was in the six- to twelve-year-old age group twenty years ago, has matured to become the parents of today. Similarly, those in middle childhood today will soon need the skills necessary to disseminate the faith to yet another generation. The lifestyle they are learning will determine to a large extent the nature of that faith.

Another axiom of systems theory as it has been applied to human communication supports most carefully the concept of lifestyle content. That principle, articulated by Watzlawick, Beavin, and Jackson, is "one cannot not communicate" (1967, p.51). The truth of the axiom is obvious. While one may refuse to speak, lack of verbalization itself communicates. Silence may say, "I'm angry," "I don't trust you," "I have nothing to say," or "I need to cool off." At any rate it does communicate. To exist as a human being is to communicate according to the principle.

This axiom compels parents and religious educators alike to examine their lifestyles. We must ask, "What am I communicating about the faith?" and "How can my lifestyle more effectively relate my intended message?"

APPLICATIONS

As the religious educator develops his or her middle childhood program, certain parameters of that program will emerge in response to the demographics of middle childhood and the compelling mandate of religious lifestyle content for the family.

The Wholeness Parameter. Children are a subsystem of the family. In addition, the church may act as a subsystem of the same family. For this reason the middle childhood program will impact the entire family, while the general program of the church will have impact on children. This interaction underscores the need for a holistic approach to children's ministry. While specialized programs are in order, and often appropriate, churches that do not offer such programs may still have much to offer children through the general ministry of the church (Westerhoff, 1976).

One religious educator who frequently is called upon to conduct seminars in a variety of churches made it a policy not to accept an invitation unless every session was designed for the entire family. His rationale, that the church is for the entire family, not just the adults, typifies wholeness.

Incorporating children's liturgy into the morning worship service is another way to unify faith and family. Many churches already benefit from the inclusion of a children's sermon, children's choir, or reciting of scripture learned in Sunday school. These elements of worship must be thoroughly integrated into the worship service and not just add-ons to amuse the kids or their parents if the church is to take holism seriously. This also is true for religious education efforts outside the church.

The Equifinality Parameter. The term "equifinality" often is associated with systems theory approaches to the study of human behavior to indicate that in a given system there is more than one way to arrive at the same end. The successful religious educator will recognize that nowhere is that truth more evident than in the family of the 1990s. While the complexion of the family is changing, and the demographics of middle childhood are radically different from the previous generation, the mandate is still to inculcate faith to the next generation. Religious education efforts must recognize the responsibility of assisting families in discovering new ways to respond to that mandate.

One impact of the changing socio-cultural trends is the necessity of helping families understand the importance of lifestyle content. "What do we want to communicate about our faith to the next generation?" is an important question to explore with families. Simply raising consciousness about the importance of family ministry may serve a beneficial purpose in many homes, since one outgrowth of the trends is that families often acquiesce to their reduced role in child development. A review of the scriptural mandate for Judeo-Christian families may stimulate new resolve. Further, we must remain flexible enough to consider innovative approaches in activating families.

For example, one religious educator noted that families under her care were responding to the increased role of television in the home in two ways. One group seemed to say, "There is nothing we can do about the impact of television. Let them watch what they will." Another group in the same congregation took the opposite position. They argued, "There is nothing good about television. We will not have it in our homes." In an attempt to minister within the parameter of equifinality a "television monitoring corps" was established. The corps monitored prime time programing for violence, language, and sexually explicit behavior. One key to the success of this program lay in the fact that no external standard was accepted, thus the people within the church were forced to examine the norms of acceptability for their own homes. Equifinality often requires creative synergistic approaches to family issues.

The Consistency Parameter. A final parameter to the programing of the religious educator is that of consistency. The presentation of faith must coincide with what children observe. Christian educators will want to examine the liturgy, teaching material, and overall impact of the program alongside the lifestyle of the families in the congregation in an attempt to eliminate potential dissonance from inconsistencies.

In the process of such an evaluation it will be necessary to objectively examine the lifestyle of the families of the church. The religious lifestyle of people can never be assumed. A particular family may have long been in the congregation, yet their lifestyle may challenge the teaching of the church in many respects. After careful observation, the religious educator will want to tailor the program, liturgy, and general ministry of the church to accommodate realistic expectations for the lifestyle of families and the doctrinal traditions of the church.

"Fashions may come and go. Cultures and civilizations may change. The dwelling of man may alter from a sod shack on the prairie to a ranch house in suburbia, but the family remains. Parents and children together form a corporate life of their own, unique and abiding" (Werner, 1958). The content of that family lifestyle for generations to come is dependent upon today's families and the religious educators who support them. Those programs built within the parameters of wholeness, equifinality, and consistency will most effectively build the family of the future with the faith of the ages.

REFERENCES

Aries, P. (1962). *Centuries of childhood: A social history of family life*. New York: Vintage.

Balswick, J., & Balswick, J. (1989). *The family*. Grand Rapids, MI: Baker.

Barker, R.G., & Wright, H.F. (1954). *Midwest and its children: The psychological ecology of an American town*. Evanston, IL: Row and Peterson.

Barker, R.G. (1968). *Ecological psychology*. Stanford: Stanford University Press.

Bertalanffy, L. (1968). *General systems theory: Foundations, development, applications*. New York: Braziller.

Birdwhistell, R. L. (1979). *Kinesics and context.* Philadelphia: University of Pennsylvania Press.

Bonhoeffer, D. (1967). *Letters and papers from prison.* New York: Macmillan.

Brehm, J. W., & Cohen, A. R. (1962). *Explorations in cognitive dissonance.* New York: Wiley.

Bronfenbrenner, U. (1979). *The ecology of human development: Experiments by name and design.* Cambridge, MA.: Harvard University Press.

Brown, R. (1962). Models of attitude change. In *New directions in psychology.* New York: Holt, Rinehart and Winston.

Collins, W.A. (1984) Introduction. In W. A. Collins (Ed.), *Development during middle childhood: The years from six to twelve.* Washington, DC: National Academy Press.

Comstock, G., Chaffee, S., Katzman, N., McComb, M., & Roberts, D. (1978). *Television and human behavior.* New York: Columbia University Press.

deMause, L. (1974). *The history of childhood.* New York: Harper.

Epps, E.G., & Smith, S.F. (1984). School and children: The middle childhood years. In W.A. Collins (Ed.), *Development during middle childhood: The years from six to twelve.* Washington, DC: National Academy Press.

Festinger, L. (1957). *A theory of cognitive dissonance.* Stanford, CA: Stanford University Press.

Goodland, J.I. (1973). The elementary school as a social institution. In A.D. Lester (Ed.), *The elementary school in the United States.* Seventy-second yearbook of the National Society for the Study of Education. Chicago: University of Chicago Press.

Gorsuch, R.D., & Smith, C.S. (1983). Attributions of responsibility to God: An interaction of religious beliefs and outcomes. *Journal for the Scientific Study of Religion, 22*, 340-352.

Hayes, C.D., & Kamerman, S.B. (Eds.) (1983). *Children of working parents: Experiences and outcomes.* Washington, DC: National Academy Press.

Hofferth, S.L. (1985). Updating children's life course. *Journal of Marriage And the Family, 47*, 93-115.

Hoffman, L.W., & Nye, I.F. (1974). *Working mothers.* San Francisco: Jossey-Bass.

Kelly, H.H., & Michela, J.L. (1980). Attribution theory and research. *Annual Review of Psychology, 31*, 457-501.

Kreps, G.L. (1990). *Organizational communication* (2d ed.). New York: Longman.

Lee, J.M. (1982). Discipline in a moral and religious key. In K. Walsh & M. Cowles (Eds.). *Developmental discipline.* Birmingham, AL: Religious Education Press.

Lee, J.M. (1985). *Content of religious instruction.* Birmingham, AL: Religious Education Press.

Maccoby, E. (1984). Middle childhood in the context of the family. In W.A. Collins (Ed.) *Development during middle childhood: The years from six to twelve*. Washington, DC: National Academy Press.

Medrich, E.A., Roizen, V., & Buckley, S. (1982). *The serious business of growing up: A study of children's lives outside school*. Berkeley: University of California Press.

Mehrabian, A. (1981). *Silent messages*. Belmont, CA: Wadsworth.

Messaris, P., & Hornik, R.C. (1983). Work status, television exposure, and educational outcomes. In C.D. Hayes & S.B. Kamerman (Eds.), *Children of working parents: Experiences and outcomes*. Washington, DC: National Academy Press.

Moore, R., & Moore, D. (1982). *Home-spun schools*. Waco, TX: Word.

Narramore, B. (1972). *Help! I'm a parent*. Grand Rapids, MI: Zondervan.

Neuman, S.B., & Prowda, P. (1981). Television viewing and reading achievement. Paper presented at the annual meeting of American Educational Research Associates. Los Angeles, CA, April, 1981.

Newcomb, P. (1990). The brat market. *Forbes*, 145, 126-131.

O'Brien, M. (1987). *Content analysis of selected religious language on prime time television*. Unpublished Master's thesis, C.B.N. University, Virginia Beach, VA.

Pargament, K.I., & Hahn, J. (1986). God and the just world: Causal and coping attribution to God in health situations. *Journal For The Scientific Study Of Religion, 25*, 193-207.

Postman, N. (1987). The blurring of childhood and the media. *Religious Education, 82*, 293-295.

Roberts, C.L. (1985). The cultivation effects of television violence: Further testing. Paper presented at the annual meeting of the Association for Education in Journalism and Mass Communication. Memphis, TN, February, 1985.

Ruben, B., & Kim, J.Y. (Eds.). (1975). *General systems theory and human communication*. Rochelle Park, NJ: Hayden.

Rubin, V. (1983). Family work patterns and community resources: An analysis of children's access to support and services outside schools. In C.D. Hayes & S.B. Kamerman (Eds.), *Children of working parents: Experiences and outcomes*. Washington, DC: National Academy Press.

Schickedanz, J., Hansen, K., & Forsyth, P. (1990). *Understanding children*. Mountain View, CA: Mayfield.

School-Age Child Care Project (1982). In E.F. Zigler & E.W. Gordon (Eds.), *Day care: Scientific and social policy issues*. Boston: Auburn House.

Seiler, J.A. (1967). *Systems analysis in organizational behavior*. Homewood, IL: Irwin-Dorsey.

Slocumb, F.G. (1981). An attributional analysis of religious explanations. PhD dissertation, Virginia Commonwealth University. Cited in K.E. Hyde,

Religion in childhood and adolescence. Birmingham, AL: Religious Education Press.

Smith, C.S., & Gorsuch, R.L. (1989). Sanctioning and causal attributions. In M. Lynn & D. Moberg (Eds.), *Research in the social scientific study of religion*, Vol. 1, Greenwich, CT: JAI Press.

Spilka, B., Hood, R.W., & Gorsuch, R.L. (1985). *The psychology of religion: An empirical approach*. Englewood Cliffs, NJ: Prentice-Hall.

Stein, A.H., & Friedrich, L.K. (1975). Impact of television on children and youth. In E.M. Hetherington (Ed.), *Review of child development research*. Chicago: University of Chicago Press.

Thayer, L. (1968). *Communication and communication systems*. Homewood, IL: Irvin.

Thompson, J.J. (1972). *Beyond words: Nonverbal communication in the classroom*. New York: Citation Press.

Tubbs, S.L. (1988). *A systems approach to small group interaction* (3rd ed.). New York: Random House.

U.S. Government Printing Office (1989). *U.S. children and their families: Current conditions and recent trends*. Washington, DC: Child Trends.

Warren, M. (1988). The electronically imagined world and religious education. *Religious Education, 83*, 367-383.

Watzlawick, P., Beavin, J.H., & Jackson, D.D. (1967). *Pragmatics of human communication*. New York: Norton.

Weisner, T.S. (1984). Ecocultural niches of middle childhood: A cross-cultural perspective. In W.A. Collins (Ed.), *Development during middle childhood: The years from six to twelve*. Washington, DC: National Academy Press.

Werner, H.G. (1958). *Christian family living*. Nashville, TN: Graded Press.

Westerhoff, J. (1976). *Shall our children have faith?* New York: Seabury.

Wright, H.F. (1967). *Recording and analyzing child behavior.* New York: Harper & Row.

Zajonc, R. (1960). The concepts of balance, congruity, and dissonance. *Public Opinion Quarterly, 24*, 280-296.

Zill, N., & Peterson, J.L. (1981). Television viewing in the United States and children's intellectual, social and emotional development. *Television and Children, 4*, 21-28.

Zill, N., & Peterson, J.L. (1982). Trends in the behavior and emotional well-being of U.S. children (findings from a national survey). Paper presented at the American Association for the Advancement of Science. Washington, DC, January, 1982.

Zill, N., & Rogers, C.C. (1988). Recent trends in the well-being of children in the United States and their implications for public policy. In A.J. Cherlin (Ed.), *The changing American family and public policy*. Washington, DC: Urban Institute Press.

Chapter Six

Social Contexts of Children's Ministry

DONALD RATCLIFF

Passing on the faith is a crucial concern for religious education. Children are socialized within or without faith, and exposure to faith is a requirement for acceptance of belief, but how socialization into faith takes place can make the difference between acceptance or rejection. Westerhoff (1976) asked, "Will our children have faith?" Perhaps the more basic question is, "Will our faith have children?" This question is twofold: Is the church prepared to make the sacrifices of time and finances to facilitate the religious education of children? The second aspect of the question is, how does faith beget faith? How do we spiritually impregnate for potential faith, nurture embryonic faith, help deliver newborn faith, suckle a developing faith, and release a matured faith?

This chapter will consider a broad spectrum of situations for encouraging children's faith. Three general contexts are detailed: the family, the school, and the church, each entailing numerous subcontexts. However, the underlying principles of socialization and culture need to be developed as important prerequisites to the analysis of those social contexts.

Socialization

Socialization is the process in which the values, roles, and skills of a society are learned, by which individuals develop a sense of self (McCluskey, 1982). Socialization thus includes not only specific behaviors in specific situations but also important continuities of behavior which make up personality.

Children learn nearly all of their behavior. Sociologists use the term "socialization" to describe the nature of that learning. Socialization, in its

119

broadest sense, includes psychological as well as sociological processes, as evidenced by the inclusion of psychological theories in most accounts of socialization in introductory textbooks (for example, see McCluskey, 1982; Wallace & Wallace, 1989; Farley, 1990; Vander Zanden, 1990).

Hoult (1979) makes a most interesting case for giftedness being the result of socialization influences. Citing the methods of the Japanese music instructor Suzuki, as well as the child rearing used by the father of John Stuart Mill, Hoult maintains that social influences can make the difference between a child prodigy and average achievement. While Hoult's conclusions are probably exaggerated, the important influence of socialization is correctly underscored.

Hoult speaks of *sanctions* in the socialization process, the sociological equivalent of reinforcements and punishments. Sanctions differ from the latter in that they are given by others in a group context, such as the howls of laughter from peers when a child plays the clown or the frown from a displeased parent (as will be seen later, the family is the most important social group in early socialization). From the very earliest months of life, the infant receives sanctions that help mold (psychologists would say "shape") the child's behavior so that it is socially appropriate in the situation.

Not only is specific behavior learned in the process of socialization, but the self-concept is acquired as well. Sociologist Charles Cooley (1902) described the famous "Looking Glass Self" theory, which states that the child's perspective of the self is the result of how others treat that child. Family, peers, and others act as mirrors that reflect back to the child a perception of who he or she is. Others' impressions of the child become the child's understanding of self.

George Herbert Mead (1934) emphasized that *significant others* are crucial in the development of the self-concept. These individuals are people who are particularly important to the child, and thus he or she not only tries to make them happy but also develops the self-concept from their reactions to the child's behavior. Thus Mead, like Cooley, affirmed that the self emerges in the context of social interaction.

This emergence occurs in predictable stages, says Mead. The first stage occurs in infancy, where the child has no real understanding of self as a separate entity. In the second stage, during the preschool years, children develop the ability to take on the role of another person (such as playing the role of mother in playing house), allowing them to see themselves from the perspective of that other person. During the school years, role interrelationships and the coordinating of roles into a unified system is seen in game playing. The final stage is when the child moves beyond significant others to responding to the *generalized other*, made up of the expectations of society. They see themselves as a component of society at large and thus begin to internalize beliefs and standards they have long followed. Later in adolescence they will move from reasoning centered on others to reasoning centered on themselves, seeing themselves as separated from others' expectations. They analyze why others see them the way they do and begin to distinguish the personal self-image from the social self-image (Light, Keller, & Calhoun, 1989).

For example, in the first stage an infant attends church but is unlikely to reflect upon the self. During the preschool years, the child is able to play church and take on specific roles, such as usher, preacher, and so on (Ratcliff, 1985). During the school years, the reactions of others become more pronounced in the perspective of self, so that children see themselves as members of the Christian community or as basically outsiders (or perhaps as good Christians or poor Christians). This perspective is derived from the reactions of Sunday school or catechal instructors, pastor or priest, parents, church peers, and others. In later childhood, the child is more able to understand the roles of many different people in the church and how their roles relate to one another. The church as a social system is better understood, as well as the importance of his or her role within that system. Internalization of beliefs begins, while the expectations of society are increasingly taken into account, creating the potential for conflict between society's norms and the church's standards. Later in adolescence the social self-image of what others think of them as a church attender can be separated from the real self-image of how he or she personally relates to religious faith.

Culture and Ethnicity

The extent of socialization is clarified when one examines the differences in socialization cross-culturally. The child in New Guinea is raised in a manner different from American children, because the society the child is socialized into is quite different. Both process and product are distinctive. Child developmentalists have begun to acknowledge the importance of cultural distinctives in the development of the individual (see "Child Development in Other Cultures" in Dworetzky's introductory text, 1990, as well as book-length treatment of the subject in Wagner & Shepherson, 1982). Knowledge of cultural differences is important for religious educators because of the increasingly multicultural nature of the United States.

Over the last several decades it has been in vogue to minimize the differences of minority groups within the United States. Yet ethnic differences may have important pedagogical implications that should not be overlooked. Several trustworthy studies will be considered that underscore significant differences among ethnic groups which should be considered for effective religious education.

As can been seen in chapter nine of this handbook, the question-and-answer format is dominant in education. Yet there is considerable evidence that this format is not inherent in the socialization of black children (Heath, 1982). Many black parents only ask their children questions when seeking information not known by the parents. For example, when telling a story, the black parent is unlikely to stop periodically and ask about the details of what has happened thus far, while white parents are more likely to use this question-answer format with their children. When children are then taught with the question-answer format, white children are more familiar with this method of learning and assessment, while black children are more likely to see such questioning as attempting to prove the ignorance of the child. Black children often do not attempt to answer such questions because they have not been socialized into that learning process. Thus an important aspect of readiness for such children is to learn the technique and legitimacy of the question-and-answer approach, and teachers should realize that silence on the part of black students may not be ignorance or obstinance but rather unfamiliarity with the teaching method.

Historically Hispanics have been very family-oriented, and today there are indications that the family-centeredness of Hispanics is generally stronger than the mainstream American culture. In contrast, primarily due to the horrors of slavery, blacks tend to have weaker families (Mattox, 1989), manifested by high levels of illegitimacy and single-parent homes. The black family problem is perpetuated by welfare and governmental policies that encourage single parent arrangements, as well as chronic high unemployment and poverty rates. Religious educators who attempt to reach black children should provide a family-like setting in their religious education endeavors, as well as supporting and providing needed social services.

Villarreal (1982) studied low income, Mexican-American children and their learning styles. She found that these children learned particularly well through role playing and imaginative play. Playing *during* the narrative was especially effective. This is a valuable method for teaching children in general, but particularly for Hispanic children.

Scollon and Scollon (1981) compared the socialization of their own child with that of Canadian Indians among whom they lived. Their fine ethnographic study indicates that American children are customarily literate before they read; they learn many of the characteristics of reading before actually reading. For example the Scollon's preschool daughter used a different tone of voice as she pretended to read a book, periodically turned the pages as she "read," and referred to herself in the third person within the story line. In contrast, even preteen Indian children failed to use these reading conventionalities. Likewise many minority and underclass children in the United States may lack experiences in being read to and thus not have acquired reading conventionalities. This would place them at a disadvantage for learning to read and help account for deficient reading skills.

Anderson (1988) made a detailed study of two ethnic groups in the United States: Eurocentric persons (primarily white middle- and upper-class individuals) and people of color (mostly blacks, Hispanics, and high-risk students).

Anderson studied late adolescents, but many of his findings can be generalized to elementary children. For example, he found that Eurocentric persons did well in a detached mode of learning while people of color preferred more relational instruction; the teacher was effective if he or she personally related to the student both in and out of class. People of color desired stories while Eurocentrics preferred facts. Eurocentrics were more oriented toward critical thinking, while people of color were more inclined toward rote learning and needed applications provided. People of color need praise and support, Eurocentrics respond more to internal standards. Eurocentrics were more field independent, dichotomous in their thinking, oriented toward theory, time-oriented, and were more inclined toward conjunctive concepts. In contrast, people of color were more field dependent, holistic, imagery-oriented, used "elastic" time, and were more inclined toward disjunctive concepts. Anderson emphasizes that an increasing number of young people have developed these characteristics of people of color, and thus a significant percentage of children and youth have those characteristics, regardless of ethnicity or color. He also noted that some blacks are more Eurocentric than some whites.

Anderson suggests that teachers should adapt to these differences and help students adapt to the dominant culture. He states that educators need to be relational and practical, matching the teaching to the learning style of the individual. But he also suggests that while affirming their style of learning, that teachers teach another style by moving from the concrete to the abstract, back to the concrete, returning to the abstract, and so on. This coincides with Piaget's idea that the abstract must be built upon the concrete, and too often religious educators attempt to teach theological abstractions without an adequate foundation in the tangible and relational.

An understanding of ethnic distinctives is crucial for reaching those populations with religious instruction. For additional details on the learning styles and other significant differences between blacks and whites, see Hale-Benson (1986), McAdoo and McAdoo (1985), and Mitchell (1986).

Sociologists have long suggested that the most important socialization influence is the family. Second to the family is the importance of the school and one's peers. For the purposes of the present analysis, we will also consider the church and/or parachurch as a potentially important source of socialization as well. These three make up the outline for the three contexts of religious education to be considered for the remainder of this chapter.

THE FAMILY

During childhood the family has traditionally been more influential than any other aspect of society in the development of values and behavior. The home is also a key location for the internalization of what Lee (1985) terms lifestyle content, the integration of all religious education contents.

While the home has traditionally been the central locus for the child, in recent years this has changed significantly. A dramatic increase in the number of working mothers has decreased the amount of contact with the child — nearly 80 percent of the mothers of school-aged children now work outside the home (Schickedanz, Hansen, & Forsyth, 1990). In addition, fathers are more likely to take second jobs or work more hours and thus spend more time away from the family. The extended family, comprised of grandparents, cousins, and so on, are less influential today than in the past (Farley, 1990). Single-parent families have significantly increased, both due to more people having children without marriage and the increased number of divorced individuals. Thus two of the major functions of the family, emotional support and socialization (Parsons & Bales, 1955), are less likely to occur in the home and more likely to be accomplished by outsiders. The research on mother and father absence shows a number of detrimental effects (Rekers, 1982), which are likely to increase when parents are rarely available to the child. In addition, children probably become more dependent upon peers and other nonfamily members when parents are less available.

Another by-product of single parenting and increased work is the phenomenon of latchkey children (see chapter five). These children are primarily from middle-class suburban homes, not the lower class (Chollar, 1987). Religious educators should give consideration to initiating church-centered programs for these children, which can be a valuable means of reaching them with religious content, as well as providing needed care for children.

In recent years home schooling has become a phenomenon recognized as sociologically significant (Wallace & Wallace, 1989). Advantages of this approach to education include greater individualization to the needs of the child, increased leadership and achievement by children (Moore & Moore, 1979; Ray, 1990), less conformity to peers (Delahooke, 1986), and freedom from excessive competition (Holt, 1981). Contrary to some critics, home schoolers are generally not undersocialized; they are involved in many activities outside the home with other children (Rakesthaw, 1987; Schemmer, 1985), and they differ little from other children in most psychosocial areas (Delahooke, 1986).

Yet there are disadvantages to this approach as well. Not all parents have the patience and skill needed to teach academic subjects, while the inconvenience and financial sacrifice required make it untenable for most families. Barna (1989) projects that these difficulties are likely to curb future growth of the movement. Yet there is a sense in which every parent can use a limited home schooling for religious instruction. Home-centered religious programs, including those of a more formal nature, can serve as a supplement to the education received at school.

While the family has become less involved in religious education in recent decades (Farley, 1990), there is much that the family can accomplish with some planning and commitment from parents. Farley notes that many families continue to provide religious training, and children are still most likely to adopt the religion of their parents. What can parents do to provide quality religious instruction for their children? Several suggested activities can be mentioned.

Suggestions for Religious Education

Parent Education. One way of fostering religious education in the home is by helping to prepare parents for child-rearing tasks, including the important task of discipline (see chapter seven). This includes special classes for parents, prospective parents, and even teenagers. Lay-level texts that are based upon research-proven principles can help underscore key principles and serve as useful references after such a class is completed [texts written by Christian psychologists and researchers include Meier (1977), Walsh & Cowles (1982), Barber (1984), and Dobbins (1985)].

Parents should ask themselves what kind of heritage they want to give their children, what kind of memories they want them to relive throughout life, and upon what religious foundations they want their children to build. This kind of reflection may help parents focus on long-term goals, not just the immediate situation.

Media Instruction. A number of media sources are available for religious education of children at home. The popular "Superbook" and "Flying House" television series have been useful in teaching school-aged children stories from the Bible in an attractive, nonsectarian form. Parents should watch such programs with their children and use commercial breaks to discuss the content, asking questions to see if they correctly understood what occurred in the program and underscoring important ideas and values. Children will probably need help in articulating these more clearly and learning to apply what has been learned.

The same approach might be used with secular programs. Latent values may need to be specified, thus teaching the child to be more aware of the value-ladenness of events. Parents might use a nondirective mode in talking about programs and their values, using verbal probes to help the child evaluate the message of television programs and compare that message with important religious and other values.

The Family Huddle. Sociologists have long noted that ritual tends to produce cohesiveness (Gaede, 1985). A daily "huddle" or family meeting for discovery, study, and prayer can be an excellent context for socializing children into the faith. While not as immediate as "lifestyle content" (to be considered later), the family time can be a means of contextualizing faith. The best time to "huddle" may be just prior to going to bed, or perhaps at the dinner table. The family meeting, used for the purpose of religious education, could involve five steps (every step need not be used each evening and the steps do not always have to be sequential).

Discovery is the first component of the family huddle. Life events are shared freely by members of the family, making sure that each person is allowed time to talk about the events of the day. It is important to explore feelings about events as well as details of what happened. There should be reciprocity in this self-disclosure; family members, to the degree possible, need to reveal themselves at the same level of intimacy and have an equal opportunity to speak. Some parents choose to have their children say informal, short prayers to help discover what events they are thinking about.

Second, the values implicit in the disclosed events are clarified. The emphasis is that all behavior has implicit values. To the extent possible, family members should do their own clarifying, but probing by parents and other members may be appropriate. Children need to learn that all behavior involves underlying values.

Third, there is the teaching and affirmation of religious and other values. Some of the methods in chapters eight and nine may be helpful at this point. This could involve reading Bible stories or other stories that directly relate to the experiences children are likely to have. It is important not to overdo here; a short story or a verse or two from a simple version of the Bible is sufficient for younger children. A devotional booklet may be helpful.

Fourth, life experiences are triangulated with ideal values of the church, the Bible, the family, or the individual. Here the incongruence between the real and ideal is underscored; children learn that actualized values (values from daily behavior) are not always consistent with prototypical values. The parent might ask, "Is what you did in line with what God says or opposite what God says?" Sometimes there is the possibility of using "story therapy" to distance the child from the immediate event; the parent can tell a story that gets at the same principles involved in the child's situation. The goal is to affirm the transcendent values, including religious values, while acknowledging that everyone falls short of reaching perfection.

Fifth is the commitment to bring real living into greater congruence with the ideal. While the resolution between lived and ideal values is difficult and there is always some discrepancy (we are all imperfect), the transcendent is elevated because it provides meaning (Gaede, 1985). As C. S. Lewis said, religion is the "still point in a changing world." Personal need is acknowledged by each member of the family through confessional prayer and recommitment to the ultimate values in life.

The family huddle is *not* a substitute for other family rituals, such as seasonal observances (the advent wreath, for example). Family rituals and special events come closer to the lifestyle dimension of religious education, to be considered shortly.

The Checkup. Parents may elect to have a one-on-one time of evaluation with each child. This has been found to be effective with young children as early as four or five. Occasionally the parent may want to take a short walk with the child and ask, "How am I doing as a parent?" This gives the child an opportunity to freely express his feelings and give the parent a "report card." The results of the evaluation may, with some children, be an attempt to manipulate, but sometimes this direct approach can uncover long dormant problems that need airing. The checkup can also be an opportunity to correct misperceptions. The parent who becomes overly defensive in reacting to the child's critique will accomplish little and benefit little from the checkup.

Some parents use a variation of this idea by having a weekly "date" with each child, eating out or going to some event with the emphasis upon communicating with the child. This may be an opportunity to talk about the child's relationship with God. Children are more open than adults to religious questions such as "What is God doing in your life?" and "What's he teaching you?" Parents might share a bit of their own view of life by talking about the reality of death, the shortness of life, and making life count moment by moment.

Lifestyle. As mentioned earlier, lifestyle content (Lee, 1985) is central to integrating faith and life. Not only is lifestyle content the most pervasive kind of religious education, but it is the most likely to have lasting significance in the development of lifelong faith.

The key to facilitating lifestyle content is to instruct at the "teachable moment," when either a religious topic surfaces naturally, or to infuse religious concepts into the mainstream of life. It is all too easy to defer to a more convenient moment, a moment that may never arrive. Of course, this requires that parents be available to children for an adequate amount of time. Taking a walk or a drive in the country with one's children can be a prime context for lifestyle content. Observing people, objects, and events can be a pretext for conveying religious understandings and perspectives.

Lifestyle content need not rely upon a contrived context. In the everyday life at home, children are indirectly socialized into the predominant values they observe in their parents' and siblings' lives. Someone once said that children derive their worldview much as one contracts a cold; usually one is not aware of when it happens. Values are easily picked up not only from observing others in the home but also from television, music, books, and other sources of entertainment.

The key to lifestyle content is to integrate religion into life. Too often there is a compartmentalization of religion that separates it from the mainstream, making it irrelevant and insignificant. Instead, religion needs to be infused into the daily routines and rituals of the family. Orthodox Jews are well-known for family-oriented religious practices that significantly shape an identity that continues to influence even if the child comes to discard the particulars of that faith. Christians would do well to emulate this prototype of religious socialization.

THE SCHOOL

The peers in the school context and school personnel also are important in socialization. The school is a significant influence upon the child, an influence that may facilitate or impede quality religious education. Two varieties of religious education are possible in school: religious content per se (for example, Bible and theology) and religious perspectives of other subject matter (for example, a Christian view of science). Of course, the educational system is far from a monolithic entity; religious and public school systems represent very different philosophical approaches to education (although not always different in their products). In addition, there is considerable diversity within each of these two approaches to education.

Public Education

The public school system has received much criticism from both the religious and nonreligious elements of society. The nonreligious critique has tended to emphasize the poor quality of education and substandard achievement of pupils. Religious criticism has tended to focus upon the secularistic and sometimes antireligious values and curricular content.

Vitz (1986) has thoroughly documented the exclusion of religion in current elementary textbooks. For example, the Pilgrims are often described as people who came to the United States because they wanted to make long journeys; their strong religious motivation is ignored. Religion has generally been removed from curricular materials, with the exception of a few references to fringe groups such as the Amish. Generally the United States is presented as a country in which virtually no one has any religious faith or attends church, even though a large majority believe in God, over half consider religion very important in their lives, and 40 percent of the population are in church on any given Sunday morning (Barna, 1990).

Sociologists have long posited the presence of a "hidden curriculum" in the public schools (Parson, 1959). This refers to ideas that are never directly taught but are implicit from the structure and approach of the classroom. For example, the value of conformity is built into the social context but not directly taught by teachers as a curricular content. Gearing and Epstein (1982) document that children who are academically deficient learn to wait for smarter students to answer questions, then echo those correct answers. Another example of the hidden curriculum is that lower-middle-class children are socialized through external control by teachers, while internal control is emphasized to a greater extent by teachers of upper-middle-class students (Wilcox, 1982). Wilcox also noted that future aspirations and accomplishments were emphasized in the upper-middle-class classroom, and the present was emphasized by teachers of lower-middle-class children. Is not the absence of teaching about religion a hidden curriculum, an unspoken message that religion is irrelevant to modern life?

Sociologically it is also significant that American public schools are a government-sponsored and protected form of monopoly. True, alternatives exist, but only at considerable cost to the parent. Thus public education as it exists today is for all practical purposes a monopoly. Since public schools are supported by tax money, parents who wish to send their children to some alternative must pay twice for their children's education. Even an alternative public school is usually forbidden or requires the payment of tuition. Researchers from the Brookings Institution, a left-of-center think tank in Washington, have compared public schools in the United States with those of the Soviet Union in terms of their overbearing bureaucracies. The researchers called for more local autonomy, parent choice, and total decentralization (Public education perestroika, 1990).

As with all monopolies (Brown et al., 1982), this practice has produced an inferior product as well as bureaucratic decadence. The public has been convinced that public education is the only viable approach yet simultaneously told that public education continues to decline in quality. It is astounding that few ever put these two factors together. This is not, of course, intended as a blanket condemnation; good public schools are to be found in many localities, in spite of these sociological influences.

Suggestions for Religious Education

While changes in the educational system to provide for tax support of alternatives (at least a choice of alternative secular public schools, and preferably private alternatives as well) is the more ideal solution, there are also means available within the present social context for religious education. Those interested in religious education cannot afford to bemoan what should be, while ignoring the options they now have. Instead they should take advantage of strong support for religious education in public schools among churched and unchurched parents alike (Gallup, 1989) and take action in that direction.

One possibility is to educate teachers as to what religious education is legally permitted in a public school classroom. A wide spectrum of religious and educational organizations, including the National Education Association and the National Council of Churches, produced a brochure entitled "Religion in the Public School Curriculum" (1988), which provides these guidelines for such instruction:

1) be academic, not devotional
2) encourage awareness, not acceptance, of a specific religion

3) study about religion, but do not conduct religious observances in the school setting
4) expose students to different views, but do not impose a particular view
5) educate, but do not attempt to conform students to a belief
6) inform about religion, but do not indoctrinate

The September 1990 issue of *Social Education* is entirely given to integrating religion into social studies courses in public schools, while guidelines for including religion in history classes are also available (Haynes, 1989). Haynes is president of the National Council on Religion and Public Education, which also produces the journal *Religion and Public Education.*

The Williamsburg Charter Foundation has developed a public school curriculum titled "Living With Our Deepest Differences" (1990) for elementary school children in fifth grade (as well as two upper-level courses for teenagers). It describes principles that will help those of any faith (or no faith) understand diversities of belief, emphasizing mutual respect and values.

Another possibility is that of released-time instruction (Colby & Payne, 1990). This long neglected but legally protected approach to religious education, involves teaching children during school hours about their faith. By law this instruction must take place off the school grounds, in a church or other private facility. While attendance is always voluntary, this is a valuable approach that more churches should consider.

Moberg (1984) notes that while released-time religious education has its critics, it generally contributes to religious knowledge and promotes interfaith cooperation. While in general teens become more likely to leave the church as they grow older, Wright (1990) reports that released-time instruction can reverse this trend. Fifty percent of the youngsters who enroll in his program are non-churched, but a large majority are active in some church upon completion of their high-school years. He notes that overt evangelism and indoctrination are not necessary in such programs.

Religious Schools

Over the last two decades there has been rapid growth in the number of religious schools in the United States (Weldin & Weldin, 1982). About 12 percent of elementary-aged children attend private schools, about two-thirds of them going to Catholic schools (Moberg, 1984). While parochial schools have existed for a century or more, the tremendous growth in religious schools in the 1970s and 1980s has been a significant social movement. Today half the population would send their children to a private or parochial school if cost was not a factor (Gallup, 1989).

While some of these schools were developed to promote segregation, the large majority are supported by parents due to the crime, poor education quality, and antireligious sentiment in some public schools. Sometimes religious schools have been seen as Christian reformatories to which semidelinquent children are sent. Most people, however, send their children because they want them to learn religious values (Gallup, 1989).

What is the effect of religious schools upon children? Hyde (1990) has compiled a large number of resources to answer this question. Apart from the influence of parents, the effects of religious schools tend to be minimal. Of course, the influence of a particular school may be great or small, depending upon its approach. The studies cited by Hyde indicate that the atmosphere of the school, rather than the denomination, theological orientation, or even curriculum, is the most significant factor in the degree of influence it exercises upon students. Religious schools influence children most when the parents are religious.

Among Hyde's many other findings are that teachers generally become significant others to children in religious schools, and single-sex schools do not produce more religious students. Hyde cites Jarvis in noting that all schools provide religious socialization of some kind (neglect of the topic implies that it is unimportant). Sharp (1990a) notes that more legalistic schools tend to produce graduates who are less committed to their faith as adults.

In the United States, the day school is the most common variety of private education available for elementary-aged children. However, boarding schools where children live as well as study reach a small elite in the United States and a significant number of Americans overseas, including missionary children.

What are the psychological and sociological effects of boarding schools? This question rarely has been addressed. Studies of the Israeli kibbutz, a communal child-rearing and education context, may provide some clues. Generally the literature on the kibbutz suggests a lack of negative effects, although the concept of God as Father may be less developed (McCluskey, 1982). Recent research on the effects of boarding schools upon missionary children may provide more detailed conclusions.

Sharp (1990a, 1990b) sent a twelve-page questionnaire to about 500 grown children of missionaries in Brazil. Half had attended boarding schools overseas. A diverse, but not random, sample was studied. The researcher reported no negative effects of the boarding school experience but found that missionary kids (MKs) who had that experience grew up to be more conservative, more likely to be missionaries, more committed, and less open-minded about cross-cultural values.

Several problems with this study should be noted, however. First, causation cannot be affirmed from correlation research. Second, it should be noted that these MKs had an average of over twelve years in Brazil but only five years at boarding school. Most likely these five years were toward the end of their stay, perhaps in high school rather than elementary school. Third, a review of the article (Journal file, 1990) noted that the external validity of the study was in question, and the reviewer knew of many boarding students that would disagree with the overly positive conclusions. Those with negative experiences are less likely to open up old wounds by filling out the questionnaire. The reviewer also noted the research failed to address important differences between boarding schools, some of which have terrible reputations. One psychologist who has visited many boarding schools noted reports of child abuse are just beginning to surface in such schools because the topic has been so taboo (Powell, 1988).

One of the effects of boarding schools upon missionary children, noted by this writer in his counseling of a number of college-aged missionary kids, is the underlying anger so many feel. This anger is related to trauma from separation and terrible memories of the boarding school (the latter reported by one-third to one-half of MKs, in a survey cited by Tucker, 1989). Sometimes this anger is directed to the parents for their leaving the child at an early age. Occasionally this anger is directed to God, for calling their parents to an occupation that involves virtual abandonment for most of the year. At other times that anger becomes directed to authority in general (Troutman, 1974) due to transference. Sometimes anger may become submerged into identification in which the child feels compelled to follow in the parents' footsteps, becoming a missionary and likewise sending the children to boarding school. Often there is a significant overreliance upon peers due to the absence of parents. Lengthy parent-child separation can produce feelings of isolation and lack of personal intimacy that last into adulthood. This is most likely if the children enter boarding school in their early years (ages six to eight) than if they enter during adolescence (Wrobbel, 1990; Wrobble & Plueddemann, 1990).

Perhaps the best conclusion is that elementary-aged children who attend boarding schools are likely to develop problems either immediately or later in life, although some appear to cope fairly well. On the other hand the research indicates that negative effects upon the child are minimal during the high-school years, and possibly even during junior high (Pollock, 1989). Children are individuals, and some may need to remain at home until college, others may be able to live in a boarding school prior to the teen years with minimal problem. Indeed, self-esteem was higher for *adolescent* boarding students than MKs that did not board (Schipper, 1977), and self-esteem is lower with late entry (Wickstrom & Fleck, 1983).

Suggestions for Religious Education

It is crucial that the curricular content of religious schools be evaluated. It cannot be assumed that because a school is religious it will automatically have good religious instruction. Too often the author has found that religious schools dichotomize religious values from other curricula; a Bible class tacked onto a list of essentially secular courses is not sufficient as religious education. Religious schools must consistently integrate religious faith into all courses, otherwise implicit non-Christian values are unlikely to be noticed in those "secular" classes.

One danger of religious schools that is rarely addressed by writers and researchers is the possibility of being sheltered from the variety of opinions and perspectives in society (Moberg, 1984). The goal of religious education is not censoring all alternatives but rather to consider those alternatives from a position of faith. Non-Christian perspectives are not to be presented as "straw men" to be discarded without much analysis but rather as viable approaches which pale in comparison with religious alternatives. Inoculation theory from psychology (Myers, 1990) might be used expeditiously in this context, presenting anti-Christian views and having children create arguments against those views from a theistic perspective.

Other dangers from religious schools include a possible abdication of parental responsibility. Some parents may come to believe that because of the great expense of Christian schools they no longer have a role to fulfill in giving their children religious education. This point of view overlooks the primacy of the home in socialization. The child that goes to the most religious school, but comes home to a home environment devoid of religion, will most likely become indifferent to religion, as Hyde (1991) documents so well.

For the missionaries contemplating boarding schools for their children, it is strongly recommended that other possibilities be explored at least until the junior high years. Even if there were no long-term effects of early separation, it is hard to justify extended parent-child separation. Alternatives include correspondence courses, such as the famous Calvert program. Nearby national schools have distinct advantages (Kladensky, 1974), while private schools in the community may be valuable. Home schooling is a legitimate option to be considered. The Moores (1979) cite evidence that deferring school until age eight or later can improve the child's long-term performance. In the future, field education systems using satellites, computers, learning centers, and itinerant teachers may become more widely available (Tucker, 1989). This writer participated in pooled teaching with other missionaries, in which each adult spent an hour or two each week instructing one or more children. Two or three hours of individualized instruction a day can accomplish as much or more than the public school achieves in a full day.

It should be noted that the experience of children living overseas with their parents can be very beneficial. Intercultural and multiple language skills are more likely (Sharp, 1985), as well as greater appreciation for ethnic diversity (more world-consciousness). MKs often struggle with re-adjustment when they return to their home country, however (Pollock, 1989).

CHURCH AND PARACHURCH

Sociologists distinguish between transitions that build upon prior social-ization and those that involve *resocialization* which require learning new norms, values, and roles. Examples of resocialization include prisons, men-tal hospitals, and army boot camp. Six steps in the resocialization process have been identified: 1) people are made to feel they are different, 2) a discredit-ing of prior learning, 3) conflict and confusion, 4) despair, accompanied by either thoughts of leaving the group or simply doing what one is told, 5) beginning to see self as developing some of the desired attributes, and 6) reaffirmation and internalization of the group's norms and values (Light, Keller, & Calhoun, 1989, pp.130-132).

McCluskey (1982) states that an important mission of the church is reso-cialization. Probably not all of the stages listed above will be involved, but some clearly occur. The task is to instill a new set of habits consistent with Christian values and change the areas of concern for the convert. Theologically this is given the designation "sanctification" or spiritual devel-opment. Thus, McCluskey would suggest that teaching a new way of valu-ing and behaving is central to the task of the religious educator.

While many church leaders would probably endorse resocialization as one of the missions of the church, one must ask if it is actually accomplished. Is there a "hidden curriculum" that may actually counteract the resocializa-tion task? Campolo (1989), citing Durkheim's theory, suggests that the church too often socializes children to fit into society and adopt its values, rather than resocializing them into a new value matrix. If the church was really accomplishing its educational mission, Campolo suggests, it would be turning out revolutionaries rather than socially acceptable Americans.

There certainly is a tension that needs to be realized between the values of society and the values found in religion. Yet one must ask if revolution-ary religion and culturally conformed religion are the only alternatives. Stellway (1982) suggests the category of "peaceful revolutionary," which incorporates both the challenge and comfort aspects of religious faith. He admits this is "walking a tightrope," but a genuine option for church ministry. Other sociologists (Farley, 1990) contrast the revolution, which attempts to remake society, with the *reform* social movement, which works for limited changes and reforms within society. We need to teach children to work with-in the norms and structures of society (to the degree those norms and struc-tures do not conflict with religious values) but also to confront and help modify those areas of society that are in need of redemption. Working from within is more likely to effect change than imposing from the outside.

A danger in teaching children to fit in with society is the possible accep-tance of *civil religion*. This sociological concept refers to the idea that a specific country, in this case the United States, has a contract with God to play a special role in history (Bellah, 1970). National leaders often invoke civil religion in their speeches, "baptizing" their policies with divine sanction. One often hears references to God during political speeches. Civil religion is devoid of doctrine, particularly the doctrine of sin, while national heroes and ideals come to be seen as sacred (Stellway, 1982). While acknowledging the important role of religion in the development of the United States is legitimate, civil religion inevitably compromises religion.

While civil religion is considered appropriate by many in the United States, state support of a specific church body is not. This is the basis of the current separation of church and state controversy. Sociologists point to the privatization of religion as a result of this separation, in which the individual chooses a religion, constructs a belief system, and even practices faith apart from others. This produces the phenomenon of *free enterprise* religion, where the person constantly chooses from a smorgasbord of faiths. This in turn fosters competition between churches (Stellway, 1982) as prospects shop for the most attractive church in their area, often a church that fulfills their wants rather than addressing what may be the most important needs. A consequence in the near future is that people will have several church homes and on a given Sunday they will choose the one they feel best meets their desires at that moment (Barna, 1990). Membership and long-term commitment will be virtually nonexistent.

While state supported and controlled religion can have obvious drawbacks as well, free enterprise religion tends to encourage the proliferation of self-centered groups that pragmatically give people whatever they want. A consequence, which trends researchers believe will become increasingly common in the coming decade (Barna, 1990), is increasing synthesis in the development of one's personal religion, where the individual will take aspects of several faiths (Christian and non-Christian) and blend them with little concern for consistency and ultimacy.

Sociologists have noted another kind of "hidden curriculum" in the church that is generally fused with the overt religious message. Sociologists term it the "Language of Zion," a curious dialect in many churches that is a mixture of King James English and theological terms. This dialect is most often noted in public prayers, hymns, and sermons, but occasionally in other contexts as well.

Eutychus (1987), poking fun at this curious dialect, offers these creative redefinitions of Zion terminology:

Old nature: last year's leaves

New nature: this year's leaves

Justification: used to relieve stress ("just a vacation")

Sanctification: what occurred to the boat during vacation

Discipleship: Saint Peter's boat

Total commitment: dedication to a certain breakfast cereal

Religious education often imparts the Language of Zion to children. The social consequence is that children become insiders to the religious group because they are knowledgeable of the terminology, while those lacking knowledge of the dialect do not feel as welcome. While this exclusionary factor is negative enough, dialect can take the place of genuine belief — one who says the right words may be considered more spiritual than one who has not yet learned the dialect. One can sound spiritual but lack the Spirit, as can be exemplified by recent television evangelist scandals. Religious educators must be aware of this possibility and encourage children to understand religious concepts and value religious experience without overly valuing certain terminology.

Suggestions for Religious Education

The church and parachurch provide a number of different subcontexts for religious education. Indeed there are so many, one must ask if they fragment efforts. Cooperative efforts among various agencies may help to circumvent such fragmentation and the possibility of overlap of efforts, without negating the efforts of any. Perhaps genuine Christian love can help churches avoid the competitiveness made possible by "free enterprise religion." Barna (1990) suggests that churches concentrate upon specific areas in which they can excell and refer people to other churches if they have other needs.

In considering the specific areas of church ministry, the first area that should be mentioned is the catechismal and/or doctrinal classes. Some would include Sunday school in this category as well. The former would be considered preparatory for full participation in the church, a means to an end, while the latter is usually considered to be a entity in itself. Should religious education be seen as fundamentally preparatory or conversely a function that perpetuates indefinitely?

These are not mutually exclusive. Some would point out that religion in general is both preparatory (for spiritual maturity, social change, and/or for the next life) and perpetual (growth continues throughout life). Regardless of one's confession, both functions need to be addressed by religious education endeavors.

Yet this form of ministry is not without its critics. Some have accused Sunday school of being "the most wasted hour of the week," contributing to the decline of family-based religious nurture (cited by Moberg, 1984). But no empirical evidence for this conclusion is given. Indeed it is equally possible that quality instructional training of parents in Sunday school could *increase* family religious education.

One of the characteristics of catechal and Sunday school classes is age grading. While this characteristic is generally accepted in elementary schools (although a few have moved away from this), there is little or no research to indicate that age-grading is a beneficial method of grouping children. It assumes that ability is related to age, and while this is the case with many children it neglects those who are advanced or slower. Ability grouping has the advantage of allowing for a more homogeneous curriculum, but it can also foster elitism and perpetuate class structures (sociologists call this process "tracking" — Tischler, 1990). Children may also lose the challenge of keeping up with more advanced peers, although for some children having more intelligent peers causes less achievement. While there are advantages and disadvantages of age-grouping versus ability-grouping, the church has uncritically adopted the standard approach of the public school system (chapter ten also considers this subject).

The phenomenon of "junior church," where children have some form of religious education during the standard worship service can take many forms, but the designation implies a junior level of the standard church service. Here the long-term goal of preparing children for church worship needs to be underscored. Psychologically, the process of shaping should be used to help children develop the understanding and practice of corporate worship. Within the strictures of church polity, this could incorporate elements of liturgy (a mini-mass?) or a sermonette. Ideally, junior church should be phased so that the gradual shaping begins at the preschool level and is complete by adolescence, when full incorporation into the standard service is accomplished. Elements of the standard service could be introduced gradually, with explanations appropriate to the age of the child.

The concept of junior church is not to suggest, of course, that children totally be excluded from the standard service. Occasional attendance at regular church worship is certainly acceptable, particularly if children are curious and interested. Some churches creatively provide simplified songs and a children's sermon at the beginning of the service, then dismiss the children for junior church. But if a church makes no provision for something more age-appropriate, one must ask if that church really has an interest in children. Wiggling, noisy children can disrupt a formal service and ruin any sense of worship for their elders. This is because sermons that are formal operational in content, and thus more likely to be challenging for adults, will probably be boring for children who are at the concrete operational level of thinking. We must consider the undesirable conditioning of children that can come from attending uninteresting services, conditioning that will result in avoidance of church later in life (Dobbins, 1975).

Churches often have other kinds of special groups as well. These include Boy and Girl Scouts, which offer religious merit badges that can be general in nature or specifically keyed to one's denomination. Churches may offer mid-week meetings for children. Vacation Bible schools are popular in some areas in which children assemble for several hours a day over the period of a week, for religious training as well as craft and recreational activities.

Groups such as Child Evangelism offer series of classes to children within a community, rather than working within a single church affiliation, with the goal of conversion. Perhaps a proliferation of approaches makes it more likely that most children will receive *some* kind of religious education. This may be one possible advantage of free enterprise religion.

In addition, churches often make use of church or denominational camps and special outings, in which religious education is combined with recreational activities. The children's or youth camp has gained considerable popularity, and is an outgrowth of the nineteenth-century campmeetings (Moberg, 1984). Parachurch groups offer camps, sometimes to specific churches and sometimes for needy children with or without church affiliation. The camping experience may be a valuable context for integrating life and faith, or lifestyle content as Lee (1985) describes it. The interpersonal struggles and joys in an around-the-clock context can be a means of applying faith dynamically, as well as encouraging wholesome interests and hobbies (Moberg, 1984). There is also the possibility of spiritual evaluation of self, as well as evaluation by religious education leaders in such contexts. The author recalls his oldest son, at six- and-one-half years, attending a church retreat. One evening he stared at the campfire wistfully. He commented that the log was like Jesus, the fire like the Romans who crucified Jesus, and the stones around the fire were like Mary looking at Jesus on the cross. This spontaneous remark indicated not only that he had acquired theological content, but also suggested the genesis of allegorical reasoning.

As noted earlier, short-term commitments to a church are more likely than long-term membership in the near future. People are more likely to commit themselves to attending for five Sundays than they will for six months or a year. The church needs to adapt to this fact by concentrating attention on short series of lessons (perhaps five to ten weeks) for adults, and corresponding series for children.

CONCLUSION

Religious education of children involves multiple contexts and multiple educators. It is imperative that parents, schools, and church educators coordinate their efforts for children to be maximally influenced toward religious faith. Will our children have faith? Only if we work effectively within all of the contexts available to nurture that faith in an appealing manner.

REFERENCES

Anderson, J. (1988). Cognitive styles and multicultural populations. *Journal of Teacher Education, 39*, 2-8.

Barber, L. (1984). *Teaching Christian values*. Birmingham, AL: Religious Education Press.

Barna, G. (1989). *America 2000*. Glendale, CA: Barna Research.

Barna, G. (1990). *The frog in the kettle*. Ventura, CA: Regal.

Bellah, R. (1970). *Beyond belief*. New York: Harper & Row.

Brown, S., et al. (1982). *The incredible bread machine* (rev. ed.). San Diego: World Research.

Campolo, A. (1989). *Growing up in America*. Grand Rapids, MI: Zondervan.

Chollar, S. (1987). Latchkey children. *Psychology Today, 21*, 12.

Colby, K., & Payne, R. (1990). Religious released time education. *The Journal for Weekday Religious Education, 1*, 1-29 (center insert).

Cooley, C. (1902). *Human nature and the social order*. New York: Scribners.

Delahooke, M. (1986). *Home educated children's social/emotional adjustment*. Unpublished doctoral dissertation, Los Angeles: California School of Professional Psychology.

Dobbins, R. (1975). Too much too soon. *Christianity Today*, (October 24) 99-100.

Dobbins, R. (1985). *Venturing into a child's world*. Old Tappan, NJ: Revell.

Dworetzky, J. (1990). *Introduction to child development* (4th ed.). St. Paul, MN: West.

Eutychus (1987). Corn again. *Christianity Today* (April 3), 8.

Farley, J. (1990). *Sociology*. Englewood Cliffs, NJ: Prentice-Hall.

Gaede, S. (1985). *Belonging*. Grand Rapids, MI: Zondervan.

Gallup, G. (1989). *The people's religion*. New York: Macmillan.

Gearing, F., & Epstein, P. (1982). Learning to wait. In G. Spindler (Ed.), *Doing the ethnography of schooling*. New York: Holt, Rinehart and Winston.

Hale-Benson, J. (1986). *Black children* (rev. ed.). Baltimore: Johns Hopkins University Press.

Haynes, C. (1989). *Religion in American history: What to teach and how*. Alexandria, VA: Assn. for Supervision & Curriculum Development.

Heath, S. (1982). Questioning at home and at school. In G. Spindler (Ed.), *Doing the ethnography of schooling*. New York: Holt, Rinehart and Winston.

Holt, J. (1981). *Teach your own*. Boston: Holt Associates. Also see *Phi Delta Kappan* (February, 1983) for a series of articles on potentially positive relationships between public schools and home education.

Hoult, T. (1979). *Sociology for a new day* (2d ed). New York: Random House.

Hyde, K. (1990). *Religion in childhood and adolescence*. Birmingham, AL: Religious Education Press.

Journal file. (1990). *Journal of Psychology and Theology, 18*, 184-185.

Kladensky, G. (1974). The advantages of going to national schools. *Evangelical Missions Quarterly, 10,* 154-159.

Lee, J. (1985). *The content of religious instruction.* Birmingham, AL: Religious Education Press.

Light, D., Keller, S., & Calhoun, C. (1989). *Sociology.* New York: Knopf.

Living with our deepest differences (1990). Boulder, CO: Learning Connections.

Mattox, W. (1989). Restoring the black family. *Family Policy* (September-October), 1-7.

McAdoo, H., & McAdoo, J. (1985). *Black children.* Beverly Hills, CA: Sage.

McCluskey, R. (1982). Socialization. In S. Grunlan & M. Reimer (Eds.), *Christian perspectives on sociology.* Grand Rapids, MI: Zondervan.

Mead, G. H. (1934). *Mind, self, and society.* Chicago: University of Chicago Press.

Meier, P. (1977). *Christian child-rearing and personality development.* Grand Rapids, MI: Baker.

Mitchell, E. (1986). Oral tradition: Legacy of faith for the black church. *Religious Education, 81,* 93-112.

Moberg, D. (1984). *The church as a social institution* (2d ed.). Grand Rapids, MI: Baker.

Moore, R., & Moore, D. (1979). *School can wait.* Provo, UT: Brigham Young University Press.

Myers, D. (1990). *Social psychology* (3d ed.). New York: McGraw-Hill.

Parsons, T. (1959). The school class as a social system. *Harvard Educational Review, 19,* 297-318.

Parsons, T., & Bales, R. (1955). *Family, socialization, and the interaction process.* Glencoe, IL: The Free Press.

Pollock, D. (1987). Welcome home! Easing the pain of MK re-entry. *Evangelical Missions Quarterly, 23,* 278-283.

Powell, J. (1988). Counseling missionaries overseas. International Congress on Christian Counseling, Atlanta, GA (November 10).

Public education perestroika. (1990). Reported in *Family Research Council Washington Watch* (July), 2.

Rakeshaw, J. (1987). *An analysis of home schooling.* Doctoral dissertation, Tuscaloosa, AL: University of Alabama.

Ratcliff, D. (1985). The use of play in Christian education. *Christian Education Journal, 6,* 26-33.

Ray, B. (1990). Review of home-school research. *The Teaching Home* (August/September), 29-30. Dr. Ray is president of the Home Education Research Institute (25 W. Cremona, Seattle, WA 98119) and edits the *Home School Researcher.*

Rekers, G. (1982). *Shaping your child's sexual identity.* Grand Rapids, MI: Baker.

Religion in the public school curriculum. (1988). [A brochure jointly sponsored by 14 national organizations.] Available from the First Liberty Institute at George Mason University, 4400 University Dr., Fairfax, VA 22030. The guidelines were originally developed by the Public Education Religious Studies Center at Wright State University.

Schemmer, B. (1985). *Case studies of four families engaged in home education.* Doctoral dissertation, Muncie, IN: Ball State University.

Schickedanz, J., Hansen, K., & Forsyth, P. (1990). *Understanding children.* Mountain View, CA: Mayfield.

Schipper, D. (1977). *Self-concept differences between early, late and non-boarding missionary children.* Unpublished dissertation, Rosemead Graduate School of Psychology, LaMirada, CA.

Scollon, R., & Scollon, S. (1981). *Narrative, literacy and face in interethnic communication. Advances in discourse processes* (Vol. 7). Norwood, NJ: Ablex.

Sharp, L. (1985). Toward a greater understanding of the real MK. *Journal of Psychology and Christianity, 5,* 73-78.

Sharp, L. (1990a). Boarding schools: What difference do they make? *Evangelical Missions Quarterly, 26,* 26-35.

Sharp, L. (1990b). How missionary children become world Christians. *Journal of Psychology and Theology, 18,* 66-74.

Stellway, R. (1982). Religion. In S. Grunlan & M. Reimer (Eds.), *Christian perspectives on sociology.* Grand Rapids, MI: Zondervan.

Tischler, H. (1990). *Introduction to sociology* (3d ed.). Forth Worth: Holt, Rinehart and Winston.

Troutman, C. (1974). Family security. *Evangelical Missions Quarterly, 10,* 146-152.

Tucker, R. (1989). Growing up a world away. *Christianity Today* (February 17), 17-21.

Vander Zanden, J. (1990). *The social experience* (2nd ed.). New York: McGraw-Hill.

Villarreal, B. (1982). *An investigation of the effects of types of play.* Ph.D. dissertation, Pennsylvania State University.

Vitz, P. (1986). *Censorship.* Ann Arbor, MI: Servant.

Wagner, D., & Stephenson, H. (Eds.). (1982). *Cultural perspectives on child development.* San Francisco: Freeman.

Wallace, R., & Wallace, W. (1989). *Sociology* (2nd ed.). Boston: Allyn and Bacon.

Walsh, K., & Cowles, M. (1982). *Developmental discipline.* Birmingham, AL: Religious Education Press.

Weldin, M., & Weldin, C. (1982). Education. In S. Grunlan & M. Reimer (Eds.), *Christian perspectives on sociology.* Grand Rapids, MI: Zondervan.

Westerhoff, J. (1976). *Will our children have faith?* New York: Seabury.

Wickstrom, D., & Fleck, J. (1983). Missionary children. *Journal of Psychology and Theology*, *11*, 226-235.

Wilcox, K. (1982). Differential socialization in the classroom. In G. Spindler (Ed.), *Doing the ethnography of schooling*. New York: Holt, Rinehart and Winston.

Wright, K. (1990). Personal interview, Toccoa, GA (August 9). He is editor of *The Journal for Weekday Religious Education*, published by the National Association for Released Time Christian Education, 400 S. Main, Ellijay, GA 30540.

Wrobble, K. (1990). Adult MKs: How different are they? *Evangelical Missions Quarterly*, *26*, 164-170.

Wrobble, K., & Plueddemann, J. (1990). Psychosocial development in adult missionary kids. *Journal of Psychology and Theology*, *18*, 363-374.

Chapter Seven

Discipline, Development, and Spiritual Growth

CARY A. BUZZELLI AND KEVIN WALSH

The aim of religious education is development, which includes the intellectual, social, emotional, and moral growth of children. Development results from interactions embedded in a social community. Through deep and significant relationships with others we come to know ourselves and orient our lives and actions toward what is moral and ultimate in life.

Judgments of what is right or wrong, of how one treats others and hopes to be treated by others are issues of morality and form a basis for spiritual development. Discipline is the process of learning the behaviors, values, and attitudes which form the foundations of morality upon which such judgments are made. Thus, discipline is intimately embedded in the process of development, most significantly, in the development of morality. One specific goal in the process of development is autonomy—the ability to think for oneself while remaining aware of and responsive to the needs and feelings of others. The transcendence implicit in spirituality is influenced by prior interpersonal relationships as well as autonomous choosing of one's relationship with the divine. Mature faith is at once autonomous and relational.

Children's reasoning about what is right or wrong and the standards upon which they base their judgments are formed through interactions with their peers and with adults who are important to them. It is commonly held that morality arises neither from the mere internalization of cultural values nor from the gradual unfolding of innate emotions but rather is developed as the result of interactions between an individual and others within the social environment. This includes the religious aspects of one's environment.

Children's social interactions with peers and with adults require a knowledge of the principles, rules, and dynamics which govern relationships. Participation in social relationships also requires discipline. Through discipline individuals bring their behavior under control and use it for positive social ends. Discipline is genuinely educative when children control their behavior based upon standards they have internalized through interactions with peers and adults.

Growth toward maturity in self-discipline and morality occurs when discipline is fully integrated into the life of the children's community, be that home, school, or church. This involves the complementary processes children experience during interactions with peers and adults (Youniss, 1980). Through interactions with peers children develop notions of reciprocity and cooperation which deepen their knowledge and awareness of others. Moral development is further enhanced by allowing children opportunities to engage in discussion, compromise, and negotiation with peers as a part of problem solving and conflict resolution. Such experiences, guided by adults, nurture moral and spiritual growth.

Discipline promotes moral development, and specifically the development of autonomy when:
- It occurs within and as part of the social community; it is relationally embedded in the fabric of the child's social experiences with others.
- It focuses upon the child's ongoing development of character.
- It presents to the child the relationship of his/her own behavior to the thoughts, feelings, behaviors, and circumstances of others.
- It facilitates mutual respect, reciprocity, and cooperation.
- It encourages the continued movement toward more sophisticated and advanced levels of thought rather than merely sanctioning behavior.

Parents and religious educators guide and support children's development through their interactions with children and the discipline methods they use at home and in church. The discipline children experience in the school classroom also influences their moral development. Sensitive and skillful adults encourage children's moral development through discipline by providing children with opportunities to:
- Take perspectives of others by focusing on the emotions and points of view of others.
- Consider fairness by looking at how they treat others and are treated by others.
- Examine decisions as moral rather than as pragmatic, legal, or procedural.
- Consider higher levels of moral reasoning which are modeled by the teacher, parent, and other significant adults.

Through such experiences children acquire the behaviors, values, and attitudes upon which they base moral judgments of justice and caring. Thus, these experiences also play a vital role in the development of young children's spirituality. Understanding how discipline promotes moral development, and in turn how moral development is fundamental to spiritual development, is central to this chapter.

The models described in this chapter are representative of several theories of child development and their accompanying views of discipline. We believe the methods of discipline which include all the criteria outlined above are those that most nurture the moral and spiritual development of young children. These ideas, although discussed in the context of religious education, can be adapted by parents as they seek to teach their children about religion and faith.

The first two models presented, the Assertive Discipline model of Lee and Marlene Canter and the Behaviorist/Punishment model of James Dobson are based upon the behavioral theory of child development. Children's development and behavior are shaped by external forces through reinforcement and punishment (Skinner, 1971). The remaining three models, William Glasser's Reality model, the Social Discipline model of Rudolf Dreikurs, and Kevin Walsh's Developmental Discipline, all derive their theoretical framework from the social interaction theory of child development which views children's development as a continual process whereby children influence their social environment while being influenced by others in that social environment (Bronfenbrenner, 1979).

LEE AND MARLENE CANTER:
ASSERTIVE DISCIPLINE MODEL

Assertive Discipline is based on the following premises: 1) that people can choose to respond to conflict with others in three ways: assertively, nonassertively, or with hostility; 2) that teachers must attend to their own needs and rights if they are to provide optimum instruction for all children; and 3) that teachers can maintain appropriate behavior through the systematic use of behavioral principles such as reinforcement and punishment (Canter & Canter, 1976).

How religious educators respond to students' misbehavior sets expectations for acceptable behavior. Nonassertive teacher behavior involves pleading with students to obey, or timidly ignoring unacceptable behavior. Hostility toward students is marked by overly emotional reactions which can include belittling or berating children. According to the Canters, assertive teachers clearly and unambiguously state their rights, needs, and wishes. Assertive statements are not aggressive, obnoxious, or vengeful, nor are they vague, apologetic, or "wishy-washy" (Canter & Canter, 1976). Applied to the religious education situation, the Canters emphasize that teachers claim the following rights:

1) The right to establish a structure and routine that provides the optimal learning environment in light of your own strengths and weaknesses.

2) The right to determine and request appropriate behavior from the students which meets your needs and encourages the positive social and educational development of the child.

3) The right to ask for help from parents, supervisors, and others, when you need assistance with a child (1976, p. 2).

The Canters believe that the best approach is through the selective use of rewards and punishments of children's behavior. To this end, teachers are responsible for establishing a plan or list of rules based upon their needs, desires, and the limits of student behavior permissible to them, but which still allows for optimal instruction and learning. The rules should be specific and easily understood by the students. Children, once they have heard or read the rules, know what is expected of them. One plan might include the following examples: Always walk in church; keep your hands to yourself; do not take other people's property; always raise your hand to talk. A second equally important part of the plan is the consequences for violations of or compliance with the rules. Again these are clearly stated and might include the following examples:

Violations:

1. First violation, name on board.
2. Second violation, check next to name and ten-minute detention.
3. Third violation, second check next to name and note sent to parents.
4. Fourth violation, third check and isolation (Wolfgang & Glickman, 1986, p. 155).

Compliance:

1. Each student without a violation that day earns one point.
2. Students may "cash in" points at a specified time.
3. Students may "buy" recreation time, church library time, or items such as records, books, and so on.

The Canters caution that children's behavior not be attributed to causes beyond the teacher's control, such as family conditions, hyperactivity, or socio-economic background (Canter & Canter, 1976). All children are to be treated alike. All are expected to comply with the rules and to succeed.

For a teacher to devise and implement a plan, the teacher must have the approval and support of the religious education director and perhaps the church board and/or pastor or priest. Although the values in local communities may vary "the teacher has the right to teach and for the student to behave" (Wolfgang & Glickman, 1986, p. 156). Once all aspects of the plan are acceptable to those in charge and the teacher, the plan is ready to be implemented. The teacher ensures that all children are aware of and understand the plan. When misbehavior occurs the teacher can proceed through the four levels and strategies of intervention.

At the first level, when a teacher sees misbehavior, a general statement is made to the entire group. A nondirective comment such as, "We all should be on page 12," is intended to alert the misbehaving student without being singled out. If the misbehavior continues, the teacher moves to the second level strategy of questioning. The question, "Would you start work on page 12?" might be directed to the offending child. The teacher asks such a question with the purpose of redirecting the student's behavior without being directly confrontational. The student has been alerted, indirectly, as to the expected behavior. The student can now choose to comply or continue misbehaving.

Direct, confrontational statements are necessary in step three. The teacher clearly states what is expected of the student: "I want you to stop playing with that pencil and get to work on page 12." Failure to comply to direct statements leads to the final level of intervention, demands. Demands are presented to the student as a choice just as in the previous level. Demands are not threats, nor are they negotiated with the student. They are clear statements about expectations and consequences. The student's refusal to comply at this point means the student is choosing the consequences. For the Canters, teachers must be prepared to enforce the demands by presenting the student with the consequences. In the plan noted above, the student's name is written on the board. Subsequent violations will lead to subsequent consequences (i.e., check marks next to name, notes home, isolation). The Canters believe this method gives students the choice to behave or to be punished. The punishments outlined above are only examples and others might include depriving a child of participation in an outing or activity, or staying with parents.

As is evident in Assertive Discipline, the student may choose, by continuing to misbehave, to accept the consequences, namely punishment. In severe cases it might be necessary to remove the student from the learning situation. This can take the form of isolation where the student goes to a prearranged room for a period of time. The Canters emphasize that the teacher has the right to request the assistance of parents and designated leaders in extreme circumstances.

Much has been said concerning the consequences of misbehavior, but it is important to include in this discussion the consequences of compliance to the rules. Clearly, students who behave should be rewarded. The Canters view rewards as positive reinforcers. Teachers may reward the entire group noting their good behavior with points. When a predetermined number is reached the class may choose to see a video or have a popcorn party during the week. Similarly, as stated above, individual students can earn points or tokens which can be exchanged for certain desired activities (Canter & Canter, 1976).

Implications

It is difficult, and at times might be impossible to aid spiritual development in a chaotic situation. The Canters' approach can be used so teachers achieve and maintain a controlled context for learning. It is important to consider, however, that the style of discipline is a content in its own right (Lee, 1985). The use of rewards and punishments by teachers, parents, and others responsible for children's spiritual growth can influence children's conceptions of God. Careful consideration should be taken so that children do not come to envision God as a Santa Claus-type person who dispenses "goodies" as rewards and punishments for wrong-doings. Although the Canters' techniques may be effective in maintaining control, they may not engender the types of experiences which nurture the higher levels of thinking and ways of acting toward others which lead to the understanding of others' thoughts and feelings and promote higher levels of moral development.

JAMES DOBSON: DARE TO DISCIPLINE

Although James Dobson's method of discipline is derived from behavioristic theory, he deviates from the views of the Canters in two important areas: 1) the use of Christian principles, as he interprets them from the Bible, as guidelines for working with children; and 2) the use of corporal punishment.

For Dobson, religious values cannot and should not be separated from the standards and boundaries parents establish for children. In his book *Hide or Seek*, Dobson asks, "Why do I stress the role of Christian faith so strongly in reference to our children's self-esteem and worthiness? Because this belief offers the only way of life which can free us from the tyranny of the self" (1974, p. 157). Dobson then specifies a value system for raising children drawn from the Bible. "It is composed of six all-important principles: 1) devotion to God; 2) love for mankind; 3) respect for authority; 4) obedience to divine commandments; 5) self-discipline and self-control; and 6) humbleness of spirit" (1974, p. 158). As is evident, Dobson's focus is clearly on children's moral and social development.

Central to Dobson's model is belief in the proper combination of love and discipline. "Although love is essential to human life, parental responsibility extends far beyond it" (1970, p. 7). Similarly he states, "Love in the absence of instruction will not produce a child with self-discipline, self-control, and respect for his fellow man" (1970, p. 7). From this perspective Dobson recommends the restrained use of corporal punishment but only if the teacher has genuine affection for the child.

Dobson (1970) provides five guidelines for parents and teachers: "1) Developing respect for the parents is the critical factor in child management" (p.11). Parents and teachers must decide whether undesirable behavior is a direct challenge to their authority. Decisions to punish a child depend on this evaluation. "2) The best opportunity to communicate often occurs after punishment" (p. 21). Warmth and affection from parents and teachers show the child that it is the behavior and not the child that is objectionable. "3)

Control without nagging" (p. 23). Successful control techniques manipulate something that is important to the child, either as a reward or punishment. "4) Don't saturate the child with excessive materialism" (p. 29). Children given everything on demand will not learn the necessary lesson of delayed gratification. Children may only come to feel pleasure if a need is satisfied. By temporarily depriving the child of something, a need is generated which can later be fulfilled thus teaching the child important lessons about the value of things. "5) Avoid extremes in control and love" (p.32). The over-controlled child, under extreme parental authority, may never develop decision-making abilities, creativity, or self-identity. Nor will the child who is over-indulged, over-protected, and over-loved ever learn to take risks in relationships or the physical world and thereby will remain forever emotionally immature.

Dobson does advocate the use of corporal punishment, but for specific reasons and within specific guidelines. Corporal punishment should never be used on children over the age of ten. For Dobson, spanking and other forms of corporal punishment are a means of getting the child's attention on what has occurred. In effect it is a way to "teach the child a lesson" (1970). Special importance, in Dobson's view, is placed on parents and teachers establishing authority and maintaining respect. Dobson cites defiance as one situation warranting corporal punishment, as children must learn the consequences of open defiance to legitimate adult authority. "Spankings should be reserved for the moment a child expresses a defiant, 'I will not!' or 'You shut up!' When a youngster tries this kind of stiff-necked rebellion, you better take it out of him, and pain is a marvelous purifier" (1970, p. 13). A second instance is when children are destructive toward other people or the property of others. A pat on the hand or a few smacks on the rump informs the child that if one hurts others or their things, one can expect to be hurt. Another behavior which may deserve corporal punishment is if a child knowingly lies to a teacher or other person in authority. While an advocate of corporal punishment, Dobson repeatedly cautions that it be used only for specific violations and always with restraint. He also believes it should never be used in infancy and be tailored to different ages (Dobson, 1978). While Dobson is very direct about the reasons for and uses of corporal punishment, he is equally adamant that the teacher show genuine love, respect, and concern for students. "Discipline and love are not antithetical; one is a function of the other" (1970, p. 15). The parent or teacher "must convince himself that punishment is not something he does *to* the child; it is something he does *for* the child" (1970, p. 15). Part of caring is serving as a good model by displaying acceptable behavior. It also includes the appropriate use of positive reinforcement such as tokens.

Like the Canters, Dobson believes that at the beginning of the year the teacher should set down clear expectations for children's behavior. Rules are presented matter-of-factly. They are neither discussed nor negotiated with the children. The teacher ensures that all children understand the rules and that those who break the rules can expect to receive the consequences. These consequences may include being deprived of a favorite activity, isolation, and corporal punishment (spanking). For those who abide by the rules there are positive consequences or rewards such as tokens, more time in favored activities, or serving as the teacher's helper.

Dobson advocates several of the same teacher behaviors outlined by the Canters, but with minor variations. Silently looking on is used primarily to gather information about the child's behavior. By observing, the teacher may discern the environmental conditions which reward the child's misbehavior while gathering data for making changes which could lead to environmental reinforcement of appropriate behaviors (Dobson, 1970).

If the behavior continues the teacher must act immediately but in a calm manner. The child is told of the misbehavior and that the consequence is punishment. The student who is showing off or is so disruptive that instruction is impossible should be removed to an isolated area for a specified time. In this way Dobson differs from other writers who allow the children to decide when they should return. Unacceptable behavior upon return to the room is cause for longer periods of isolation. Those children who do show improved behavior upon return should be rewarded (Dobson, 1970).

In those cases where corporal punishment is deemed necessary, the teacher removes the child from the room. The teacher tells the child why the punishment is occurring and then proceeds to spank the child. Following the punishment, the teacher is to offer consolation and affection to the child. As noted above, it is important for the child to know that the behavior is unacceptable, not the child.

Implications

Dobson presents to religious educators a view of discipline that goes beyond merely manipulating or controlling behavior. Dobson's central goal is to achieve a balance in the proper combination of love and discipline. Within this context, children may come to develop a concept of God as one who balances love and justice. However religious educators must carefully consider the use of corporal punishment. Although the dictum of "sparing the rod, and spoiling the child" is still held in high regard by some, others regard the use of corporal punishment as an act of violence. Children are entrusted to the care of the adults in their community. Children learn through what they experience and what they observe. Is the use of corporal punishment, most evident in a hand raised to strike another, usually smaller, weaker individual, an image we want to instill in our children about how we hope they will attempt to solve their conflicts?

RUDOLF DREIKURS: SOCIAL DISCIPLINE MODEL

Rudolf Dreikurs based his theories of children's behavior on the writings of social psychologist Alfred Adler. Adler postulated that "the need to belong or to be accepted is the basic human motivation" (Dreikurs & Grey, 1968a, p. 26). From this Dreikurs derives his central theme that all behavior, including misbehavior, is purposeful, orderly, and directed toward a goal. The goal is social recognition—the feeling that one belongs as part of a group. Thus, children's behaviors are based upon decisions they make about how they can belong to a group.

Dreikurs believes that parents and teachers may not always provide enough appropriate opportunities for children to gain social recognition. As a result children learn alternative ways based upon mistaken goals about how to belong and gain status from others. "Even though the behavior is inappropriate, it is based upon the belief that it is the only way to be significant to others" (Dreikurs, Grunwald, & Pepper, 1971, p. 13). Parents and teachers unaware of the meaning of children's behavior may reinforce the mistaken goals. To change children's behavior parents and teachers must recognize the faulty goals of misbehavior and provide positive ways of group acceptance. Dreikurs identifies four goals underlying misbehavior: 1) attention-getting; 2) power and control; 3) revenge; and 4) show of helplessness (Dreikurs & Cassel, 1972, p. 41).

Each goal will be described followed by a discussion of how teachers and parents can recognize children's goals.

1) *Attention-getting.* Children who fail to receive social recognition in positive ways may seek proof of acceptance through what they can get from others, especially others' attention. These children need constant validation of their belonging. Through their behavior they say, "Hey notice me! I'm here and I'm important!" (Dinkmeyer, McKay, & Dinkmeyer, 1980, p. 10). Children use a variety of behaviors to gain attention. Some children use active strategies such as excessive talking, fighting, or clowning. Others use passive means to get noticed such as requiring constant reminders to complete assignments, dawdling, or withdrawing so as to be coaxed to participate. The repeated attempts of teachers and parents to punish or persuade children to end such behaviors only meet the children's goal of getting attention.

2) *Power and control.* Power struggles may follow adults' attempts to stop a child's annoying, attention-getting behavior. Adult demands for control are met head-on by the child's resistance. It is the child who seeks to control the adult, for feelings of acceptance and worthiness come by doing whatever one wants, by challenging authority, resisting rules, and refusing to do what others want. A battle of wills ensues. When adults fight power with power they unknowingly play into the child's hands. "Once the battle has been joined the child has already won it" (Dreikurs & Grey, 1968a, p. 38).

3) *Revenge*. The rejected child who has lost faith in self and others, whose sense of belonging remains unfulfilled by attention-getting or gaining power, may seek revenge. Hope of attaining worthiness through cooperative behavior is abandoned. Hurt and feeling isolated the child seeks to hurt others through retaliation. "The only role that such a child can play is to get even with those who hurt him" (Dreikurs et al., 1971, p. 18). A child may pursue revenge actively by physically or verbally attacking the teacher or other children. At other times revenge may be passive through defiant, hateful looks, or indirectly by damaging others' property (Dinkmeyer et al., 1980, p. 13).

4) *Helplessness*. The child who is completely discouraged may choose to withdraw from further attempts to gain recognition and acceptance from others. Overcome by feelings of hopelessness, the child wants only to be left alone. For such a child, significance lies in hiding behind real or imagined inadequacies and in the adults' acceptance of the inadequacies (Dreikurs et al, 1971, p. 19). Often the inadequacies appear in one specific area, such as mathematics or writing.

To deal with misbehavior, knowledge of the child's goal is necessary. How do adults recognize the goals of misbehavior? Dreikurs offers three approaches to diagnosing the child's goal (Dreikurs & Grey, 1968a). The first means is observation. The reactions the child evokes from others may give some indication of the goal. Dreikurs' second method is "corrective feedback." The teacher observes the child's reaction to attempts to stop the child's behavior. For example, bids for attention may cease temporarily if the child is reprimanded. However, if the goal is revenge the behavior may escalate. The third approach focuses on adults' emotions. Feeling annoyed means that the child has gotten our attention. Anger toward the child indicates a power struggle. Hurt feelings may result from a child's revengeful attack. Inability to help a child may stir feelings of despair and helplessness (Dinkmeyer et al., 1980). By recognizing their feelings, adults can avoid meeting the child's goal of misbehavior.

Children can change their behavior if they are shown better alternatives for attaining acceptance and recognition. For Dreikurs this involves the identification of the faulty goal, the use of natural/logical consequences rather than punishment, and encouragement.

Discipline is necessary for effective teaching and learning to occur in religious education contexts. Dreikurs states that many adults confuse discipline with punitive means by using punishment for discipline. Dreikurs believes that not only does punishment deter children's ambition, it simply does not work (Dreikurs & Grey, 1968b). Natural and logical consequences are positive ways of providing discipline. A natural consequence is defined as the normal or inherent result of one's behavior. A logical consequence is arranged by adults but is directly related to the child's behavior. For example, a child hurrying in the hallway to be first on the playground may trip and fall whereas another who rushes and pushes others may be removed by the teacher to the end of the line. The first child experienced a natural consequence; the second, a logical consequence. By experiencing the natural and logical consequences of their behavior, children come to assume responsibility for their own behavior (Dreikurs & Grey, 1968b).

For Dreikurs there are important differences between punishment and use of natural/logical consequences. Punishment is rarely related to the child's behavior, whereas natural/logical consequences have a direct relationship to behavior. Punishment may involve moral and value judgments about the child's behavior. Logical consequences, by distinguishing between the child and the behavior, between doer and deed, avoid such judgments. The child can feel worthy of acceptance regardless of behavior, for it is the behavior that is not acceptable (Dreikurs & Grey, 1968a). Punishment can be used in retaliation and in anger, "to teach a child a lesson." Logical consequences are not emotionally laden because adults are not emotionally involved. Adults acting as "friendly bystanders are not personally engaged and therefore do not feel threatened or defeated" (Dreikurs & Grey, 1968a, p.77).

Children can begin feeling acceptance and may be more likely to change their behavior in a climate of respect and optimism (Dinkmeyer & Dreikurs, 1963). Adults can create such an environment through encouragement. For Dreikurs, it is crucial for adults to recognize the differences between encouragement and praise. "Encouragement involves the ability to accept the child as worthwhile, regardless of any deficiency" (Dreikurs & Grey, 1968b, p. 26). Encouragement as an acknowledgement of effort can be given freely to all children. Praise given for satisfying the demands of others can invite a sense of failure for tasks attempted but not completed. Encouragement focuses on children's strengths and their ability to evaluate their own efforts. Praise is judgmental because it relates children's value to their work. Finally, encouragement shows adults' faith in children and enables children to have faith in themselves.

Implication

One of Dreikurs' central themes is the importance of social recognition. For religious educators this means that each child wants and needs affirmation as a worthwhile and valued person. Affirmation and worthiness of personhood are central tenets of the Christian message. God freely gives these to all. Often, however, within families and religious contexts some children may not feel valued. Children's mistaken goals about how to receive recognition result in their misbehavior. Religious educators can provide a climate where all children feel affirmed and worthy. Through their interactions with children, religious educators can practice and model Christian behaviors such as not "fighting force with force," withdrawing from power struggles with children or by reaffirming children who feel inadequate. As Christians we are called to encourage one another. Encouragement through affirmation of one another is sharing God's love.

WILLIAM GLASSER: REALITY MODEL

William Glasser is a psychiatrist whose initial training was in Freudian psychoanalysis. However, Glasser's early experiences in psychiatry led him to question some of Freud's major tenets. Traditional psychoanalysis emphasizes the unconscious and seeks answers to the "why" of people's behavior. Glasser's interest is in "what" people do, the behaviors of people, especially actions used to meet their needs. Glasser acknowledges the unconscious, but it is not a necessary part of the process of helping people fulfill their needs. Helping must be consciously undertaken to be effective.

All people have the same basic physiological and psychological needs but we vary considerably in our ability to meet them. According to Glasser there are two basic psychological needs: "The need to love and to be loved and the need to feel that we are worthwhile to ourselves and to others" (1965, p. 10). The inability to meet these needs leads to aberrant behavior and in the case of children, misbehavior. In Glasser's view children's misbehavior is denying the reality of the world around them, the world of home and church and their rules. Misbehavior indicates an unwillingness or inability to take responsibility for meeting one's basic needs (Glasser, 1965).

The goal of Reality Therapy is to lead people to meet their needs successfully, that is, "toward grappling successfully with the tangible and intangible aspects of the real world" (1965, p. 6). In essence, we fulfill our needs by acting with a conscious awareness of reality, responsibility and knowledge of right-wrong (1965). Acting upon this awareness forms the foundation of discipline.

In his book *Schools Without Failure*, William Glasser (1969) states that much of the emphasis placed on failure in general and upon educational failure in particular is misleading. Viewed from the perspective of Reality Therapy there are only two kinds of failure; failure to love and the failure to achieve self-worth. Children do want and need to feel love, to feel self-worth and to experience success. But meeting these needs is a difficult task especially for children. Children who cannot meet their needs experience failure, a failure resulting in misbehavior and feelings of loneliness. Misbehavior also results from the failure of teachers and organizations to meet the needs of children and to provide the means for children to meet their own needs. The application of Reality Therapy is best understood through examining the role of reality, responsibility, and right-wrong.

In Glasser's view, one role of educators and parents is to help children understand and accept the reality that each one of us has needs and that it is our responsibility to fulfill our needs. Meeting our needs is a necessary part of developing feelings of love and self-worth. Children's misbehavior is one way for them to deny this reality.

A second task for educators and parents is to help children take active responsibility for fulfilling their own needs. They are responsible for their behavior and must bear the consequences regardless of how dependent they claim to be. To Glasser, "Students are responsible for fulfilling their needs; they are responsible for their behavior" (1969, p. 19). But as we live in the world with other people and expect children to fulfill their needs, we must also demand that when they do so they not infringe upon the rights of others. By acting responsibly, children gain feelings of self-worth and of being worthwhile to others.

The third aspect of Reality Therapy is the recognition that fulfilling our needs also involves an understanding of morals, standards, values, and of right and wrong behavior. These, too, are a necessary part of feelings of love and self-worth. Children begin to feel worthwhile through behaviors which meet the standards of behavior of themselves and others and by learning to evaluate their behavior in regard to those standards.

Implementing the principles of Reality Therapy in religious education contexts involves the use of: 1) directive statements; 2) questions; 3) realistic consequences; and 4) group meetings. For Glasser the successful implementation of these strategies is based upon a caring and personal relationship between the educator and the children. Glasser believes that "we gain self-respect through discipline and closeness to others through love. Discipline must always have within it elements of love" (1965, p. 22). Children begin to learn about responsibility and right-wrong in relationship with someone who they know cares about them. With this in mind we will examine the four strategies.

Educators must establish clear and definite boundaries of acceptable behavior. These limits must be enforced. When a child transgresses the boundaries a teacher is to confront the child directly. The teacher should tell the child to stop the irresponsible, inappropriate behavior and then explicitly describe the appropriate behavior. These actions do not belittle the child but rather focus the child's attention on the irresponsible behavior and the responsible behavior.

In situations when directive statements do not result in behavior changes, Glasser's second strategy is for the teacher to follow directive statements with questions. By asking, "What are you doing?" the teacher is forcing the child to focus on "what" is happening in the present situation. The teacher is not concerned with "why" questions. "Why" implies that the reasons for a behavior make a difference in the child's behavior. Glasser believes they do not make a difference but only offer an opportunity for the child to give excuses as a way of disowning the behavior (1965). The teacher can follow the "what" question by asking the child, "How does (talking, pushing, hitting, and so on) help you?" This question asks the child to think about the consequences of the behavior. Often the child cannot answer this question. At this point the teacher can ask the child for a plan and a commitment, "What do you plan to do so you won't break the rule again?" or "What can you do so that you can (finish your work, and so on)?" These questions place the responsibility for the child's behavior with the child not with the teacher. Further misbehavior will be dealt with according to the child's plan. The teacher, rather than being an adversary becomes a partner with the child in devising and implementing the child's plan for responsible behavior which reflects the child's thoughts and feelings.

Glasser, like Dreikurs, strongly believes that the child should experience the consequences of all behavior. The consequences are usually based upon the plan the child has outlined. This allows the child, not the teacher, to decide what the positive or negative consequences of the behavior will be. In some cases a child may choose not to devise a plan and wait for the teacher to assume the responsibility. The teacher can suggest a plan that the child can accept or send the child somewhere until the child plans an acceptable alternative. Glasser suggests that the teacher have the child sign the plan as a pledge to honor it. By doing this the child is making a commitment to abide by the agreed-upon plan.

Glasser does not advocate punishment because he believes it is ineffective. Instead, Glasser suggests a three-step process of removal and isolation of children who misbehave. Removal and isolation are not seen as punishment, but as opportunities for children to reconsider their plans and begin again.

The first step is "in-class" (or in-group) isolation in which the child is able to observe but is not to interfere with religious instruction. As noted, the teacher may ask the child while in isolation to reformulate a plan acceptable to both child and teacher. If misbehavior persists during "in-class" isolation the next step in the isolation process is warranted. The child is removed from the group to a designated area for suspension. For Glasser, such treatment represents the reality of societal expectations for all to abide by rules and laws. "In-church" suspension further reinforces for the child the necessity to plan and act responsibly in the group. At this point, Glasser believes it is still not necessary to involve the parents. Warning notes that ask or demand that parents punish the child only serve to make parents responsible for that which they cannot take responsibility, the child's behavior. The final step of isolation is suspension from the religious education program. Return is contingent upon the child making a mutually acceptable plan.

At each step the teacher continues to be personally involved with the child. This involvement is expressed to the child as a caring attitude and willingness to help. "I care enough about you to force you to act in a better way, in a way you will learn through experience to know, and I already know, is the right way" (Glasser, 1965, p. 19). Thus, the caring teacher cares enough to make the child do what he has committed to do in the plan. In Glasser's words, "Before one can successfully change behavior one must be involved" (1969, p. 124).

Group meetings afford another opportunity for teacher-student involvement. During the meetings there are no wrong answers, so each participant can feel successful. Teachers and students are free to express feelings, ideas, and opinions. Glasser describes three types of meetings: 1) social problem-solving meetings; 2) open-ended meetings; and 3) educational diagnostic meetings (1969).

During social problem-solving meetings the group deals with a real problem in their context which affects them. The problem may cover rules, such as taking turns using limited educational resources. The meetings may also serve to address any subject that might be important to any individual child, such as disruptive behavior, stealing, or fighting. Glasser stresses that the focus must always remain on solving the problem and finding better ways to behave rather than on punishment (1969).

Open-ended meetings provide a forum to discuss students' interests and questions related to specific topics or anything of general interest in their lives. The purpose is to stimulate students' thinking on the subject and to help them relate what they may already know to the topic under discussion. Glasser sees the meetings as a time for children to use their brains to address and solve problems. To Glasser this is a necessary departure from curricula which may emphasize only the learning of facts.

Educational-diagnostic meetings are directly related to what the students are studying at the time. One purpose is to help the teacher evaluate the students' progress in the subject, such as what they already know, what they don't know, and what they might like to know. A second purpose is to evaluate teaching procedures to gauge their effectiveness. Both processes gather information teachers could use to make curriculum decisions. (Assessment in religious education, to be considered in chapter ten, might also make use of this kind of meeting.)

Implications

Glasser calls to the attention of religious educators two basic psychological needs we all have: The need to love and be loved, and the need to feel valued by ourselves and others. By taking responsibility for meeting these needs children come to feel self-love and self-worth. God's love and affirmation, freely given to all, is received by us through our faith in God. But Christian life is lived through faith and behavior. As a matter of behavior, Christian maturity means assuming the responsibility and autonomy to seek answers to questions and problems through the use of one's skills, abilities, and available resources. This can mean seeking the counsel of a priest or minister, but not relying exclusively on their answers. Fulfilling needs within a faith community also requires an understanding of the community's values. The plans children construct should be consistent with the values of the specific faith community. As a matter of faith, we rely on God's love and mercy as we pray for our needs and those of others. In this regard religious educators must respect the autonomy of each child's relationship with God.

KEVIN WALSH: DEVELOPMENTAL DISCIPLINE MODEL

Developmental Discipline is based upon two fundamental premises. First, that the developmental nature of the child plays a major role in the enactment of a successful discipline process. Second, that the disciplining of the child must be perceived as a moral and social experience that ends in the development of character.

Concerning the former, Developmental Discipline emphasizes the importance in having knowledge of development to successfully discipline the child. In short, it stresses that in order to provide the proper discipline of the child at any age, the adult must understand the nature of the child during that age. By assimilating the thoughts of such psychological theorists as Piaget, Erikson, Freud, Kohlberg, and Maslow, Developmental Discipline attempts to prove that nature, through development, sets forth a plan by which the young establish conscience. Showing the relationship between and among the different theories, Walsh (& Cowles, 1982) presents a portrait of development which is unified and whole.

By showing the interdependent relationship among the various theories Walsh concludes that the child between the ages of birth and twelve is driven to find safety—which is only found through limits, a properly constituted authority, and consistency. He believes that the child develops the foundation of a conscience directly and indirectly through the limits encountered consistently from a properly constituted authority. In this way nature provides the opportunity for each generation to help set in place those morals and values it deems important for the young to possess for their good and the good of their culture.

Concerning the latter premise of Developmental Discipline, Walsh believes that the laying of the foundation of conscience is in fact the developing of character in the child. Therefore, he believes that the end result of the discipline of the child must be the development of character, which includes development of a social conscience. He stresses that a generation does not successfully discipline its children unless they come to maturity realizing that they live in a society with others and that they have a responsibility to that society and to those others. To Walsh, discipline is not what you do to children when they misbehave nor what you do to children when they behave or even the combination of these two. Discipline is in essence, the process by which children learn, through experience, the morals and values of their culture.

Walsh fuses the two major premises of Developmental Discipline by focusing on the origin and nature of the development of conscience. Through the intricate weaving of the work of psychological theorists with that of philosophers such as Hegel, Dewey, and Teilhard de Chardin, he introduces what he calls nature's plan.

Walsh explains nature's plan as an upward progression of life. He believes that discipline is the primary process by which all cultures inculcate their vital morals, values, and attitudes within the young. However, he perceives discipline as merely one aspect of the overall plan of nature by which all cultures are provided with a way to continue to renew and improve themselves through their young. For Walsh, the process of culture is in fact the process of life itself (Walsh & Cowles, 1982). As a result of this concept he believes that the American culture must initially focus upon what it wants to become, for the process of culture is reflected in its process of education (including its religious education), and its process of education is reflected in its method of discipline. Therefore, he strongly argues that discipline by its very nature must always be envisioned as the means by which the American culture helps to establish a foundation of conscience which includes the morals and values that result in a social conscience. To this end, Developmental Discipline concedes that there are universal morals such as truthfulness, honesty, respect for human life, and respect for human dignity that must be established in the foundation of conscience during the developing years of the young. However, Walsh stresses that his intention is not only to develop universal morals but also to direct the attention of all those who work with the young to what he terms the five hidden elements of morality that are essential to the American culture: 1) the work ethic; 2) perseverance; 3) constructive self-criticism; 4) cooperation; and 5) responsibility toward family. He believes that these five elements of morality provide the means of shared interest by which the continuity of national character is developed within the culture.

Walsh states that "the development of the five basic aspects of morality that build a sound American culture, when viewed holistically, constitutes social consciousness: the responsibility of the individual within a democratic pluralistic society and a society composed of individuals" (Walsh & Cowles, 1982, pp. 25-26).

Therefore, Developmental Discipline is presented as a process that begins with a parent or teacher who organizes a social environment appropriate to the developmental age of the child, and through the interaction of the child with that environment continually lays the foundation of his conscience.

In order to facilitate the establishment of the Developmental Discipline process Walsh presents what he calls the Trinity of Discipline—Structure,

Intervention, and Consistency. He states that "through the harmony of the Trinity of Discipline the child comes to understand both himself and his social responsibilities" (Walsh & Cowles, 1982, p. 54). He believes that "these three elements, when rhythmically enacted, are a part of the transformation the child makes from being self-centered and uncontrolled to becoming socially conscious and self-disciplined" (p. 54).

Structure. To Walsh, "Structure is that element which provides the overall limits to the child's environment. Through it comes the reality of social living as it comes to bear on the child" (Walsh & Cowles, 1982, p. 54). He believes that a structured environment allows the child to utilize his natural impulses, appropriate to his age of development, but also guides and directs him in the use of those impulses.

In Developmental Discipline, a structured environment has four interacting components: 1) psychological; 2) physical; 3) content; and 4) process. Walsh believes that an environment, involving social interactions of children, is not structured unless the child's psychological needs for safety through limits, a properly constituted authority, and consistency are first met. Following along the lines of his theoretical base, Walsh urges parents and teachers to realize that if the child's basic need for safety is not satisfied, all learning is relegated to a secondary status by the child.

In order to assist in meeting the primary need for psychological structure Walsh introduces the physical component. It is his belief that a structured environment is all too often perceived as purely a physical component. That is to say, when most people speak of a structured environment they are referring only to how it is physically arranged. Developmental Discipline promotes the idea that if the child's need for safety (a psychological structure) is satisfied, no matter what physical arrangement is employed, the environment is structured. However, Walsh is quick to point out that some physical arrangements are inherently more likely to satisfy the child's safety needs than others. For example, if a room is too small for the number of assigned children, it is a liability; or if it is an open space with too many distractions it also is a liability to establishing structure. However, Walsh believes that almost any environment can be structured by an insightful adult who understands that children need psychological safety and that they find it primarily in the physical limits of the environment.

Walsh presents the third of his four interacting components, content, as the means by which a parent or teacher develops the aforementioned psychological and physical components. He considers the content of a structured environment to be its limits, which when analyzed include six elements: rules, responsibilities, love, modeling, consequences, and manners. He believes that by establishing these elements of content within the structured environment the child's need for safety is met. In addition the elements become the means by which the child's foundation of conscience is laid.

Walsh emphasizes that each one of these elements must be implemented in such a way as to help develop an individual who can regulate his or her own actions. To use his words, "Limits should not be seen, except in dangerous situations, as a means of immediate control but rather as a way of providing needed guidance for the child as he is growing into responsibility for his own behavior" (Walsh & Cowles, 1982, p. 54).

It is Walsh's contention that it is the adult's responsibility to prepare the child for living and thus, it is vital that limit setting be a developmental process directed toward this end. He believes that the child must participate in the limit-setting process for two important reasons: First, the child, as a member of a democratic society, must eventually participate in rule making; and second, the child will tend to see rules in which he has participated in establishing as being his own, not merely rules someone else is forcing on him. However, Walsh clearly indicates that having the child participate in the establishing of the limits in no way should be interpreted as allowing the child to set his own limits. He states that "young children often set unrealistic limits with extremely harsh physical or humiliating consequences, while the adolescent in his drive for adulthood often will abolish all controls" (p. 57).

Following his presentation on the establishing of the content of a structured environment Walsh discusses each of the six elements of the content of an environment in detail; most specifically he focuses on what each element is and how the adult is to introduce it into the child's life. Included within this are suggested manners to be learned as well as suggested consequences the teacher or parent can use to successfully help the child develop into a productive adult.

The fourth and final interacting component of a structured environment process Walsh presents as being the transformation from an adult-controlled environment to that of a child-responsible environment. It is within this component that he draws the aforementioned elements of content into workable educational or home situations. Put quite simply, the adult must initially be in charge. If begun in any other way the environment will become uncontrolled and totally unproductive for the child. Walsh believes that it is from routine that responsibility is formed. However, he is quick to point out that the transformation from an adult-controlled environment to a child-responsible one must be undertaken, even if it is not as easy and as simple as maintaining control, because for Walsh the goal of discipline is that of developing adults who possess morals and values rather than those who are possessed by them. The goal is to produce adults who think for themselves not merely about themselves.

Intervention is the second aspect of the Trinity of Discipline. Intervention is the means by which an adult maintains or makes adjustments in the structured environment. Developmental Discipline presents intervention as having two principles and eight different techniques.

The two principles are given as overriding rules for the utilization of the eight techniques. The first principle is to always use the least intervention necessary to succeed. Whenever an adult can achieve a desired result by merely giving a hand signal, for example, it is better than having to firmly say something to the child. The second principle is whenever the child can help to determine the outcome, there is a greater chance of success with the problem situation. This emphasizes a key idea which is presented throughout the entire process of Developmental Discipline. That is, whenever the child helps to create the desired environment or a desired outcome, success is achieved more often because of his personal perception of and responsibility in that outcome.

Developmental Discipline includes eight intervention techniques: 1) physical; 2) verbal; 3) nonverbal; 4) positioning; 5) removal of seductive objectives or activities; 6) observation and recording; 7) humor; and 8) positive intervention.

Positive intervention is given special status as it is a major part of the other seven techniques. In short, intervention as part of the Trinity of Discipline describes the interactive tools to be used by the adult for successful discipline.

Consistency is the third and final aspect of the Trinity of Discipline. Walsh reiterates the importance of consistency in successful discipline, detailing seven practical applications. Walsh includes consistencies such as those within ourselves, that is, consistency between what we say and what we do, and among properly constituted authorities, and discusses how to develop such consistencies within a discipline process. More than anything else, this aspect of the trinity is an attempt to show that no matter what structure an adult establishes with a child or how many intervention techniques the adult knows, if he is inconsistent in his behavior toward the child, true discipline is totally impossible. For Walsh, inconsistency breeds insecurity and insecurity breeds discipline problems.

In concluding the Trinity of Discipline, Walsh states that the trinity describes the elements of discipline and how they work. Yet another trinity also helps make the discipline process successful: thought, love, and patience. He believes that it is only through all of these factors that the social conscience of the child can be brought to a sufficient level that will enable him to be a productive member of society.

Implications

Walsh focuses on the development of social conscience. This idea has long been neglected in discussions of discipline. For religious educators the recognition of the development of conscience as an important guide of personal behavior is crucial. Conscience develops through interactions with others, and reflection upon those interactions. For Walsh the foundation of social conscience is based upon the trinity of discipline of structure, intervention and consistency. For religious educators, the trinity of discipline while forming the foundation of social conscience provides the central core of spiritual development. Spiritual development is not possible without a structure within which one acts, nor is it possible solely as an individual activity; nor is it possible without consistent effort of all involved in our spiritual formation. We need the support, affirmation, and guidance of others.

REFERENCES

Bronfenbrenner, U. (1979). *The ecology of human development: Experiments by nature and design.* Cambridge, MA: Harvard University Press.

Canter, L., & Canter, M. (1976). *Assertive discipline: A take-charge approach for today's educator.* Seal Beach, CA: Canter and Associates.

Dinkmeyer, D., & Dreikurs, R. (1963). *Encouraging children to learn: The encouragement process.* Englewood Cliffs, NJ: Prentice-Hall.

Dinkmeyer, D., McKay, G.D., Dinkmeyer, D. Jr. (1980). *Systematic training for effective teaching - Teacher's handbook.* Circle Pines, MN: American Guidance Service.

Dobson, J. (1970). *Dare to discipline.* Wheaton, IL: Tyndale House Publishers.

Dobson, J. (1974). *Hide or seek.* Old Tappan, NJ: Revell.

Dobson, J. (1978). *The strong-willed child: Birth to adolescence.* Wheaton, IL: Tyndale House.

Dreikurs, R. (1958). *The challenge of parenthood.* New York: Hawthorn.

Dreikurs, R., & Cassel, P. (1972). *Discipline without tears.* New York: Hawthorn.

Dreikurs, R., & Grey, L. (1968a). *A new approach to discipline: Logical consequences.* New York: Hawthorn.

Dreikurs, R., & Grey, L. (1968b). *A parents' guide to discipline.* New York: Hawthorn.

Dreikurs, R., Grunwald, B.B., & Pepper, F.C. (1971). *Maintaining sanity in the classroom: Illustrated teaching techniques.* New York: Harper & Row.

Glasser, W. (1965). *Reality therapy.* New York: Harper & Row.

Glasser, W., (1969). *Schools without failure.* New York: Harper & Row.

Lee, J.M. (1985). *The content of religious instruction: A social science approach.* Birmingham, AL: Religious Education Press.

Skinner, B.F. (1971). *Beyond freedom and dignity.* New York: Knopf.

Walsh, K., & Cowles, M. (1982). *Developmental discipline.* Birmingham, AL: Religious Education Press.

Wolfgang, C.H., & Glickman, C.D. (1986). *Solving discipline problems: Strategies for classroom teachers.* Boston, MA: Allyn & Bacon.

Youniss, J. (1980). *Parents and peers in social development.* Chicago: University of Chicago Press.

Chapter Eight

General Procedures of Teaching Religion

JAMES MICHAEL LEE

"Blessed be childhood, which brings down something of heaven into the midst of our rough earthliness."

Henri Frédéric Amiel

INTRODUCTION

This chapter deals with generic principles and procedures of teaching religion to children of elementary school age. The chapter which follows this one is devoted to specific strategies, methods, and techniques.

A brief note on terminology is in order at this point. Every science creates or appropriates special technical language in order to delineate clearly defined parameters and to give precise meanings to the words or phrases which it uses. Thus, for example, theological science employs technical terms like "epiphany," "eucharist," and "metanoia," terms which have special meaning to persons who know something about theological science but which inherently mean little or nothing to persons ignorant of theology. Medical science also has many technical terms, such as "biopsy" for example. Computer science utilizes a host of technical terms; "cache memory" is one such example. Educational science also has its own set of technical words and phrases. I will use technical educational terms in this chapter because these terms are or at least should be an integral part of the childhood religious educator's professional vocabulary.

Sometimes a technical term has one meaning in everyday usage, or one connotation in some sector of the general public, but has a far different meaning in scientific vocabulary. In everyday parlance, for example, a bus is a large streetbound motorized vehicle capable of transporting a relatively large number of people. In computer science, however, a bus is a set of parallel conductors in a computer system that forms a main transmission path for data. For some persons, the term "instruction" connotes a highly stylized, didactic, cognitive, verbal form of teaching conducted in a formal setting such as a classroom. Despite the fact that Webster's Third Unabridged dictionary equates the term "instruction" with the entire practice of teaching, some general educationists (Eisner, 1979, pp. 158-159) and some religious educationists (Westerhoff, 1976b, p. 76) still cling to the highly restrictive meaning of instruction. In this chapter I am using the word "instruction" as I have always used it, namely, as a synonym for teaching in its totality with no restriction as to environment, subject-matter, or product. I prefer the word "instruction" because the term underscores the fact that teaching is an art/science, namely, a well-honed skill deployed intentionally from a scientific base. The term "instruction," then, gives a certain scientifically laden and process-based valence to the term "teaching."

GENERIC TEACHING PRINCIPLES AND PROCEDURES

There are some religious educators who believe that instructional principles and procedures are *fundamentally* different for religion teaching than for other nonreligious substantive contents such as history, theology, or mathematics. This view is erroneous (Dunkin & Biddle, 1974, pp. 26-27). Teaching principles and procedures are by and large generic, much as surgery principles and procedures are typically generic. The way in which a surgeon cuts, separates, and sutures the stomach is basically the same as the way in which he/she cuts, separates, and sutures the arm or the thigh. There are, of course, specific differences in the way a religion teacher deploys a teaching procedure at a given time and circumstance. These specific differences are instances of the generic procedure.

The point I am making is that specific teaching procedures are not fundamentally different from the *applicable* generic pedagogical principles or procedures. Rather, specific teaching procedures fall under the overall umbrella of an appropriate generic principle or procedure. Every genus contains within itself a wide variety of derivative specific differences. Indeed, one sure-fire test of the richness and fecundity of a generic principle and procedure is the number of specific procedures which flow from it.

Consequently a chapter on general principles and procedures of teaching religion to children is justified. But more than this, the fact that there are indeed general principles and procedures of religious instruction suggests that to be truly effective the childhood religious educator should first master the applicable generic teaching principles and procedures before attempting to master one or another specific teaching method or technique which flows from, and thus depends on, the adequate understanding of the generic principle or generic teaching procedure. There are particular pedagogical techniques with various kinds of learners much as there are specific differences in the way a surgeon operates on different patients and on different body parts. Questioning skills, for example, with their various targets and complexities and cognitive levels, are generically the same 1) for all cognitive portions of all subject-matter contents ranging from religion to theology to history, and 2) for persons of different ages and socio-economic backgrounds. This is not to say that the childhood religious educator asks the same specific kinds of questions that the science teacher or the reading specialist asks, or that the childhood religious educator asks the same specific kinds of questions to first graders and to fourth graders and to sixth graders in a religious education classroom setting. The principles and procedures of questioning are generic for the domain or area in which they are relevant. (Questioning is by and large useful only for cognitive learnings since questioning is a cognitively grounded technique. Questioning is therefore generally inappropriate or unworkable in noncognitive areas such as affective or lifestyle learnings— Lee, 1985, pp. 196-275, 608-735). Also the principles and procedures of questioning are generic regardless of whether they are asked in a formal instructional environment such as a classroom or in an informal instructional environment such as the church playground.

Successful religious instruction requires that the teacher possess subject-matter competencies and generic teaching skills as well as specific teaching skills. Therefore it is imperative that childhood religious educators be adequately trained to teach religion regardless of whether such instruction takes place in formal environments such as the classroom or in informal environments such as the street. Since the 1960s, educational research has exploded the erroneous belief that extensive and intensive preservice and inservice training in teaching skills is unnecessary for effective education. The research overwhelmingly concludes that educators who have received adequate preservice and inservice preparation both in relevant subject-matter content and in teaching skills are significantly more successful in facilitating desired learning outcomes than educators lacking such preparation (Darling-Hammond, 1990, p. 287; Everton, Hawley, & Zlotnik, 1985, pp. 2-12). Relating this well-established research finding to the generic teaching skill of questioning, a review of twenty-six empirical research studies (Gliessman et al., 1988, pp. 25-45) concludes that training in how to ask questions not only results in more effective use of this generic skill but also causes teachers to use this generic skill more frequently and at a higher level. Furthermore, the empirical research suggests that there is a significant positive correlation between the time spent practicing the generic pedagogical skill of questioning and subsequent ability in questioning, especially with respect to higher-order questions.

The previous paragraph has important practical ramifications for persons teaching religion to children of elementary school age. Most programs in religious education housed in seminaries or in graduate schools, while offering courses in the substantive content of religion teaching and in the foundations of religious education, nonetheless are very seriously deficient in providing courses or other kinds of training experiences both in the general underlying principles of how to teach and in extensive concrete theory-and-research-based practice sessions in which a wide repertoire of teaching skills can be acquired. To be effective, the childhood religious educator must be competent not only in religious substantive content but also in the conceptual foundations of pedagogical procedure (Gliessman & Pugh, 1987, pp. 41-49; Wagner, 1973, pp. 299-305) and, I maintain, in the actual conceptually guided practice of concrete pedagogical procedures. All effective religious education has not only a substantive content base but also 1) an empirical knowledge base of pedagogical practice plus 2) the enactment of the practice itself. Because seminary and graduate programs are by and large deficient in adequately training religious educators both in the conceptual instructional base and in the practical teaching skills requisite for effective religious instruction, dioceses, judicatories, and even clusters of parishes will have to provide childhood religious educators with the basic principles and practices of effective teaching. Failing this, childhood religious educators will have to acquire for themselves the principles and practices of teaching.

TEACHING AS AN ART/SCIENCE

All teaching, including the teaching of religion, is simultaneously an art and a science.

Teaching as an Art

As an art, religion teaching is the concrete enactment of an intentionally structured set of facilitational procedures deliberatively designed to bring about a desired learning outcome. The word art is derived from the Latin *ars* which means making, doing. As an art, religion teaching is the concrete doing of those things which make learning occur. As an art, religion teaching consists in the intentional control of those technical skills of instruction which actually facilitate learning (Cooper, 1982, p. 6). As an art, religion teaching means that the educator analyzes what is occurring in the instructional dynamic (Jackson, 1986, p. 86) and on the basis of this analysis adjusts or strengthens his/her pedagogical procedures in such a way as to bring about the intended learning outcome.

As an art, then, religion teaching consists in placing the teacher's personality and skills at the direct disposal of the instructional task (Lee, 1973, pp. 225-229). Consequently, every preservice and inservice program designed to help religious educators master the art of teaching must perforce include a strong and pervasive element of practice—the practice of the act of teaching in different settings and under different conditions and with different kinds of learners. Like all members of the helping professions, practitioners of the pedagogical arts must ceaselessly strive to refine and improve their technical skills of facilitation.

Teaching as a Science

The art of teaching is not free-floating. It is, rather, based on and shot through with scientific principles and findings (Gage, 1978, pp. 17-20). Teaching is preeminently an empirical process conducted in an artistic fashion. In other words, teaching is a process based on scientifically derived data, laws, and theory rather than a matter of teacher opinions or hunches rooted in sources other than data, laws, and theories concerning the teaching-learning process. As a science, religion teaching is a process in which the educator explains, predicts, and verifies the effectiveness of one or more instructional practices (Lee, 1973, pp. 216-217).

A working knowledge of the scientific base of the art of teaching enables the religious educator not only to be effective but also to be an artist, namely, a person in control of the fluid dynamics which transpire in the instructional process. It is a working knowledge of the scientific base of the art of teaching that enables the religious educator to make crucial adjustments during the instructional event, adjustments which change the contours of and components within the instructional act while still preserving its fundamental axis and goal-thrust. It is a working knowledge of the scientific base of the art of teaching that prevents the religious educator from deploying pedagogical procedures in a cookbook fashion, namely, using a particular instructional procedure inflexibly, mindlessly, "according to the cookbook." A major difficulty inherent in the cookbook approach is that when a specific pedagogical procedure fails, the religious educator has no pedagogical alternatives because the cookbook approach deals in absolutes. The cookbook approach to teaching explicitly stipulates that if such-and-such happens, then the religious educator automatically does so-and-so—hardly an artistic way of teaching. Drawing on the scientific basis of the art of teaching, if such-and-such does transpire in the instructional event, the religious educator has a whole range of options to do this-or-that, options directly generated by the scientific base. Thus, if one particular this-or-that fails, the religious educator reanalyzes the teaching-learning dynamic and selects another pedagogical procedure from a variety of other scientifically generated instructional alternatives (Weber, 1982, pp. 308-309). It is the working knowledge of the scientific basis of the art of teaching that prevents the religious educator from becoming rattled by unexpected or lateral developments in the instructional act. It is the scientific base which enables the religious educator to be highly resourceful about pedagogical procedures, not in the sense of thinking about more of the same pedagogical procedures, but rather in the sense of devising different pedagogical procedures which can effectively yield the desired learning outcomes (Jackson, 1986, p. 87).

A working knowledge of the scientific basis of the art of teaching is absolutely indispensable for effective and intentional religious instruction. The available empirical research supports this statement. Thus A. C. Wagner's study concludes that practicing a particular teaching skill in the absence of the knowledge of the scientific base of this skill did not of itself lead to mastery of that teaching skill (Wagner, 1973, pp. 299-305). Furthermore, a study by David Gliessman and his associates reported that conceptual training in the scientific basis of the pedagogical procedure of questioning, plus a demonstration by the trainer of how the questioning technique is successfully enacted, is sufficient to enable teachers to significantly change and improve their use of questioning techniques. Actual practice of questioning skills by the teachers-in-training was not part of the training package (Gliessman et al., 1988, pp. 25-46). I mention the Wagner study and the Gliessman study to highlight the importance of every childhood religious educator possessing a working knowledge of the scientific base of the art of teaching. These empirical studies do not in any way minimize the importance of practicing one or another teaching skill during the religious educator's preservice and ongoing inservice efforts to improve his/her instructional skills. Indeed, Gliessman and his associates concede that the fact that Gliessman's research subjects were experienced teachers who had used questioning skills regularly might well account for the fact that these persons did not require additional practice to upgrade their questioning skills (Gliessman et al., 1988, p. 39).

Gliessman and his associates also point out that while there is little direct empirical evidence to support the claim that the practice of a pedagogical skill is essential for the acquisition and improvement of that skill, nonetheless there are three very important lines of indirect empirical evidence to support the contention that conjoining instruction in the principles underlying a particular pedagogical skill with the actual practice of that skill will result in greater gains in successfully deploying that skill. First, there is the accumulated experience of professors who teach preservice and inservice teachers how to teach. On the basis of their professional experiences with these teachers (soft empirical data), these professors typically state that practice is indeed an essential component in the acquisition and improvement of teaching skills (Bush, 1977, pp. 5-9). Second, the many empirical research studies in microteaching conducted from the late 1960s onward suggest that improvements in various pedagogical skills can be explicitly or at least implicitly attributed to repeated practice of these skills together with appropriate feedback (McKnight, 1980, pp. 214-217). Third, a legitimate inference from the research studies on the acquisition of nonpedagogical skills in which practice is a central component is that practice is similarly important in the acquisition of pedagogical skills (Stones, 1979, pp. 238-239; Gliessman et al., 1988, p. 31).

Theory

A necessary and all-pervasive dimension of the scientific base of the art of teaching is theory. The practice of any art, including the art of teaching, is fundamentally the practice of a theory. The more important the art, the greater is the role of theory in its concrete enactment. Also, the more effective and successful the art, the greater is the conscious and pervasive use of theory in its here-and-now deployment. Theory enables the practitioners of an art to move away from "seat-of-the-pants" enactment and toward validated procedures which make it more probable that the desired outcome is attained.

A theory of teaching is different from a principle of teaching. A theory of teaching delineates the general structural and interactive relationships which exist among all the major variables in the instructional act. A principle of teaching, on the other hand, delineates the general structural relationship between one specific pedagogical procedure or one set of interrelated specific pedagogical procedures and the proven consequences of that procedure or set of procedures. A principle flows from theory and receives its explanatory and predictive power from theory. A teaching principle can be either descriptive or prescriptive. A descriptive teaching principle is explanatory: It delineates and identifies the likely results which can/should flow from the deployment of a particular pedagogical procedure or set of interrelated procedures. A prescriptive principle of teaching designates when and how and under what conditions a particular procedure or set of pedagogical procedures is likely to produce the desired learning outcomes. The practical value of both descriptive and prescriptive principles lies in the degree to which they are supported by the relevant empirical research and the degree to which they are grounded in theory (Reigeluth, 1987, pp. 1-3; Reigeluth, 1983).

Theory also differs from tract and from speculation. A tract is a short motivational piece of writing designed to bring about action of one kind or another. A tract is based on the personal opinions and ideology of the tractarian rather than on validated empirical research on the effectiveness of the particular views and practices that are presented. A tract might be helpful to get religious educators interested in some phase of teaching practice. But because a tract is based primarily on the tractarian's own personal opinion and ideology, it is not helpful in delineating either the principles of effective teaching or the ingredients of successful pedagogical practice. One of the finest tractarians in the modern era is John Westerhoff (Westerhoff, 1976a).

Much the same may be said for the pedagogical usefulness of speculation. For its part, speculation consists in armchair musings and conjecture. Thus, speculation is the opposite of empiric. Though speculation is somewhat more refined and sophisticated than tract, it nonetheless relies heavily on the personal opinion and ideology of the speculator. Though speculation may at times incorporate validated empirical research data, it does so more in a sporadic way than in a manner whereby the entire piece of speculation as a whole and in its parts rests upon validated research findings. Hence, speculation tends to be an unreliable and chancey guide to either delineating the principles of effective teaching or specifying the ingredients of successful practice.

Theory, on the other hand—and most notably theory of practice—is based on actual concrete practice. Theory is drawn from practice and is validated by practice. Theory has the power to explain and predict practice because it is in constant dialogue with practice. Whereas practice as a here-and-now datum is factually certain, theory is always tentative. Because it is tentative, theory is continuously being extended and refined by practice (Lee, 1982, pp. 117-121).

Unfortunately, most of religious instruction practice has been based on tract and speculation. Tractarians such as John Westerhoff (Westerhoff, 1980) and speculationists like Gabriel Moran (Moran, 1989) have been widely read and admired, even though tracts and speculations are not structurally or essentially based on the practices with which they occasionally deal. Theoretical writings in religious education have been few and far between. Even though theory is based on practice and exists for the purpose of improving practice, religious educators by and large seem to believe that theory is fundamentally unrelated to practice. Yet the very purpose of theory is the enhancement of practice by explaining why a particular practice works or does not work, by predicting when, how, and under what conditions a particular practice will probably work or will probably not work, and by verifying the degree to which a particular practice has or has not worked. Theory, then, is highly practical (Eisner, 1979, pp. 155-157). Indeed, a theory of teaching is more practical than a particular practice because theory is inherently capable of generating a whole host of different practices whereas a particular practice is only applicable to itself at a particular time and under a particular set of conditions. Furthermore, a particular teaching practice is blind; it cannot explain why it worked, predict when it will be likely to work again in the future, or even verify the degree to which it has worked.

In general education (Ginsburg & Clift, 1990, p. 454) as well as in religious education (Lee, 1977, pp. 119-121) there has been a heavy antitheoretical bias among teachers. This strong antitheoretical bias among preservice and inservice teachers (Crittenden, 1973, pp. 1-11; Bullough, 1982, pp. 207-212; Lanier & Little, 1986, pp. 542-543; Grossman & Richart, 1988, pp. 53-62; Thies-Sprinthall & Sprinthall, 1987, pp. 44-47) results in teachers grounding their practice in trial-and-error rather than in that systematic and comprehensive explanation and prediction of instructional events afforded by theory. Teachers who neglect or disvalue theory are at best technicians rather than artists, at worst bumbling hacks rather than reflective practitioners.

Possibly the most practical thing that childhood religious educators can do over the long term is to consciously radicate their concrete pedagogical procedures in theory, for only then will childhood religious educators be able to reliably and consistently explain, predict, and verify their religious instruction efforts.

Procedurism and Procedurology

Because religious instruction is an art, the teacher is a procedurist, namely, a person who enacts a procedure in an intentional and coordinated manner so as to successfully facilitate the acquisition of a desired learning outcome. Because religious instruction is a science, the teacher is a proceduroligist, namely, a person clearly conversant with the scientific data, laws, and theories upon which all consistently effective facilitation rests. To be a consistently successful procedurist, one must also be a procedurologist. Unfortunately many persons in the field of religious instruction disvalue procedure. Religious educators who place much attention on teaching procedure are often denigrated as "procedures persons," "methods men," "techniques women." But this mentality is a false and debilitating one. Procedures are extremely important and necessary in all religion teaching. Without procedures there would be no religion teaching. Indeed the test of effective teaching is not how much the teacher knows, how deeply the teacher feels, or how admirable a lifestyle the teacher has. Rather, the test of successful teaching lies in how well the religion teacher has actually facilitated desired learning outcomes. In other words, the universally recognized test of teaching consists in the fruits of the facilitational procedure, fruits which are the direct result of procedure.

There are some religious educators who seem embarrassed at being called procedurists/procedurologists because they regard procedure as a low level of human activity. This view is erroneous. Surgeons, for example, are basically procedure persons and certainly they enjoy great prestige. Indeed, surgeons are paid higher fees than most medical practitioners precisely because their work centers around a set of highly detailed and carefully executed procedures. If religious educators of children of elementary school age are to become consistently successful, they must not only regard themselves primarily as procedures persons but prize the incontrovertible fact that at bottom they are indeed procedurists. It is procedure based on procedurology which causes things to happen in a consistently effective way. Without procedure, the world would be inert and lifeless. In religious terms, procedure is incarnation.

Content

There are two primary, overarching contents a religious educator teaches when that individual is engaged in religious instruction. These two fundamental contents are substantive content and structural content, and I will treat each of these in the following two sections of this chapter. What is important to keep in mind is that substantive content and structural content always exist together in the concrete, here-and-now religious instruction act.

SUBSTANTIVE CONTENT

Substantive content, which is often called subject-matter content, is that which we teach. My own empirical analysis of the teaching act has revealed that there are nine molar substantive contents (Lee, 1985). These nine molar substantive contents are always present in every teaching/learning act. These molar substantive contents are product content, process content, verbal content, nonverbal content, cognitive content, affective content, conscious content, unconscious content, and lifestyle content. In the next few pages I will briefly describe all of these substantive contents.

Product Content

Product content is an easily seen, more or less tangible substantive content. Product content is typically the result of some activity (Lee, 1985, pp. 35-77). Consequently, product content is typically static. In the example 2 x 2 = 4, the number 4 is the product content, the result of the particular act of multiplying. There are many kinds of product content in religious instruction, as for example learning a particular biblical doctrine, acquiring a more favorable attitude toward persons of other religions, and so forth.

Process Content

Process content is the obverse of product content. Process content is a generalized, dynamic, and usually intangible content (Lee, 1985, pp. 78-128). Thus process content is not the result of something, but rather is the flow of activity involved in the getting of something. In the example of 2 x 2 = 4, the activity of multiplying is itself the process content. Because process content is intangible, many persons fail to realize that process content is a true content, a real substantive content in its own right. Process content is often more important than product content in religious instruction because process content is generalizable whereas product content is nongeneralizable. In the example of 2 x 2 = 4, the product content of 4 can be gained only by multiplying 2 x 2. If we were to substitute 3 x 1, 2 x 9, or 4 x 6, we would be unable to arrive at a solution because all we know is that 4 is the result of 2 x 2 since 4 is a particularized content having no generalizeability in our case. But if we acquire the generalizable process content of multiplying, then we can use this process content in every instance in which multiplication of any sort is involved. In teaching religion to children, for example, it is more important to help learners live biblically (process content) than to know a biblically based doctrine (product content). The overall goal of religious instruction is religious living, a goal which, while containing a certain amount of essential product content, is nonetheless far more of a process content than a product content.

Verbal Content

Verbal content is the set of words we use when teaching religion. Verbal content is a content in its own right and not just a vehicle for communicating other content (Lee, 1985, pp. 276-377; Spolsky, 1973, pp. 81-93; Atkinson, Kilby, & Roca, 1988). Verbal content is artificial in that its meaning is a contrived convention of a particular group or society. Let us use the word "white" as an example. The French word *blanc*, the Italian word *bianco*, the German word *weiss*, and the English word *white* are not of themselves white but are only artificial linguistic designators constructed by and agreed to by different societies as meaning white. An obscene word is not obscene in and of itself. It is a social group which artificially attaches an obscene meaning to this or that word which it then labels as obscene. A word only points to a reality; it is not that reality itself. Thus a word is at once a linguistic reality having logical existence and an artificial symbol pointing to some other reality. Because verbal content is artificial and symbolic, the religious educator has to take care that the word he/she chooses most effectively points to the real reality which it artificially symbolizes.

Nonverbal Content

Nonverbal content is the set of physical expressions, motions, or noises which the religious educator uses while teaching. Nonverbal content is a content in its own right and not just a bearer of other kinds of content (Lee, 1985, pp. 378-474). All human communication, including religious instruction, takes place on two simultaneous channels, namely, the verbal channel and the nonverbal channel. The verbal channel is primarily but not exclusively tied in with what the communitor thinks (cognitive content). The nonverbal channel is primarily but not exclusively tied in with what the communicator feels (affective content). There are many types of nonverbal content (Klinzing & Tisher, 1986, pp. 89-133). There is paralanguage, namely, the sounds which are admixed with the words used when speaking, sounds which may nuance, accentuate, or contradict the meaning and especially the affective correlates of the words to which they are conjoined. Tempo, pitch, and accent of words are other examples of paralanguage. Then there are the facial expressions which the religious educator uses: smiles of various kinds, eyebrow flashes, frowns, gazes, and more. Each of these communicates a powerful affective message to learners. Then there is kinesic behavior (known popularly as body language). Examples of kinesic behavior include posture, hand movements, arm movements, and movement of the torso and legs—all of these communicate substantive content in and of themselves.

Conscious Content and Unconscious Content

Conscious content is that content of which we are aware, whereas unconscious content is that content which falls below the level of our awareness (Lee, 1985, pp. 475-607). The writings of Sigmund Freud (Freud, 1989), Carl Jung (Jung, 1959), other depth psychologists (Caputi, 1984) show the great power unconscious content exerts throughout human life. Unconscious content such as that revealed in free association exercises, dreams (Sanford, 1968), and in certain kinds of personal depth journaling (Progoff, 1980) forms an important content of religious instruction since the unconscious is frequently tied in with the deepest personal structure and thrusts of religious existence.

Cognitive Content

Cognitive content is intellectual content (Lee, 1985, pp. 129-195; Dodd & White, 1980). Cognitive content encompasses both the process content of intellectualizing and the product content which is yielded by the intellectualizing process.

Cognitive content can be rational and extrarational. Rational cognitive knowing is that power by which, through the use of an objective system of intellectual logic, inferences are made and conclusions are drawn from phenomena, premises, or various kinds of data. Extrarational cognitive knowing is that power by which, through the use of means which lie outside of any objective system of logic, inferences are made and conclusions drawn from phenomena, premises, or various kinds of data. Extrarational knowing is quite different from irrational; the latter is an invalid form of rational knowing and hence invalid. Two important types of extrarational knowing are symbol (Jung, 1967, pp. 515-523 [#s 894-908]) and myth (Eliade, 1963, pp. 139-143; Campbell, 1964, pp. 519-521).

Cognitive content can be ratiocinative or intuitive. Ratiocination is the gathering into the mind of the intelligible forms of reality and the subjective judgment and reasoning about these forms by the mind. Intuition is the direct, nonsen-sory, immediate, intellectual apprehension of a reality without any intermediary. Intuition is direct and immediate knowing, as contrasted with ratiocination which slices up reality by abstraction, judgment, and reasoning.

Cognition can be convergent or divergent. Convergent thinking is linear thinking in which intellection proceeds according to well-defined, logically ordered steps. Areas like accountancy place a high premium on convergent thinking. Divergent thinking is lateral thinking which goes outside the normal boundaries and sources of the available data to generate innovative ways of thinking. Divergent thinking is an important process and font of creativity (Guilford, 1967; De Bono, 1970).

There are three levels of cognitive content. The lowest level, knowledge, is the simple apprehension concerning the facts basic to a given reality. Knowledge tells a person the that of a given reality. Understanding is the grasp of the elementary and the penultimate principles underlying a given reality. Understanding comes about only through experience. (First-hand experience is unnecessary for knowledge.) Understanding tells a person the immediate why of a given reality. Wisdom, the highest level of cognitive content, is the comprehension of the ultimate principles underlying a reality. Like understanding, wisdom requires experience. Wisdom tells a person the ultimate why of a given reality.

Affective Content

Affective content refers to any kind of content which is characterized by feeling. Affective content can be a positive force (such as trust, feeling accepted, love) or a negative type (such as fear, anxiety, or hatred). There are four major types of affects: emotions, attitudes, values, and love (Lee, 1985, pp. 196-275).

Emotion is generally acknowledged to be one of the most complex of all psychological phenomena. Its complexity derives from the fact that emotion involves so many aspects of the organism at so many levels of psychological, neural, and chemical integration (Thompson, 1988). Most psychologists agree that emotion is molar—it is a big, massive event involving a full rush of feeling. Emotion admits to many varieties such as fear, terror, anger, rage, joy, ecstasy, sadness, grief, surprise, disgust, and the like.

An attitude is an affective, acquired, and relatively permanent disposition or personality-set to respond in a consistent manner toward some physical or mental stimulus. An attitude, then, is a psychologically organized feeling-tone about a stimulus, together with a preconceived judgment about that stimulus and a prepared reaction toward it. Attitudes influence and condition nearly all learning. They determine for an individual what he/she will see and hear, what he/she will think and do (Allport, 1935, p. 806).

Value is the affective attachment which a person has to the perceived worth of a reality. There are many kinds of value, such as aesthetic value, social value, utilitarian value, religious value, and the like.

Love has never been adequately or satisfactorily defined. Many scholars believe that love is a set of interpersonal learned behaviors which seeks union with the beloved and which is characterized by self-giving, not for personal gain, but for the good of the beloved. Love has been shown to be the most powerful human motivating force and is the center of most religions.

Lifestyle Content

Lifestyle content refers to the overall pattern of a person's activities. Lifestyle content is integrative in that it meshes the myriad kinds of human activities and behaviors into one overall relatively congruent pattern of human functioning. Lifestyle content is the holistic living-out of the combination of one's "inner" and "outer" behaviors (Lee, 1985, pp. 608-735).

STRUCTURAL CONTENT

Structural content is the set of teaching procedures which the religious educator employs in formal or informal settings to bring about desired learning outcomes. The term "structural content" is a more pedagogically accurate term than the term "a set of teaching procedures" because the term "structural content" directly points to the all-important fact that teaching procedures are themselves a powerful content in their own right. Pedagogical procedures are not just a means of producing content; rather pedagogical procedures themselves comprise a content of their own, a content which is directly taught and directly learned.

Viewed globally, the total content which is directly taught and directly learned is a compound of substantive content and structural content. In the concrete here-and-now religious instruction act, substantive content dynamically and integratively interacts with structural content in such a way that a new entity is produced. The developmental interactive emergence of the new mediated entity (Lee, 1982, pp. 165-172) called the religious instruction act means that neither substantive content nor structural content exist in themselves but only as they participate in the new sublated reality of the concrete religious instruction act. Thus religion (substantive content) changes in the act of teaching (structural content) it.

Another way of asserting that instructional procedure is a content in its own right is to state that the way we teach is what we teach. Indeed, the way a religious educator teaches often is a more powerful content than what the religious educator teaches. For example, a lesson in which the Ten Commandments are taught in a juridical fashion will tend to yield a far different learning outcome than a lesson in which the selfsame Ten Commandments are taught in a loving manner. Or again, an instructional event characterized by a question-and-answer discussion on the nature of Christian charity will tend to yield significantly different learning outcomes than a lesson in which the learners actually participate in distributing soup to homeless persons in a church-operated soup kitchen.

THE FOUR MOLAR INTERACTIVE VARIABLES

There are four molar interactive variables present in each and every religious instruction act, namely, the teacher, the learner, the subject-matter content, and the environment.

These four variables are molar because they are massive and irreducible. They are massive because each embraces a whole host of constitutive elements. They are irreducible because the myriad elements and dynamics of what transpires in the religious instruction act cannot be reduced to any more basic categories.

The four molar variables are variable because they continually change their force, hue, and configuration as they interact in the ongoing concrete dynamic of the religious instruction act.

The way these four molar variables are continuously structured and restructured (structural content) by the religious educator plays a major role in determining what is learned (Lee, 1970, pp. 56-64).

In order to tap into the rich inclusiveness of each of the four molar variables it is well to briefly delineate the meaning of each. A *teacher* is one who intentionally facilitates the acquisition of desired learning outcomes in any way, shape, or form. Thus childhood religious educators are teaching when they structure a situation in which the children visit residents of a nursing home, when they work with children to write letters to state senators to influence legislation, when they interact sensitively with a girl who has been treated badly by some adults, when they help children see the application of a biblical text on fair play to last Friday's athletic contest, when they discuss with the children the meaning of God's love within the framework of God's law, and so forth. A *learner* is a person who engages in an activity which is capable of yielding a desired learning outcome. Thus, in childhood religious education the boys and girls are learners whenever or wherever they are learning something as a result of their participation in religious instruction activity on the playground, in a classroom, in worship services, on a field trip, on a hike, visiting the sick in a hospital, and so forth. *Subject matter* is that which is taught. Subject matter is more or less identical to substantive content. It is important to realize that subject matter is far wider than just cognitive subject matter such as the understanding of a biblical text or verbal knowledge about one or another point of liturgy. As noted earlier in this chapter, other key subject-matter (substantive) contents include affective contents such as feelings, attitudes, and values, and also lifestyle contents such as various concrete ways of religious living. And finally, *environment* is the milieu in which the instructional event takes place. Environment is both psychosocial and physical. Psychosocial environment is the aggregate, thrust, and coloration of the psychodynamics encasing and swirling through the religious instruction act. Socio-emotional climate is a prime example of this kind of environment. Physical environment is the sum total of all the elements singly and in concert which comprise the material setting in which the instructional event occurs. Examples of physical environment include the playground, the classroom, the church building, fieldtrips, the decoration and temperature of a room, and so forth.

The fact the religious instruction act is everywhere and always composed of four interactive molar variables shows religion teaching is essentially contextual in nature. All four molar variables operate in a somewhat different fashion depending on the here-and-now interactive context in which they take place. The interactive contextual character of religious instruction is best illustrated in a pictorial model which I devised in 1973 and which over the years has consistently proven to be very useful in understanding the inner dynamic structure of the teaching-learning act (Lee, 1973, pp. 233-236).

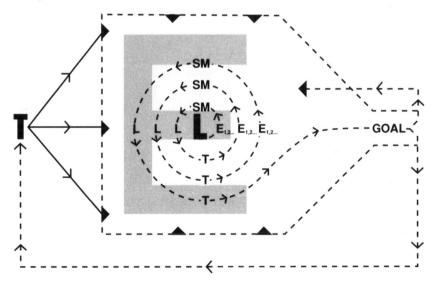

In this model, T stands for the teacher—in our case, the childhood religious educator. L stands for learner, E for environment, and SM for subject-matter content. The large square circumscribed by dotted lines represents the learning situation. As the diagram indicates, the learning situation as a whole converges toward a focused, open-minded funnel, suggesting that the dynamics of the learning situation are targeted toward a desired outcome or goal . The diagram also depicts a large shaded-in E which covers the entire learning situation; this shows that the learning situation is a psychosocial/physical environment and therefore all four independent variables (causative factors) in the learning situation have their locus in the environment. Put another way, it indicates that everything contained within the large dotted-line square comprises an interactive aspect of the learning situation (the instructural environment). Learning takes place within an environmental context and is therefore being constantly modified by the dynamic ongoing interaction among all the relative variables inside and outside it (Garner, 1990, pp. 517-529).

Now that I have limned each of the four molar variables always present in every teaching act, and now that I have delineated the pattern of the dynamic interaction among these variables, it will be helpful to devote somewhat more extended attention to each of these molar variables.

THE TEACHER

I will devote more space to a consideration of the religious educator's processive role in the instructural act than to the other three ever-present interactive molar variables because this chapter deals with the general procedures of teaching.

Before dealing with some of the major dimensionalities of teaching, it is essential to reinforce once again the central axis of this chapter, namely, that effective teaching is necessarily an art/science, the practice of an art based on and shot through with scientific principles. Art is the enfleshment of scientific principles put into an effective medium—in our case, the medium of teaching.

Religious instruction is the deployment of a technical skill. It is the fluid, concrete, here-and-now enactment of a set of teaching practices which the educator predicts will result in the attainment of a desired learning outcome (Lee, 1972, pp. 43-54).

There are two essential and interactive elements in the exercise of a technical skill, especially in a professional technical skill such as teaching. *First,* technical skill involves proficiency, the efficient and effective exercise of an activity in such a manner that the intended outcome of the skill is produced as successfully as possible. Among the general technical skills which the religious educator should be able to proficiently deploy are planning, implementing, and evaluating (Cooper, 1982, p. 14). Among the specific technical skills which the religious educator should be able to implement are writing instructional objectives in performance terms (Mager, 1962, p. 13); enacting various methods of affective teaching (Case, 1975; Miller, 1976; Cohler, 1989, pp. 41-45); deploying effective questioning skills (Wilen, 1987, pp. 173-193; Hunkins, 1989, pp. 171-223; Dantonio, 1990); utilizing an appropriate repertoire of formative evaluation devices (Baker, 1974, pp. 533-585); and so forth. *Second,* technical skill is the practice of a theory, a theory which perforce is supported by the available research and which is congruent with the field of activity in which the practice occurs. A technical skill is not at all the same as activity. Technical skill denotes that kind of activity which has a good probability of success because the theory which it practices suggests why that skill will be effective under a set of given conditions and how it can be effectively deployed. It is theory with its research support which gives both the practitioner and the practitionee reasonable assurance that the result of the exercise of the technical skill will be what they both expect. Without theory, technical skill collapses and disappears, being replaced by hit-or-miss activity.

Structuring the Learning Situation

The Lee model depicts the teacher first and foremost as the structurer of the pedagogical situation. By structuring the situation I mean the deliberative arrangement of the appropriate conditions in such a way that the probability of attaining the desired learning outcome is thereby enhanced. To be sure, it is through the initial structuring of the pedagogical situation and the continuous subsequent restructuring of parts or even the whole situation that the religious educator fulfills his/her primary role as facilitator of desired learning outcomes.

Awareness of the central fact that all genuine effective teaching essentially consists of structuring the pedagogical situation enables the religious educator to alter his/her basic instructional perspective in at least three fundamental ways. *First,* it shows the religious educator that he/she must be constantly mindful of a whole range of ever-changing conditions, each of which separately and interactively demand his/her attention during the planning and enactment of the instructional event. *Second,* it accentuates the fact that the instructional process is not simply selecting the subject-matter content to be delivered to the learner but rather choosing, deploying, and adjusting whole processive frameworks within which this content is interactively embedded (Jackson, 1986, pp. 18-19). Teaching is not the delivery of subject-matter content from teacher (sender) to receiver (learner) as the radio model of transmissionist religious instruction erroneously claims (Lee, 1970, pp. 56-58; Hofinger, 1962, p. 17). Teaching is organizing the entire instructional situation in such a way as to facilitate the acquisition of desired learning outcomes—outcomes which include but, because of the intrinsic nature of the religious instruction act, cannot possibly be restricted to intended subject-matter outcomes. As has been shown earlier in this chapter, the concrete instructional act is a here-and-now mediator between substantive content on the one hand and structural content on the other hand, a mediator which produces a new entity of which subject matter is only a part—and, as a result of its participation in the concrete instructional act, a significantly changed part at that. Furthermore, in planning the instructional event, the religious educator does not aim to teach subject matter in and of itself. Rather, the religious educator carefully picks and chooses certain aspects of the subject matter, aspects which he/she predicts will be both important for the learner to learn at this particular time and which also are capable of being taught/learned by the learner. Once the subject matter has been selected by the religious educator on the basis of its pedagogical worthwhileness, the religious educator then organizes this content on the basis of what he/she deems is the most effective way of successfully facilitating the acquisition of that content. As a crucial part of this organization process, the religious educator juxtaposes subject matter with other appropriate conditions and variables so that a whole pedagogical architecture emerges as a fruit of the planning process. *Third,* the fact that teaching is first and foremost a structuring activity rather than merely a unilinear relationship between educator and learner prompts the religious educator to renounce undue attention to himself/herself or to any one or another of his/her actions such as talking. To structure the pedagogical situation is to see oneself not as oneself but as one of many dynamic variables in a whole network of interactive conditions, a variable which becomes salient or recedes depending on the instructional exigencies of the moment.

Reflective Teaching

In order for the childhood religious educator to purposively structure the learning situation and to continuously restructure it during the teaching event it is necessary that he/she be a reflective teacher. To be a reflective religious educator means to be continuously aware of what is actually transpiring in the here-and-now instructional dynamic. This continuous instructional awareness, which I have been stressing over and over again in my writings since 1973 (Lee, 1973, pp. 279-286), was given the formal name "reflective teaching" by later specialists in the instructional process. As Bernice Wong observes in a related context, reflective teaching can be regarded as a form of self-questioning by the educator as to what is occurring or what could occur in the teaching-learning dynamic (Wong, 1985, pp. 229-230). Reflective teaching means that the religious educator is an on-the-hoof researcher, namely, a practitioner who is always seeking during the enactment of the here-and-now instructional dynamic to find out what is happening in the teaching event so as to make necessary adjustments in the way he/she is teaching (Kincheloe, 1991, pp. 1-25; Grant & Zeichner, 1984, pp. 4-5; Webb, 1990).

Reflective teaching sometimes concentrates on one or another particular aspect of the religious instruction event. Thus in one instance reflective teaching might concentrate on the religious educator's specific pedagogical behavior during the teaching/learning act, as for example the observable effects which the deployment of this or that teacher nonverbal behavior had on the learner. Or obversely, reflective teaching might concentrate on the overall sequence of pedagogical events which took place in the teaching/learning act, such as: 1) "What did I do in the instructional act?" 2) "What does this or that element of the instructional act mean?" 3) "How did I come to take this pedagogical action?" 4) "How might I do things differently in a similar instructional event the next time around?" (Smyth, 1989, pp. 2-9). But no matter what axis or emphasis the childhood religious educator uses in reflective teaching, he/she should always place the object of reflection within the global context of the instructional situation as a whole. Teaching is structuring the whole pedagogical situation. Hence each condition and every variable in the instructional situation gains salience, coloration, force, and even in a sense its own special existence as it is in itself and as it interacts in the whole pedagogical situation.

Preservice and inservice religious educators can learn to enhance their reflective teaching skills (Posner, 1988, pp. 21-35; Zeichner, 1987, pp. 565-575). Interaction analysis systems such as the famous one devised by Ned Flanders (1965) have been very helpful in this regard. In the graduate religious education program at the University of Notre Dame, Eugene Hemrick (1971) used the Flanders system successfully in his efforts to enable religious educators in the Midwest to engage more wholeheartedly in reflective teaching and thereby improve the quality of their religious instruction endeavors. In his doctoral dissertation, and later in his activities in the Midwest, Hemrick invited religious educators to voluntarily have their classes videotaped. After taping, Hemrich showed the videos to the teachers, using the Flanders system to explain in a factual, nonjudgmental way what happened pedagogically during the lesson. The Ohio State University has developed a series of reflective-teaching lessons which are geared to assisting preservice and inservice educators enhance their reflective-teaching skills (Cruikshank et al., 1981, pp. 26-32; Troyer, 1988).

Prediction

Effective religious instruction for children of elementary school age requires that the educator be able to predict which teaching practices will tend to yield specified learning outcomes. Prediction is important because without it the religious instruction of children would necessarily degenerate into a hit-or-miss affair.

The Lee model clearly shows that customary successful prediction flows from the effective arrangement (structuring) of all the molar variables in the instructional act and not from just one or two of these variables (Lee, 1973, pp. 212-215). Successful prediction involves what Donald Schön (1983, p. 40) calls problem setting, namely, "the process by which [the practitioner] defines the decision to be made, the ends to be achieved, the means which may be chosen." Problem setting consists in identifying the four molar variables together with the goal/objective, and then framing the instructional context in which the childhood religious educator will attend to these four molar variables and to the desired goal/objective.

The religious educator's prediction of which specific instructional procedures he/she will use in a given pedagogical event is ultimately based on a combination of three factors: 1) his/her own past experiences as a participant in instructional events; 2) his/her knowledge of the relevant empirical research; and 3) his/her own theory of teaching.

From past experience, childhood religious educators know which facilitational procedures have worked for them and which have not. Religious educators know that because of their personalities and their own personal lives (Pajak & Blase, 1989, pp. 283-310), some facilitational styles have in the past proven successful and others unsuccessful for them (Brown, 1981, pp. 94-100). But past experience of successful or unsuccessful facilitational procedures, considered solely from the perspective of past experience, is not a generally trust-worthy guide to the prediction of future teaching success. Past experience qua past experience is valid for present prediction only when the learning goal/objective and all four molar variables in past instructional events are sufficiently similar to the learning goal/objective and to the four molar variables in the present pedagogical situation.

While past experience can be a helpful guide to present prediction, more helpful still is the empirical research base of the particular facilitational procedure which the childhood religious educator predicts will lead to the attainment of the desired goal/objective. Sometimes the childhood religious educator's interpretation of his/her past facilitational experience is faulty because of selective memory, wishful thinking, defense mechanisms, incomplete information, latent ideology, and so forth. At other times the past instructional situation is inapplicable to the present teaching event. The advantage of relying on empirical research is that this kind of research shows with requisite definitiveness and objectivity whether a particular teaching procedure will likely be effective or ineffective in a certain kind of instructional situation. As noted earlier in this chapter, all art, including the art of teaching, rests upon a scientific research base, a base absolutely necessary for consistently adequate prediction (Lee, 1972, pp. 53-54). Knowledge of the relevant empirical research enables childhood religious educators "to base their artistry on something more than hunch, feeling, intuition, unaided insight, or raw experience" (Gage, 1985, p. 6). An active, working knowledge of the relevant empirical research requires that the childhood religious educator keep abreast of this research. He/she can do this by attending first-rate professional conferences, and especially by reading top-notch books and articles which detail and discuss this research.

Though informed past experience is helpful and necessary for successful prediction, and though a working knowledge of the relevant empirical research is even more helpful and more necessary, by far the most helpful and most necessary of all is the continuous and conscious use of theory before, during, and after the religious instruction act. As indicated earlier in this chapter, a theory is a tentative statement which attempts to make comprehensive and systematic sense out of the facts from which it is constructed. Facts recollected from past experience or derived from empirical research have no meaning or significance in and of themselves. A theory does three large-scale, practical things to facts: It explains facts, it predicts facts, and it verifies facts. The more reflective the childhood religious educator is, the more probable it is that he/she consciously grounds his/her prediction and global pedagogical practice in theory. The kind of theory which every childhood religious educator wittingly or unwittingly employs before, during, and after the instructional act can be called "theory in use" (Agyris & Schön, 1974, pp. 6-19).

Prediction is highly practical and thus requires practical knowledge. In essence, practical knowledge is knowledge of practice—why practice works (theory), how practice works, and how to predict the efficacy of future practice. In a case study of a particular teacher, Freema Elbaz (1983, p. 134) identified three ascending levels of generality in the organization of an educator's practical knowledge. The first and lowest level consists of rules of practice, a sort of cookbook type of specific actions which one might take in those particular pedagogical situations characterized by clear purpose. The second level consists of practical principles of teaching which Elbaz identifies as broader statements which are useful both in analyzing instructional situations and in selecting from an array of pedagogical practices those which apply to specific instructional circumstances. The third and highest level is that of generalized orienting frameworks—images, to use Elbaz's terminology. These images include the teacher's past experiences (including personal needs, beliefs, and educational folklore), a knowledge of the relevant empirical research, and a theory of instruction.

Hypothesis Making

Closely and indeed inextricably related to prediction is hypothesis making. From a procedural perspective, every religious instruction act first presents itself as a problem. This problem consists of the difficulty of ascertaining which of a wide number of various pedagogical procedures will in all probability be optimally effective in successfully yielding the desired learning outcome in this particular situation. To solve this pedagogical problem the childhood religious educator makes a hypothesis that teaching procedure X will likely be more effective than teaching procedure Y as he/she deals with a particular subject-matter content with these particular learners in this particular environment. Thus the childhood religious educator is essentially and always a hypothesis maker and also a hypothesis reviser (Lee, 1973, p. 215). Past experience, relevant empirical research, and especially instructional theory are guides to the religious educator in shaping and reshaping a viable hypothesis about which teaching procedure will in all probability work in such-and-such a situation.

Antecedent-Consequent Behavioral Chaining

Accurate prediction and subsequent deployment of effective pedagogical procedures require the childhood religious educator to be continuously aware of the dynamic uninterrupted flow of antecedent-consequent behavioral chaining which is constantly occurring throughout the instructional dynamic. Antecedent-consequent behavioral chaining is a term referring to the dynamic sequence of cause-effect behaviors which occur in each and every teaching/learning event regardless of the environment in which this event takes place. (Lee, 1973, pp. 196-197). As was demonstrated in several places earlier in this chapter, all teaching occurs as a structured learning situation in which the childhood religious educator makes the first pedagogical move. The learner then responds in one way or another to the childhood religious educator's initiatory move. The learner's response-move is influenced by the shape, flow, and content of the educator's previous move. The childhood religious educator then responds to the learner's move. The thrust and texture of the childhood religious educator's response to the learner's response to the educator's initiatory move is almost totally influenced by the educator's reflective awareness of the degree to which the learner's response is leading the learner toward or away from the attainment of the desired outcome. The learner then responds to the educator's move, and so it continues.

I have coined the term "antecedent-consequent behavioral chaining" to describe the sequence of reciprocal instructional moves for two reasons. First, all educator and learner moves are, at bottom, behaviors. A behavior may be defined as anything which a human being does and which can be directly or indirectly observed by someone, including the person engaging in that behavior. Thus an act of thinking or an act of feeling is just as fully and authentically a behavior as an act of walking or an act of talking. Childhood religious instruction, like all other forms of intentional education, is a series of interactive behaviors. Second, the behaviors which occur in a religious instruction event are necessarily chained in an initiatory-response fashion. The childhood religious educator makes the iniatory first move. The child then responds. Precisely because the religious instructional event is interactive, the child's response is both a response and an initiation. It is a response because it is the child's reaction to the educator's prior behavior. It is also an initiation because it causes the childhood religious educator to respond in a deliberative fashion to the child's behavior. The childhood religious educator's response in turn becomes an initiatory behavior which itself invites a response from the child. These initiatory-response behaviors form a chain of interlocking behaviors, each one dependent upon and linked to the prior behavior.

Supportive of Lee's earlier conceptualization of teaching as antecedent-consequent behavioral chaining, Christopher Clark and Penelope Peterson (1986, pp. 257-258) state that the degree to which the learners in an instructional event are actually learning tends to influence their responses to the educator. Furthermore, continue Clark and Peterson, the educator's response to the learners is largely determined by the degree of learning which the learners exhibit in their responses to the educator.

Focusing intently and continuously on antecedent-consequent behavioral chaining during the religious instruction event is one of the quickest and most effective ways in which childhood religious educators can improve the dynamics of their pedagogical ministry. This is especially true for those religious instruction activities carried on in informal settings, settings which often lack some of the built-in facilitational valence and explicit intentionality as do many formal settings.

Decision Making

Continuous awareness of antecedent-consequent behavioral chaining, of intentionality, of prediction—these and the other basic functions of childhood religious education already discussed in this chapter all flow into decision making. All teaching, all childhood religious instruction, is primarily a process of deciding how/when to structure the learning situation, and how/when to intervene during the instructional event so that the desired learning outcome will be achieved (Orlich et al., 1985, pp. 2-8). Childhood religious educators, then, are first and foremost persons of action because they decide when and how to do something educationally worthwhile in a given situation and then implement this decision in action (Pasch et al., 1991). The role of constant awareness, of what is happening instructionally, of intentionality, of prediction, and so on, is to transform uninformed decision making into informed decision making. This information which the childhood religious educator gains from awareness, prediction, hypothesis making, and so on, serves to transform uninformed decision making into informed decision making. This information which the childhood religious educator gains from awareness, prediction, hypothesis making, and so on enables the teacher to make those instructional decisions which are effective in the here-and-now and which are wise over the long term.

The kind of knowledge outlined in the previous paragraph is knowledge about the present or predicted instructional process itself. To this knowledge must be added other background kinds of knowledge such as knowledge of the empirical research data on learning, motivation and facilitation, knowledge of the principles and theory of teaching, knowledge of a wide repertoire of teaching procedures, knowledge of religious subject-matter content, and so forth.

It must be underscored that the varieties of knowledge discussed in the foregoing paragraphs do not comprise inert knowledge but rather active, working knowledge. Such working knowledge enables the childhood religious educator to constantly alter his/her pedagogical procedures during the ongoing religious instruction event to ensure that the desired learning outcomes are attained in an optimally effective manner.

Teacher education programs in general education have been developed to enable preservice and inservice educators to sharpen and otherwise improve their skills in instructional decision making (Feiman-Nemser, 1991, pp. 224-225; McNergney et al., 1988, pp. 37-43). Many of these preservice programs place decision making within a holistically structural framework. This framework includes many of the basic ingredients of effective instructional decision making, namely a knowledge of goals and terminal objectives, relevant information on structural and substantive content, practice of different teaching procedures, task analysis, and evaluation. This holistic framework is interfaced with a parallel framework dealing with the relevant empirical research on teaching/learning and with the theory of teaching. Preservice educators thus learn to make productive instructional decisions while actually engaged in making decisions, decisions guided by and shot through with appropriate working knowledge (Feiman-Nemser & Buchmann, 1989, pp. 365-377).

Productive decision making also includes the all-important element of evaluation. Before deciding which general instructional style or particular technique to deploy at a given moment (Mosston & Ashworth, 1990), the childhood religious educator must evaluate the probable effectiveness of enacting this general facilitational style or that particular technique (Lee, 1973, pp. 32-33). As is consistently noted in the educational literature, the whole purpose and thrust of evaluation is to help the educator to make informed decisions about some aspect of instructional activity (Galluzzo & Craig, 1990, pp. 599-616). The evaluation which the childhood religious educator makes of past (and probable) effectiveness of an instructional procedure should not only be summative but even more importantly formative (Scriven, 1967, pp. 55-66; Scriven, 1981, pp. 244-271; Bloom, Hastings, & Madaus, 1971). The evaluation should be summative in that it assesses the effectiveness of that large or small phase of the completed teaching event, formative in that it seeks to improve the quality and productivity of the childhood religious educator's series of present and future instructional interventions. If it is to be an effective dimension of the decision-making process, the evaluation should not be simplistic or two-dimensional but should be richly detailed as suggested in the Lee model of the teaching act. Such inclusiveness perforce embraces what Robert Stake (1967, pp. 523-540) calls the general pre-existing conditions antecedent to the instructional event, the transactions during the event, and the outcomes which flow from each general and specific portion of the event. Evaluation in religious instruction exists not only to ascertain what the learner has actually learned but also to help the religious educator decide more effectively and more wisely what to do processively in the religious instruction act, when to do it, and how to do it.

THE LEARNER

The second of the four molar variables present in every religious instruction act is the learner. Since this chapter deals primarily with general teaching procedures, my treatment of the learner, the subject-matter content, and the environment will, for reasons of space, be briefer than my discussion of the teacher. The briefer consideration of the three nonteacher molar variables in no way suggests that these three variables are less important than the teacher. Space limitation, not importance, is the overriding determinant of the degree of expansiveness accorded in this chapter to the learner, the subject-matter content, and the environment.

The various personality characteristics of the learner have been dealt with in other chapters in this volume, so there is no need to repeat these here. Furthermore, virtually all the available empirical research studies conducted on the religious life of children have been brilliantly summarized in Kenneth Hyde's (1990) book, *Religion in Childhood and Adolescence,* a book which surely should be on the active shelf of every childhood religious educator.

Because religious instruction by definition is the facilitation of desired religious outcomes in the learner, it stands to reason that the learner is at once the focus and the axis of all the educator's activity. The effective childhood religious educator takes the child very seriously because only then can the religious educator do what it takes pedagogically to facilitate a desired learning outcome. The age of the child is a critical variable which must be factored into the overall equation on how to teach in the here-and-now situation (Elkind, 1964, pp. 36-40). The child's gender is also another highly significant variable which the religious educator must seriously consider when devising a general teaching strategy (Hyde, 1990, pp. 198-201). The child's socio-economic background exerts significant impact upon the way the individual learns (Ornstein & Levine, 1989, pp. 406-443). Childhood religious educators must also tailor their general teaching procedures to the ethnic background of the child (Slaughter, 1969, pp. 105-111; Cureton, 1978, pp. 751-756). For example, children from an African-American culture tend to have a significantly different cognitive learning style than do persons of Caucasian ancestry; the former tend to be more person-oriented in the way they learn while the latter tend to be more object-oriented, to mention just one of the empirically demonstrated differences (Shade, 1982, pp. 219-244).

The major point I would like to emphasize in this abbreviated section on the learner is that during the planning, implementation, and evaluation phases of his/her instructional activity, the childhood religious educator must constantly strive to operationally link the empirical research data derived from social-scientific studies of learning with the design and enactment of the teaching process (Glaser, 1982, pp. 292-305). Thus, for example, the childhood religious educator knows from Ronald Goldman's (1965) research that religious learning depends on the child's cognitive, affective, and lifestyle readiness to learn religious subject matter (see chapter ten). Thus children up to eleven or twelve years of age will typically reduce to gross trivialities and irrelevancies, or fail to see the essentials of biblical stories like Moses encountering the burning bush, the crossing of the Red Sea, or the temptations of Jesus. What the childhood religious educator must do is to operationally link Goldman's research findings with teaching procedure. One obvious consequence of this operational linkage is to place the teaching of the Bible to children on a noncognitive axis, such as affective- or lifestyle-based teaching procedures. (This would be quite a revolution for many childhood religious educators. But it is a needed revolution if teaching the Bible is to truly address the child where the child is developmentally and thus to make a real difference in the child's religious life.)

THE SUBJECT-MATTER CONTENT

The subject matter of religious instruction is religion. Religion may be defined as that form of lifestyle which expresses the lived relationship which a person enjoys with a transpersonal being or ultimate process as a consequence of the actualized fusion in one's self-system of that knowledge, belief, feeling, experience, and practice that in one way or another are connected with what the individual perceives to be divine (Lee, 1985, p. 3).

This definition of religion is helpful to the childhood religious educator in two important respects.

First, this definition shows that religion is substantively different from theology. Religion is a way of life. Theology, in marked contrast, is the cognitive investigation and reflection on God and his activities in the world. Virtually all theologians accept the fact that theology is a cognitive science. This holds true for major theologians coming from the Roman Catholic tradition (Rahner, 1965, p. 14), from the mainline Protestant tradition (Tillich, 1951, p. 28), and from the evangelical Protestant tradition (Thielicke, 1977, p. 3). This sharp and very real distinction between religion and theology suggests to the childhood religious educator that to teach theology is not to teach religion. Religion is a way of life, while theology is one kind of cognitive reflection on that way of life. The empirical research suggests that the acquisition of theological subject-matter content is neither a guarantee or even a probability that the learner will lead a more religious life (Hightower, 1930; Simpson, 1933, pp. 223-230). The ontic and pedagogic ground for this empirical research finding is that theological content by its nature can only yield theological consequences; it cannot directly yield religious consequences. While childhood religious educators should bring theology into the religious instruction event as appropriate, they should do so in a manner that theology supports the acquisition of desired religious outcomes rather than being an outcome in its own right. The importance of theology in religious instruction, whether modest (Moran, 1982, pp. 42-70) or robust (Lee, 1982, pp. 100-197), stems from the degree to which theology cognitively illumines and makes more meaningful a person's religious living.

Second, the definition of religion directly suggests that the subject matter of religion is necessarily holistic. Thus the subject-matter content includes all of the nine molar contents which go to make up substantive content. The subject matter which the childhood religious educator teaches is not only cognitive content but also, and even more importantly, affective content and lifestyle content. The subject matter which the childhood religious educator teaches is not only product content but also process content, not only verbal content but also nonverbal content, not only conscious content but also unconscious content. A failure to accord due pedagogical attention to any of these nine molar variables inevitably leads to defective religious outcomes. Indeed, one of the major causes of the relative lack of success of many childhood religious instruction activities over the long term stems from the overemphasis on cognitive, verbal, and product contents to the concomitant neglect of affective, lifestyle, nonverbal, and process contents. Effective childhood religious instruction requires that the teacher possess both the knowledge of these molar substantive contents (Wittmer & Myrick, 1974, pp. 45-46) plus the facilitational skills necessary to deploy these contents effectively in the religious instruction act.

THE ENVIRONMENT

The environment in which religious instruction occurs consists of that aggregate of external physical, cultural, and social stimuli and conditions with which a person consciously and unconsciously interacts.

The environment is a potent force in influencing a person's cognitive, affective, and lifestyle behaviors. Many developmental philosophers (Dewey, 1938, pp. 34-45) and developmental psychologists (Kohlberg, 1980, p. 51) go so far as to assert that every human being is basically an interactive emergent, that is to say a composite of the biological organism and the environment with which it continuously interacts (Lee, 1980, pp. 326-355).

Despite the empirically supported research evidence which indicates that the environment is a powerful influence on human learning, religious educationists, especially those adhering to the theological approach, typically pay scant attention to the all-important environmental variables which help shape what is actually learned in the religious instruction act (Burgess, 1975, pp. 119-120).

The physical environment is a very important variable which influences learning (Lee, 1973, pp. 70-72). The arrangement of furniture in the formal or informal religious instruction setting (Lee, 1985, p. 444; Loo, 1977, pp. 153-158; Sommer, 1969), the color of the walls and flooring (Bakos, Bozic, & Chapen, 1987, p. 273; Birren, 1961), the acoustics of the room (Black, 1950, pp. 174-176)—these and all the other physical characteristics of the immediate physical environment exert significant impact on learning. Hence the childhood religious educator should carefully prepare the physical environment so that it furthers in its own unique way the attainment of desired learning outcomes.

The socio-cultural environment in which the religious instruction act occurs also greatly influences the type and texture of learning (Parke, 1978, pp. 33-81; Lee, 1973, pp. 66-67). Lawrence Kohlberg and his associates had some success in their efforts to transform the immediate socio-cultural environment of a school into a "just community," namely a socio-cultural environment which itself, in cooperation with the three other molar variables always involved in the educational process, contributes toward teaching justice to learners in an experiential manner (Kuhmerker, 1991, pp. 123-145).

The socio-emotional environment also exerts a profound impact on the shape and flow of the religious instruction event. Often called socio-emotional climate or even just simply teaching/learning climate, the socio-emotional climate can be effectively structured by the childhood religious educator to enhance the probability that the desired learning outcomes will be achieved (Breckenridge, 1976, pp. 314-318). Thus the childhood religious educator can structure a socio-emotional climate which is warm or cold, rigid or relaxed, open or closed, affiliative or nonaffiliative, and the like. Instruments such as the Learning Environment Inventory (Anderson, Walberg, & Fraser, n.d.) and the Classroom Environment Inventory (Moos & Trickett, 1974) can assist the childhood religious educator to improve the quality of the socio-emotional climate in which teaching occurs (Raviv, Raviv, & Reisel, 1990, pp. 141-145; Moos, 1975; Moos & Insel, 1974). An exhaustive review of over 200 empirical research studies suggests that there are many different kinds of mechanisms whereby the educator can develop that kind of socio-emotional climate which brings about desired learning outcomes (Anderson, 1982, pp. 368-420).

Socio-emotional climate is present and operative regardless of whether the religious instruction act occurs in formal settings such as in the classroom or in informal settings such as the playground or home. Consequently the childhood religious educator should work diligently in both kinds of settings to develop that kind of socio-emotional environment which will facilitate the acquisition of desired learning outcomes.

The Lee model highlights the fact that the environment in which the religious instruction act occurs is no mere appendage to the teaching event, but is an ever-present powerful interactive variable in this event (Dunkin &

Biddle, 1974, pp. 93-97; Berry, 1980, pp. 83-106; Lowenthal & Prince, 1976, pp. 117-131; Little, 1987, pp. 205-244; Mazzuca et al., 1990, pp. 473-488).

THE GOAL

The Lee model of the teaching/learning act shows that the instructional dynamic is wholly thrusted toward the attainment of an educational goal. Childhood religious instruction, therefore, is primarily and essentially a goal-directed activity. Thus effective childhood religious instruction requires that the activities of the learners and most especially of the teacher be consciously directed toward the acquisition of the desired goal. Effective learning is always a task, the task of attaining a goal.

Successful teaching, therefore, exists for the accomplishment of a task, a desired goal. Conversely, successful teaching does not exist principally for the sake of any one particular molar variable, including the learner. Though this fact might at first blush seem to be antipersonalistic, in fact it is very personalistic. If the religious instruction act were geared entirely or even primarily toward the here-and-now learner, then the whole thrust of the teaching act would be directed to meeting this want or this desire of the learner—and not only directed to one individual learner, but in cases in which the religious instruction act is conducted in groups, to all the other learners as well. The result would be bedlam, and the teaching/learning dynamic would completely disintegrate. In the instructional act, the learner sacrifices some of his/her immediate wants and desires in order to attain an outcome of value, an outcome which could not be achieved by task-dissipating self-indulgence or personal wants and desires. This willing sacrifice on the learners' part will make them better and fuller persons through the process of self-discipline, namely, the discipline required to attain the desired learning outcome (Lee, 1991, pp. 139-213). This sacrifice will also help the learners become better and fuller persons because this goal, when once attained, will add new cognitive, affective, or lifestyle contents to their lives.

A goal is typically a general statement about a broad learning outcome. For example, the goal of a particular childhood religious instruction event might be "to help the learner grow in love for Jesus" (Del Prete, 1990, p. 55). This goal, like any other goal statement, provides little direction for determining and sequencing appropriate learning experiences. Thus a general statement, or goal, must be sharpened, operationalized, and concretized if it is to be helpful to the teacher and attainable by the learner. The best way to sharpen, operationalize, and concretize a goal is to formulate specific objectives which flow directly from this goal and which in turn will enable the goal to be achieved (Lee, 1973, pp. 270, 272, 276-277). The most useful kind of objectives for religious instruction purposes are performance objectives.

Performance objectives describe the desired learner performance and indicate the way in which this performance is to be achieved and evaluated. Performance objectives are learner-centered, not teacher-centered. Performance objectives specify what the learner will do, not what the childhood religious educator will do (Davies, 1981, pp. 128-140).

There are three main steps in preparing an effective performance objective: performance, conditions, and criteria. First, the childhood religious educator identifies the terminal behavior by name, that is, specifies the particular performance or kind of performance which will be accepted as evidence that the learner has achieved the objective (*performance*). Second, the childhood religious educator defines the desired performance outcome by further describing the important and significant conditions under which the performance can be predicted or expected to occur (*conditions*). Third, the childhood religious educator specifies the criteria of acceptable performance by describing the level of performance which is considered acceptable (Mager, 1962).

Religious instruction is a creative activity, an activity in which the educator creatively fashions general goals and specific objectives (as well as particular pedagogical procedures). Creativity is exciting—but it is also exacting. Because of laziness, pompousness, or just simply inattention to detail, some childhood religious educators evade their responsibility to create teachable goals and objectives for learners in formal and informal settings. The result is often ineffective religious instruction. In the religious instruction event, as in architecture, God lies in the details—and the devil lies in the neglect of details. Careful and unrelenting attention to instructional details, including the fashioning of performance objectives, is at once the price and the reward for effective religious instruction.

As was indicated earlier in this chapter, the substantive content of religious instruction is religion. Hence adequate performance objectives in any childhood education which is truly religious must perforce include all nine molar contents which are always present in living religion. For example, the objectives of the cognitive portion of religious instruction might be any of the six levels of intellection suggested by Benjamin Bloom and his associates, namely, knowledge, comprehension, application, analysis, synthesis, and evaluation (Bloom et al., 1956). Affective performance objectives would vary depending on whether the desired learning outcome was one or another attitude, emotion, value, or form of love. Performance objectives in the lifestyle domain admit of an almost infinite variety. The key point of this paragraph is that performance objectives in religious substantive content must be holistic and not unidimensional.

There have been some persons within and without religious education who have roundly criticized performance objectives as nonpersonalistic and positivistic (Boys, 1976, pp. 505-507) or as neglecting the artistic and contemplative dimensions of religious education (McBrien, 1976, p. 175). These demurrers are uninformed and misguided. Far from being nonpersonalistic, performance objectives are highly personalistic because without performance objectives there is simply no way that the teacher can make his/her instructional efforts intentional and there is no way that the educator or his/her learners can adequately assess what if anything has been learned. Depriving the religious educator and the learners of these kinds of information is antipersonalistic; conversely, mechanisms which provide these kinds of information to the educator and the learners are necessarily personalistic. There is nothing positivistic about performance objectives; indeed performance objectives are common sense and are used by everyone in all sorts of personal as well as professional activities much of the time. Performance objectives do not neglect the artistic or contemplative dimensions of religious instruction because artistically and contemplatively thrusted performance objectives can be and have been composed and taught. If this or that set of performance objectives does not include the contemplative or the artistic, it is not the fault of the performance objectives; rather the fault lies with the religious educator who did not compose his/her performance objectives holistically with respect to subject-matter content.

There are two views about the Bible's direct relationship to religious instructional procedure, including the composition and enactment of performance objectives. The first view is that the use of a particular teaching procedure in the Bible *eo ipso* bestows a divine stamp of approval on that procedure (Richards, 1982, p. 204; LeBar, 1958, pp. 50-51). The second view is that the Bible is a divinely inspired revelation about religious truths and not an infallible revelation about which teaching procedures are ideal from God's perspective, which engineering procedures are specifically approved by God as the divine way of doing engineering, and so forth. In this view, the intrinsic merits and extrinsic effectiveness of one religious instruction procedure over another are due to the basic appropriateness of that procedure in a given set of conditions rather than to revealed divine approbation (Lee, 1983, pp. 38-47). But regardless of which of these two competing views the childhood religious educator holds, it is a fact that those instructional procedures used by Jesus and his apostles are saturated with performance objectives in the finest, most concrete, and most specific sense of the term performance objectives. Over and over again, the fundamental criterion which Jesus used for evaluating learning—cognitive, affective, and lifestyle—is performance: A tree is known by the fruit it yields (Mt 7:20). Jesus follows up this statement by indicating that not everyone who talks a lot about God or even exclaims "Lord, Lord" will enter the kingdom; only those who perform the will of God will attain salvation (Mt 7:21). In the final analysis, supreme love is not notional, but instead actually laying down one's life (performance) for one's friend (Jn 16:13). A person is Jesus' friend if that individual performs what Jesus has commanded the individual to do (Jn 16:14). There are levels of performance delineated in the New Testament. Thus Jesus was pleased at the rich young man who obeyed (performed) all the Ten Commandments but was sad when the rich young man would not attain even higher perfection by selling all his goods and following Jesus—the performance objective which Jesus set before the rich young man (Mt 19: 16-22). The apostle James puts the whole area of religion—the substantive content which religious educators teach—in performance terms when he defines religion as caring for orphans and widows in their affliction and keeping oneself unstained by the world—performances all (Jas 1:27).

A TAXONOMY OF RELIGIOUS
INSTRUCTIONAL PROCEDURES

There are many kinds of instructional procedures which are used in a wide variety of formal and informal environments with learners ranging from preschoolers to adults. Some of these teaching procedures are quite specific, such as praising a learner, while others are more general, such as the discovery strategy.

In order to assist religious educators to make their teaching efforts more effective, in 1973 I composed a taxonomy of the teaching act (Lee, 1973, pp. 28-38). The Lee taxonomy identifies and classifies discrete categories of teaching behavior logically arranged on a generality-specificity continuum. The childhood religious educator ought to use this taxonomy in the planning and enactment of religious instruction activity in order 1) to come to a deeper knowledge and understanding of the teaching/learning act; 2) to design an optimally effective instructional procedure; 3) to develop more effective models of teaching; and 4) to help insure a consistency among all the levels of the teaching act so that each level will reinforce the others instead of working at cross-purposes. An important by-product of this taxonomy is that it will liberate many childhood religious educators from the notion that instructional practice is just a bag of pedagogical tricks or consists mainly of following in cookbook fashion the recommendations given by a curriculum textbook guide.

In the following brief sections, I will outline the primary features of the Lee taxonomy of the instructional act considered in itself. The taxonomy enumerates discrete classes within the instructional act, beginning with the most general and ending with the most specific.

Approach
Approach is the primary, fundamental orientation of the teaching/learning act. It flows naturally out of the context of theory. An approach provides the most fundamental matrix which conditions the direction which the teach-

ing/learning act will take in its actuality and in its operations. The approach underlying and permeating the teaching/learning act cannot be directly observed; it can be inferred by synthesizing the diverse activities involved in a particular instructional act. In religious instruction the two principal approaches are the theological approach (Miller, 1982, pp. 153-164; Wyckoff, 1978, pp. 173-175) and the social-science approach (Lee, 1971, pp. 182-224; Lines, 1987, pp. 211-240).

Style

Style is the basic, overall pattern or mode which serves as the indicator of the specific direction which the activities of the teaching/learning act will take. Style is the main thread with which the cloth of the concrete teaching/learning act is woven. It is from this thread that strategies, methods, and techniques at once flow from and return to. There are many examples of style as an overall pattern in religious instruction, including the following pairs of opposite modes: teacher-centered versus learner-centered, didactic versus heuristic, logical versus psychological, theological-content-cnetered versus experience-centered, and preservation-oriented versus reconstruction-oriented.

Strategy

Strategy is the comprehensive, systematized, concrete scaffolding on, around, and through which are placed the more specific methods and techniques of the teaching/learning act. Strategy provides the overall plan and concrete operationalized blueprint for the deployment of pedagogical methods and techniques. Primary examples of strategy include the transmission strategy and the discovery strategy.

Method

Method is the internally ordered set of pedagogical procedures which are arranged in discrete generalized bodies or classes. Method serves to furnish the larger tactical unit of the teaching/learning act. Examples of method are problem-solving, teacher-learner planning, socialized teaching, and affective teaching.

Because method is not the whole of teaching enactment, but is only one of six elements within the whole taxonomy, childhood religious educators would do well to use the term "procedure" when referring to the teaching process as a whole, and use the term "method" in its precise taxonomic sense.

Technique

Technique is the concrete, tangible, and specific way in which a pedagogical event is structured in a given teaching/learning situation. Technique functions as a specific procedure which is actualized in a definite instructional circumstance. Lecturing and telling, role playing, project, discussion—these are all examples of technique.

Step

Step is the highly specific behavioral unit or behavioral sequence through which here-and-now instructional practice is enacted. Step is the most directly observable feature of the pedagogical act and serves as the particularized antecedent teacher behavior upon which depends the particularized consequent learner response. Examples of step include such specific teacher or learner behaviors as praise, offering verbal support, asking questions, giving directions, and so forth. Because the effective exercise of step is most immediate to the religious educator, and because the systematic investigation of teaching step has classically been one of the most neglected areas in instructional practice, there has been considerable research since 1960 into this most specific and focused of all taxonomic categories.

Of the many immediate and practical advantages of the Lee taxonomy for childhood religious educators, one is deserving of special mention. By using the taxonomy, the childhood religious educator will be able to optimize internal pedagogical harmony within the instructional event. By this I mean that the childhood religious educator will make sure that all the instructional procedures he/she uses during the pedagogical event reinforce each other rather than work at cross purposes. For example, if the method to be deployed is that of affective teaching, the childhood religious educator will choose a technique such as role playing or trust walk which are affective in texture rather than a technique such as lecturing/telling or asking questions, both of which are cognitive in hue. Much of the ineffectiveness in religious instruction can be traced to an unwitting disharmony among the various elements in the taxonomy of instructional practice.

CONCLUSION

There was a time that the name and thought of John Dewey were rejected out of hand, or at least were seriously suspect, in Christian religious education circles, especially among Catholics and conservative Protestants. A former Sunday school teacher, Dewey came to reject Christianity and all other particularized forms of religion, claiming that these groups clung to outmoded beliefs and practices which retard the growth of the distinctly human in persons (Dykhuizen, 1973, pp. 261-264). Though rejecting institutional religion of every kind, Dewey stressed the importance of what he called "the religious," namely, the deepest processive set of naturalistic human values which satisfy and are satisfied "by all human concerns and arrangements" (Dewey, 1934).

Since 1970 Dewey has made something of a comeback with Christian thinkers in general and with religious educators in particular. Thus religious educators increasingly abandoned negative prejudgments about Dewey and let his ideas speak to them on their own merits. It is in this open and professional spirit that I wish to close this chapter with some thoughts from John Dewey which are quite relevant for today's childhood religious educators.

In 1903 Dewey was invited to speak at the first annual convention of the Religious Education Association which had been founded earlier that year. It is well to remember in this connection that one of the most important promotional pieces sent out by William Rainey Harper, a key founder of the new organization, characterized the R.E.A., not as a society which would take the lead in the improvement of the Sunday school, but rather a society which would heal the divorce between religious instruction and the other branches of education (Schmidt, 1983, pp. 19-20). Dewey closed his address by telling general educators that they cannot afford to neglect the most fundamental of all educational issues, namely, the moral and the religious, and by telling religious educators that they cannot afford to neglect the careful and systematic scientific study of teaching procedures (Dewey, 1977, p. 215).

What Dewey said to the R.E.A. in 1903 has acute relevance for today. If childhood religious educators are to be effective, they must use all the social-scientific theory and research at their disposal to 1) analyze and 2) improve their teaching procedures. Nothing less will do.

REFERENCES

Allport, G. W. (1935). Attitudes. In C. A. Murchison (Ed.), *A handbook of social psychology*. Worcester, MA: Clark University Press.

Anderson, C. (1982). The search for school climate: A review of the research. *Research of Educational Research, 52*, 368-420.

Anderson, G. J., Walberg, H. J., & Fraser, B. J. (n.d.). Assessment of learning environments: Manual for learning environment inventory (3d ed.). Unpublished document.

Argyris, C., & Schön, D. (1974). *Theory in practice: Increasing professional effectiveness*. San Francisco: Jossey-Bass.

Atkinson, M., Kilby, D., & Roca, I. (1988). *Foundations of general linguistics* (2d ed.). London: Unwin Hyman.

Baker, E. L. (1974). Formative evaluation of instruction. In W. J. Popham (Ed.), *Evaluation in education*. Berkeley, CA: McCutcheon.

Bakos, M., Bozic, R., & Chapen, D. (1987). Children's spaces. In C. S. Weinstein & T. G. David (Eds.), *Spaces for children: The built environment and child development*. New York: Plenum.

Berry, J. W. (1980). Cultural ecology and human behavior. In I. Altman, A. Rapoport, & J. F. Wohlwill (Eds.), *Human behavior and environment*, vol 4. New York: Plenum.

Birren, F. (1961). *Color psychology and color therapy.* New Hyde Park, NY: University Books.

Black, J. W. (1950). The effect of room characteristics upon vocal intensity and rate. *Journal of the Accoustical Society of America, 22,* 174-176.

Bloom, B. S., et al. (1956). *Taxonomy of educational objectives: Handbook I: Cognitive domain.* New York: McKay.

Bloom, B. S., Hastings, T. J., & Madaus, G. F. (1971). *Handbook of formative and summative evaluation.* New York: McGraw-Hill.

Boys, M. C. (1976). Supervision in religious education: Selected models. *Living Light, 13,* 505-507.

Breckenridge, E. (1976). Improving school climate. *Phi Delta Kappan, 58,* 314-318.

Brown, C. C. (1981). The relationship between teaching style, personality, and setting. In C. C. Brown & L. Peck (Eds.), *Flexibility in teaching.* New York: Lippincott.

Bullough, R. V. (1982). Professional schizophrenia: Teacher education in confusion. *Contemporary Education, 53,* 207-212.

Burgess, H. W. (1975). *An invitation to religious education.* Birmingham, AL: Religious Education Press.

Bush, R. N. (1977). We know how to train teachers: Why not do so. *Journal of Teacher Education, 28,* 5-9.

Campbell, J. (1964). *The masks of God.* New York: Viking.

Caputi, N. (1984). *Guide to the unconscious.* Birmingham, AL: Religious Education Press.

Case, L. (1975). *The other side of the report card: A how-to-do-it program for affective education.* Pacific Palisades, CA: Goodyear.

Clark, C. M., & Peterson, P. (1986). Teachers' thought processes. In M. C. Wittrock (Ed.), *Handbook of research on teaching* (3d ed.). New York: Macmillan.

Cohler, B. J. (1989). Psychoanalysis and education: Motive, meaning, and self. In K. Field, B. J. Cohler, & G. Wool (Eds.), *Learning and education: Psychoanalytic perspectives.* Madison, CT: International Universities Press.

Cooper, J. M. (1982). The teacher as decision maker. In J. M. Cooper (Ed.), *Classroom teaching skills* (2d ed.). Lexington, MA: Heath.

Crittenden, B. (1973). Some prior questions in the reform of teacher education. *Interchange, 4,* 1-11.

Cruikshank, D., et al. (1981). Evaluation of reflective outcomes. *Journal of Educational Research, 75,* 26-32.

Cureton, G. O. (1978). Using a Black learning style. *Reading Teacher, 31,* 751-756.

Dantonio, M. (1990). *How can we create thinkers: Questioning strategies that work for teachers.* Bloomington, IN: National Education Service.

Darling-Hammond, L. (1990). Teachers and teaching: Signs of a changing profession. In W. R. Houston (Ed.), *Handbook of research on teacher education.* New York: Macmillan.

Davies, I. K. (1981). *Instructional technique.* New York: McGraw-Hill.

De Bono, E. (1970). *Lateral thinking.* New York: Harper & Row.

Del Prete, T. (1990), *Thomas Merton and the education of the whole person.* Birmingham, AL: Religious Education Press.

Dewey, J. (1934). *A common faith.* New Haven, CT: Yale University Press.

Dewey, J. (1938). *Experience and education.* New York: Macmillan.

Dewey, J. (1977). Religious education as conditioned by modern psychology and pedagogy. In J. A. Boydston (Ed.), *John Dewey: The middle works, 1899-1924,* vol 3. Carbondale, IL: Southern Illinois University Press.

Dodd, D. H., & White, R. M. (1980). *Cognition: Mental structure and process.* Boston: Allyn and Bacon.

Dunkin, M. J., & Biddle, B. J. (1974). *The study of teaching.* New York: Holt, Rinehart and Winston.

Dykhuizen, G. (1973). *The life and mind of John Dewey.* Carbondale, IL: Southern Illinois University Press.

Eisner, E. W. (1979). *The educational imagination.* New York: Macmillan.

Elbaz, F. (1983). *Teachers' thinking: A study of practical knowledge.* New York: Nichols.

Eliade, M. (1963). *Myth and reality* (W. Trask, Trans.). New York: Harper & Row.

Elkind, D. (1964). Age and religious identity. *Review of Religious Research, 18,* 36-40.

Everton, C. M., Hawley, W. D., & Zlotnik, M. (1985). Making a difference in educating quality through teacher education. *Journal of Teacher Education, 36,* 2-12.

Feiman-Nemser, S. (1991). Teacher preparation: Structural and conceptual alternatives. In W. R. Houston (Ed.), *Handbook of research on teacher education.* New York: Macmillan.

Feiman-Nemser, S., & Buchmann, M. (1989). Describing teacher education: A framework and illustrative findings from a longitudinal study of six students. *Elementary School Journal, 79,* 365-377.

Flanders, N. A. (1965). *Interaction analysis in the classroom.* Ann Arbor, MI: School of Education, University of Michigan.

Freud, S. (1989). *Basic writings of Sigmund Freud* (P. Gay, Ed.). New York: Norton.

Gage, N. L. (1978). *The scientific base of the art of teaching.* New York: Teachers College Press.

Gage, N. L. (1985). *Hard gains in the soft sciences: The case of pedagogy.* Bloomington, IN: Phi Delta Kappa.

Galluzzo, G. R., & Craig, J. R. (1990). Evaluation of preservice teacher education programs. In W. R. Houston (Ed.), *Handbook of research on teacher education*. New York: Macmillan.

Garner, R. (1990). When children and adults do not use learning strategies: Toward a theory of settings. *Review of Educational Research, 60,* 517-529.

Ginsburg, M. B., & Clift, R. T. (1990). The hidden curriculum of preservice teacher education. In W. R. Houston, M. Haberman, & J. Sikula (Eds.), *Handbook of research on teacher education*. New York: Macmillan.

Glaser, R. (1982). Instructional psychology: Past, present and future. *American Psychologist, 37,* 292-305.

Gliessman, D. H., & Pugh, R. C. (1987). Conceptual instruction and intervention as methods of acquiring teaching skills. *International Journal of Educational Research, 11,* 41-49.

Gliessman, D. H., et al. (1988). Variables influencing the acquisition of a generic teaching skill. *Review of Educational Research, 58,* 25-45.

Goldman, R. (1965). *Readiness for religion: A basis for developmental religious education*. New York: Seabury.

Grant, C. A., & Zeichner, K. (1984). On becoming a reflective teacher. In C. A. Grant (Ed.), *Preparing for reflective teaching*. Boston: Allyn and Bacon.

Grossman, P. L., & Richart, A. E. (1988). Unacknowledged knowledge growth: A re-examination of the effects of teacher education. *Teaching and Teacher Education, 4,* 53-62.

Guilford, J. P. (1967). *The nature of human intelligence*. New York: McGraw-Hill.

Hemrick, E. F. (1971). *Modification of teacher behavior in religious education through the use of videotape feedback*. Doctoral dissertation, University of Notre Dame, Notre Dame, IN.

Hightower, P. R. (1930). *Biblical information in relation to character*. Iowa City, IA: State University of Iowa.

Hofinger, J. (1962). *The art of teaching Christian doctrine: The good news and its proclamation* (2d ed.). Notre Dame, IN: University of Notre Dame Press.

Hunkins, F. P. (1989). *Teaching through effective questioning*. Boston: Christopher-Gordon.

Hyde, K. E. (1990). *Religion in childhood and adolescence*. Birmingham, AL: Religious Education Press.

Jackson, P. W. (1986). *The practice of teaching*. New York: Teachers College Press.

Jung, C. G. (1959). *The basic writings of C. G. Jung* (V. S. DeLaszlo, Ed.). New York: Random House Modern Library.

Jung, C. G. (1967). *Psychologische typen,* zehnte, revidierte auflage, Band 6 in *Gesammelte werke*. Zurich: Rascher.

Kincheloe, J. L. (1991). *Teachers as researchers*. Philadelphia: Falmer.

Klinzing, H. G., & Tisher, R. P. (1986). Expressive nonverbal behaviors; A review of research on training with consequent recommendations for teacher educators. In J. D. Raths & L. G. Katz (Eds.), *Advances in teacher education,* vol. 2. Norwood, NJ: Ablex.

Kohlberg, L. (1980). Stages of development as a basis for moral education. In B. Munsey (Ed.), *Moral development, moral education, and Kohlberg.* Birmingham, AL: Religious Education Press.

Kuhmerker, L. (1991). *The Kohlberg legacy for the helping professions.* Birmingham, AL: Religious Education Press.

Lanier, J. E., & Little, J. N. (1986). Research on teacher education. In M. C. Wittrock (Ed.), *Handbook of research on teaching* (3d ed.). New York: Macmillan.

LeBar, L. E. (1958). *Education that is Christian.* Tarrytown, NJ: Revell.

Lee, J. M. (1970). The teaching of religion. In J. M. Lee & P. C. Rooney (Eds.), *Toward a future for religious education.* Dayton, OH: Pflaum.

Lee, J. M. (1971). *The shape of religious education.* Birmingham, AL: Religious Education Press.

Lee, J. M. (1972). Prediction in religious instruction. *Living Light, 9,* 43-54.

Lee, J. M. (1973). *The flow of religious instruction.* Birmingham, AL: Religious Education Press.

Lee, J. M. (1977). Toward a new era: A blueprint for positive action. In J. M. Lee (Ed.), *The religious education we need.* Birmingham, AL: Religious Education Press.

Lee, J. M. (1980). Christian religious education and moral development. In B. Munsey (Ed.), *Moral development, moral education, and Kohlberg.* Birmingham, AL: Religious Education Press.

Lee, J. M. (1982). The authentic source of religious instruction. In N. H. Thompson (Ed.), *Religious education and theology.* Birmingham, AL: Religious Education Press.

Lee, J. M. (1983). Religious education and the Bible: A religious educationist's view. In J. S. Marino (Ed.), *Biblical themes in religious education.* Birmingham, AL: Religious Education Press.

Lee, J. M. (1985). *The content of religious instruction.* Birmingham, AL: Religious Education Press.

Lee, J. M. (1991). The context of morality and religion. In K. Walsh (Ed.), *Discipline for character development.* Birmingham, AL: R. E. P. Books.

Lines, T. A. (1987). *Systemic religious education.* Birmingham, AL: Religious Education Press.

Little, B. R. (1987). Personality and environment. In D. Stokols & I. Altman (Eds.), *Handbook of environmental psychology,* vol. 2. New York: Wiley.

Loo, Chalsa (1977). The effects of crowding: Situational and individual differences. In D. Stokols (Ed.), *Perspectives on environment and behavior.* New York: Plenum.

Lowenthal, D., & Prince, H. C. (1976). Transcendental experience. In S. Wapner, S. B. Cohen, & B. Kaplan (Eds.), *Experiencing the environment.* New York: Plenum.

Mager, R. F. (1962). *Preparing instructional objectives.* Palo Alto: CA: Fearon.

Mazzuca, S. A., et al. (1990). Effects of the clinical environment on physicians' response to postgraduate medical education. *American Educational Research Journal, 27,* 473-488.

McBrien, R. P. (1976). Toward an American catechesis. *Living Light, 13,* 175.

McKnight, P. C. (1980). Microteaching: Development from 1968 to 1978. *British Journal of Teacher Education, 6,* 214-217.

McNergney, R., et al. (1988). Training for pedagogical decision making. *Journal of Teacher Education, 39,* 37-43.

Miller, J. P. (1976). *Humanizing the classroom: Models of teaching in affective education.* New York: Praeger.

Miller, R. C. (1982). *The theory of religious instruction practice.* Birmingham, AL: Religious Education Press.

Moos, R. H. (1975). *The human context: Environmental determinants of behavior.* New York: Wiley.

Moos, R. H., & Insel, P. M. (Eds.) (1974). *Social ecology: Human milieus.* Palo Alto, CA: National Press Books.

Moos, R. H., & Trickett, E. J. (1974). *Classroom environment scale manual.* Palo Alto, CA: Psychology Press.

Moran, G. (1982). From obstacle to modest contributor. In N. H. Thompson (Ed.), *Religious education and theology.* Birmingham, AL: Religious Education Press.

Moran, G. (1989). *Religious education as a second language.* Birmingham, AL: Religious Education Press.

Mosston, M., & Ashworth, S. (1990). *The spectrum of teaching styles.* New York: Longman.

Orlich, D. C., et al. (1985). *Teaching strategies* (2d ed.). Lexington, MA: Heath.

Ornstein, A. C., & Levine, D. U. (1989). *Foundations of education* (4th ed.). Boston: Houghton Mifflin.

Pajak, E., & Blase, J. J. (1989). The impact of teachers' personal lives on professional role enactment. *American Educational Research Journal, 26,* 283-310.

Parke, R. P. (1978). Children's home environments: Social and cognitive effects. In I. Altman & J. F. Wohlwill (Eds.), *Children and the environment.* New York: Plenum.

Pasch, M., et al. (1991). *Teaching as decision making.* New York: Longman.

Posner, G. J. (1988). *Field experience: A guide to reflective teaching* (2d ed.). New York: Longman.

Progoff, I. (1980). *The practice of process meditation.* New York: Dialogue House.

Rahner, K. (1965). *Theological investigations,* vol. 1 (2d ed.) (C. Ernst, Trans.). Baltimore: Helicon.

Raviv, A., Raviv, A., & Reisel, E. (1990). Teachers and students: Two different perspectives? Measuring social climate in the classroom. *American Educational Research Journal, 27,* 141-145.

Reigeluth, C. M. (Ed.) (1983). *Instructional design theories and models.* Hillsdale, NJ: Erlbaum.

Reigeluth, C. M. (1987). What is instructional theory? In C. M. Reigeluth (Ed.), *Instructional theories in action.* Hillsdale, NJ: Erlbaum.

Richards, L. O. (1982). Experiencing reality together: Toward the impossible dream. In N. H. Thompson (Ed.), *Religious education and theology.* Birmingham, AL: Religious Education Press.

Sanford, J. A. (1968). *Dreams: God's forgotten language.* Philadelphia: Lippincott.

Schmidt, S. A. (1983). *A history of the Religious Education Association.* Birmingham, AL: Religious Education Press.

Schön, D. (1983). *The reflective practitioner.* New York: Basic Books.

Scriven, M. (1967). The concept of evaluation. In M. W. Apple, M. J. Subkoviak, & H. S. Lufler (Eds.), *Educational evaluation: Analysis and responsibility.* Berkeley, CA: McCutchan.

Scriven, M. (1981). Summative teacher evaluation. In J. Millman (Ed.), *Handbook of teacher evaluation.* Beverly Hills, CA: Sage.

Shade, B. J. (1982). Afro-American cognitive style: A variable in school success? *Review of Educational Research, 52,* 219-244.

Simpson, R. M. (1933). Attitudes towards the ten commandments. *Journal of Social Psychology, 4,* 223-230.

Slaughter, C. H. (1969). Cognitive style: Some implications for curriculum and instructional practices among Negro children. *Journal of Negro Education, 38,* 105-111.

Smyth, J. (1989). Developing and sustaining critical reflection in teacher education. *Journal of Teacher Education, 40,* 2-9.

Sommer, R. (1969). *Personal space.* Englewood Cliffs, NJ: Prentice-Hall.

Spolsky, B. (1973). *Educational linguistics.* Rowley, MA: Newbury.

Stake, R. E. (1967). The countenance of educational evaluation. *Teachers College Record, 68,* 523-540.

Stones, E. (1979). *Psychopedagogy: Psychological theory and the practice of teaching.* London: Methuen.

Thielicke, H. (1977). *The evangelical faith,* vol . 2 (G. W. Bromily, Trans. & Ed.). Grand Rapids, MI: Eerdmans.

Thies-Sprinthall, L., & Sprinthall, N. A. (1987). Preservice teachers as adult learners. In M. Haberman & J. M. Backus (Eds.), *Advances in teacher education,* vol. 3. Norwood, NJ: Ablex.

Thompson, J. G. (1988). *The psychobiology of emotion.* New York: Plenum.

Tillich, P. (1951). *Systematic theology,* vol. 1. Chicago: University of Chicago Press.

Troyer, M. B. (1988). *The effects of reflective teaching and a supplemental theoretical component on preservice teachers' eflectivity in analyzing classroom teaching situations.* Doctoral dissertation, The Ohio State University, Columbus, OH.

Wagner, A. C. (1973). Changing teacher behavior: A comparison of microteaching and cognitive discrimination training. *Journal of Education Psychology, 64,* 299-305.

Webb, R. (Ed.) (1990). *Practitioner research in the primary school.* Philadelphia: Falmer.

Weber, W. A. (1982). Classroom management. In J. M. Cooper (Ed.), *Classroom teaching skills.* Lexington, MA: Heath.

Westerhoff, J. H. III. (1976a). *Tomorrow's church.* Waco, TX: Word.

Westerhoff, J. H. III. (1976b). *Will our children have faith?* New York: Seabury.

Westerhoff, J. H. III. (1978). *Who are we?* Birmingham, AL: Religious Education Press.

Westerhoff, J. H. III. (1980). *Bringing up children in the Christian faith.* Minneapolis: Winston.

Wilen, W. W. (1987). Improving teachers' questions and questioning: Research informs practice. In W. W. Wilen (Ed.), *Questions, questioning, and effective teaching.* Washington, DC: National Education Association.

Wittmer, J., & Myrick, R. D. (1974). *Facilitative teaching.* Pacific Palisades, CA: Goodyear.

Wong, B. Y. L. (1985). Self-questioning instructional research. *Review of Education Research, 55,* 229-230.

Wyckoff, D. C. (1978). Religious education as a discipline. In J. H. Westerhoff III (Ed.), *Who are we?* Birmingham, AL: Religious Education Press.

Zeichner, K. M. (1987). Preparing reflective teachers: An overview of the instructional strategies which have been employed in preservice teacher education. *International Journal of Educational Research, 11,* 565-575.

Chapter Nine

Specific Procedures of Teaching Religion

JOLENE PEARL

A teacher is anyone who helps others learn and behave in new and different ways. This could include anyone from parents to drill sergeants. More specifically, when we think of religious educators, we think of persons who are charged by the church with the responsibility of facilitating learning in the context of a church or parachurch setting. Religious educators should have a foundation in general education, demonstrate a minimal level of knowledge in religion and theology, understand principles of human growth and learning, and show competence in application of methods and skills in teaching. Possession of a college degree does not, however, guarantee that teachers will be effective. What is good or effective teaching? This chapter will be devoted to looking at many of the elements identified by research related to achieving the goals and objectives of religious education.

Good teaching is very difficult to define, because "good" is a value-laden concept. What is good teaching to one person may be viewed as poor teaching to another, since each may value different outcomes or methods. While one teacher may organize the learning situation in a highly structured manner, another may allow much more freedom of choice and movement among students. Observers evaluate teachers according to what is important to them. Even though it has been difficult to agree on what good teaching is, effective teaching can be demonstrated. According to Cooper (1986, p. 3), "The effective teacher is one who is able to bring about intended learning outcomes." Without objectives, student behavior becomes random and unpredictable. If students do not actually achieve the learning goals, the teacher cannot truly be called an effective teacher.

Over the years much has been written to define effective teaching. In

1884, John Milton Gregory formulated the seven laws of teaching (Shafer, 1985). Gregory was a minister and educator. His classic work has been revised several times and is now in its twenty-third printing. The seven laws can be more clearly stated as rules or guidelines.

1. Know very thoroughly the lesson material to be taught.
2. Gain and keep the attention and interest of the students, without which it is futile to continue.
3. Use clear and simple language, understandable in the same way to both teacher and students.
4. Start with what is known and proceed to new material in single, easy steps.
5. Stimulate the thinking of the pupils and encourage them to discover ideas on their own.
6. Require students to reproduce the knowledge and concepts in their own language and behavior.
7. Review, review, review. Material should be tested, corrected, completed, confirmed and applied through a systematic process of review (Shafer, 1985, pp. 18-19).

During the 1960s and early 1970s, researchers tried to identify the most effective teaching style. A flurry of studies attempted to validate theoretically derived teaching constructs, usually represented by dichotomous variables. These variables included "authoritarian" versus "democratic" (Lewin, Lippitt, & White, 1939), "teacher-centered" versus "pupil-centered" (Withall, 1949), "direct" versus "indirect" (Flanders, 1965), and "traditional" versus "progressive" (Bennett, 1976) teaching styles. These terms still have some currency among teachers and the general public, but they lack precision in definition.

Today's educational practitioners look less for prescriptions and more for principles that will increase effectiveness in the pursuit of excellence. The vigorous research on teacher effectiveness in the recent past has yielded a small but growing number of firm connections between well-defined teacher behaviors and pupil outcomes, usually in the form of achievement test scores. In a recent attempt to help teachers improve their teaching skills, researchers studied teacher planning, management of the learning environment, student socialization, and instruction in several discipline areas (McKinney, 1987). Their primary focus was on roles of teachers, with secondary emphasis on students, curriculum, or other topics. Through coordination of several studies it was possible to extrapolate general principles of effective instruction. They found that "how" teachers teach is as important to student learning as "what" they teach.

McKinney (1987) identified five elements of effective instruction which can be applied to teaching in all types of education. First, good teachers set clear goals and stick to them. Without focused goals, students may learn about many topics, but master none. Good teachers can accomplish two or more goals simultaneously. Differences in instructional goals help explain differences in teachers' effectiveness. Second, effective teachers carefully communicate expectations. They explain what students will be studying and how it can be useful. Good teachers connect new lessons to past ones and show how they relate to everyday life. They monitor students' work carefully to ensure accuracy and completion and teach strategies for learning in and out of the learning environment. Third, good instructors thoroughly understand the subjects they teach. They also know the misconceptions students bring and work to clarify and correct them. Fourth, good teachers carefully select materials to fit the curriculum and the characteristics of their students. With the abundance of religious curricula available, teachers generally should not have to create their own materials, although that may be desirable occasionally. However, it is possible to be just as creative in teaching by integrating resources as it is to start from scratch. A word of caution is in order. It is probably not in the best interest of students to focus on one sole source of information, such as a Sunday school manual. All texts can and should be supplemented with a variety of available and relevant material (Porter & Brophy, 1988). Fifth, good teachers believe that they are responsible for what is learned and how students behave, as opposed to those who hold students totally responsible for their learning. Teachers who assume that students are low achievers do little to encourage them to learn. Both teacher and student need to assess the situation and make necessary adjustments. The teacher is responsible for taking the initiative in this adjustment process.

Teacher effectiveness research in the 1970s and 1980s focused on measuring learning outcomes with much attention given to instruction and its effect on student learning. Although many things in the setting affect learning, a competent teacher makes the major difference. Researchers found that about 15 percent of the variation among children in reading achievement at the end of the school year can be attributed to factors related to the skill and effectiveness of the teacher (Anderson et al., 1985). Porter and Brophy (1988) point out that good teachers create learning situations in which students are expected to learn not only facts and how to solve problems but how to organize information in new ways and formulate problems for themselves. They continuously monitor student understanding and routinely give feedback. They also teach students strategies for monitoring and improving their own learning efforts. In addition, these teachers frequently integrate instruction across discipline boundaries so that students grasp the interrelationships existing between bodies of knowledge. Without this perception, very little transfer of learning will occur. Effective teachers take time to reflect upon and evaluate their practices and accept the responsibility for making changes necessary for improving student learning.

Other factors related to effective teaching have emerged from the research of Harris (1984), and Otto, Wolf, and Eldridge (1984). These include the elements of time, instruction, learning environment, management, and organization. The amount of time that students are actively engaged in academic tasks seems to be the best predictor of achievement. Involvement seems to be greater if teachers pace instruction according to the learning rates of students. Involvement is also higher during teacher-directed instruction than during student-centered learning when students direct their own activities (Lehr, 1986; Rosenshine & Stevens, 1984).

Teachers approach the carrying out of instructional procedures in many ways. More effective ways include demonstration (proceeding in small steps while providing many examples and asking questions to clarify understanding); guided practice (providing practice which enables students to achieve an 80 percent or higher rate of achievement); corrective feedback (affirming and correcting responses and reteaching as needed); and independent practice (supplying enough practice to ensure overlearning of skills) (Rosenshine & Stevens, 1984).

Competent teachers provide learning environments which are orderly and structured. Research confirms the superiority of highly structured, formal over informal programs in promoting achievement, developing creativity among high intelligence children, and reducing test anxiety (Harris, 1984). Structure is especially desirable in primary grades and for low ability, dependent, or overanxious children (Rupley, Wise, & Logan, 1986).

Management of the educational context and organization are closely related to teacher effectiveness. Achievement scores tend to be higher when there is less disruptive behavior. Disturbances and wasted time reduce the amount of time children are engaged in academic tasks. Skilled teachers establish guidelines and procedures for carrying out daily routines without disruptions and loss of time. They know how to prevent many problems from arising and deal quickly with those that do arise (Anderson, Hiebert, Scott, & Wilkinson, 1985; Otto, Wolf, & Eldridge, 1984).

Good teachers use results of ongoing diagnosis as a basis for instruction. They are aware of individual differences in learning styles, reading levels, and interest and make provision for accommodating these differences in learning experiences. Students placed at their instructional levels progress at rates commensurate with their ability (Blair, 1984).

Major Elements of Effective Teaching

From a comprehensive review of the literature on effective teaching, seven major associations between teacher behavior and student achievement were found. These include quantity and pacing of instruction, whole-class versus small-group versus individualized instruction, giving information, questioning students, reacting to student responses, handling seatwork and homework assignments, and context-specific findings.

Quantity and Pacing of Instruction. The most consistently replicated findings link achievement to quantity and pacing of instruction. Amount learned is related to opportunity to learn. When teachers see academic instructions as a major part of their role, expect students to master the curricula, allocate most of the available time to curriculum-related activities, and are businesslike and task-oriented, student achievement is greater than when activities with other objectives (personal adjustment, group dynamics) or with no clear objectives (free time, student choice of activities) are pursued. Key indicators of good management include installation of rules and procedures at the beginning of the year, smoothness and momentum in lesson pacing, variety and appropriate level of challenge in assignments, and what is sometimes called "withitness," teachers communicating to students that they know what is happening in every area of the learning context at all times (Charles et al., 1978). Other important factors are consistent accountability procedures, follow-up of seatwork, and clarity about when and how students can get help and what options are available when they finish. It is important to maximize content coverage by brisk pacing. However, allowances have to be made for individual needs of students. A tension exists between the need to cover content as rapidly as possible and the need to ensure mastery through adequate practice while integrating new learnings with other concepts and skills. Students achieve more in situations when they spend most of their time being taught or supervised by the teacher rather than working on their own (Brophy & Good, 1986).

Whole-Group Versus Small-Group Versus Individualized Instruction. Research is inconclusive regarding the effects of these styles of planning and implementing instruction. Certain tradeoffs are obvious. Whole-group instruction is simpler since teachers need to plan only one lesson. The small-group approach requires preparing differentiated lessons and keeps the teacher busy instructing small groups, while the rest of the whole group is left to work independently. Small groups may be necessary in extremely heterogeneous groups when some students know many religious concepts and others very few. This analysis does not apply to the use of student teams, tournaments, and other cooperative learning strategies recommended for boosting motivation and increasing prosocial peer contact during work on assignments (Slavin, 1980, 1983). Individualized instruction, which relies heavily on unsupervised independent seatwork, is not as effective as teacher-led instruction (Brophy & Good, 1986).

Giving Information. Achievement is greatest when teachers do the following: 1) actively present material, 2) structure it by beginning with overviews, advance organizers or review of objectives, 3) outline the content, 4) signal transitions between lesson parts, 5) call attention to main ideas, 6) summarize subparts as the lesson proceeds, and 7) review main ideas at the end. There needs to be a certain amount of redundancy, consistent clarity, and a generous amount of enthusiasm, especially for older students (Smith & Sanders, 1981).

Questioning the Students. There are several elements of questioning that need to be discussed. Since questioning has been included as a method of teaching in another part of this chapter, the discussion of these aspects will be reserved for that section.

Reacting to Student Responses. Although it is important for teachers to give feedback, it is usually not important to praise the student who gives a correct answer. Such praise can be obtrusive, distracting, and may embarrass the student. Teachers who maximize achievement are sparing rather than effusive in praising correct answers. Praise is more likely to be effective when it is specific rather than global and when used with low socio-economic or dependent children rather than with high socio-economic or confident students. Sometimes feedback following an incorrect answer should include not only the right answer but an extended exploration of why the answer is correct and how it can be determined from the given information. Teachers should teach students to respond overtly to questions, even if only to say, "I don't know" (Brophy & Good, 1986).

Seatwork. Even though seatwork provides needed practice and application, it is probably overused and for the wrong reasons. Ideally, seatwork assignments should be varied and interesting enough to engage student interest, yet easy enough to ensure near 100 percent success rate. Effectiveness of seatwork increases when the work is thoroughly explained. Once it is begun, the teacher should circulate to monitor progress and provide help when needed. Feedback and follow-up are more closely related to achievement on seatwork than is praise or reward (Brophy & Good, 1986).

Context-Specific Findings. Even the best methodological research findings must be qualified by understanding the context in which the interaction occurs. These have to be taken into account when interpreting and applying the findings of research results. Low socio-economic and low achieving students need more control and structure, more active instruction and feedback, more redundancy, and smaller steps with a higher success rate. This means more review, drill, practice, and lower-level questions. Across the year, it also means exposure to fewer materials. Students from higher economic levels are likely to be more confident, eager to participate, and more responsive to challenge. They do not require a great deal of praise nor the same degree of warmth and support as do students from low socio-economic levels.

Summary

While the last twenty years have produced an orderly knowledge base linking teacher behavior to achievement, it is really only a beginning. There are obvious limitations. Causal relationships are not always clear, and the research base is limited in some areas. These conclusions are not meant to be translated into overly rigid or generalized prescriptions, but rather to provide general guidelines and stimulate further examination of effective teaching.

METHODS AND STRATEGIES OF TEACHING

Several methods of teaching are legitimate and effective ways of teaching. Methods and strategies range from highly structured ones to those that are very loosely organized and open-ended. They promote several kinds of thinking and produce a range of outcomes ranging from academic achievement to a change in social-emotional behaviors.

Generally, methods are large, over-arching global ways of organizing and presenting information. This would include planning in large segments, organizing the learning environment and materials for instruction, and deciding about evaluation, record keeping, and interactions with students. In contrast, strategies are more specific, direct, and designed to produce a given behavioral outcome. One may use several strategies in the context of a single method of teaching.

Theorists continue to experiment with different instructional approaches as research discovers how people learn. Different methods lend themselves better to certain types of content than others. No one method or strategy combination can accomplish all outcomes at one time. When selecting a method, teachers have to consider several things, including the nature of the content to be learned, the age and developmental needs of the students, and the nature of the goals. If teachers are teaching a fact-oriented lesson, they would probably select a method which lends itself to structured, sequentially arranged content. If the goal is to develop a clear understanding of relational content, a method providing group interaction and discussion might best serve to accomplish the objectives. Each method and strategy has both strengths and weaknesses and must be selected on the basis of how learning objectives can best be accomplished. As the following methods and strategies are discussed, there is an attempt to present them in sequential order from the most highly structured to the more informal, open-ended approaches.

Diagnostic-Prescriptive Teaching

Diagnostic-prescriptive teaching is a highly structured method consisting of three parts: diagnosis, prescription, and assessment of results (DPT). It is appropriate when skills and knowledge are emphasized, such as using a concordance or reciting the Lord's prayer. DPT results in rapid learning of such skills. The teacher's role includes developing a comprehensive list of skills and knowledge objectives, preparing the diagnostic procedures for evaluating skills, and identifying strengths and weaknesses. They must also develop learning activities designed to enable students to accomplish desired objectives, implement post-assessment activities and record student achievement. Students take the criterion test to determine if they are ready to move on to a new prescription (Charles et al., 1978).

Competency-Based Instruction

Like the diagnostic-prescriptive method, competency-based education is highly structured and is planned, organized, and controlled by the teacher. However, students are allowed some flexibility in choosing learning activities. Nagel and Richman (1972) describe the method as consisting of essentially two strategies: mastery learning and individualized instruction. It is good for the application of knowledge. The teacher's role involves selecting the topic and organizing the instructional package and support materials. Teachers must also prepare the pre- and post-assessment instruments, administer the assessment, provide corrective feedback, confer with students to clarify assessment, and keep records of student progress.

Read, Review, Recite

This approach has a long history in American education. Students are given reading assignments over a textbook or reference materials. After completing the assignments, students review the information. This can be done in many different ways (for example, recitation, outlining, summarizing, and so on). Once review exercises are completed, students must demonstrate mastery of the material. In the early days of our country, this was done by recitation. Now, testing is more common. Teachers select and assign the required reading, plan and direct review activities, and prepare the recitation or evaluation. Students complete the assignments and demonstrate acquisition of the knowledge and information. This approach can be boring or lively, depending upon the philosophy and personality of the teacher. It falls in the middle of the road between highly and loosely structured methods. Read, review, recite is good for acquisition of subject matter, developing interpersonal relations, application of knowledge, and developing creativity. It can be especially useful for teachers who feel insecure about their own competence.

Direct Instruction

This approach was originally aimed at low-income children who lacked language skills to succeed academically. The goal of the direct instruction approach is to assist all students in acquiring skills. Lessons are highly structured, teacher-directed, and provide immediate feedback. Direct instruction rests on the learning theories of Pavlov and Skinner, primarily on Skinner's operant conditioning theory. Inherent in the approach is the belief that any normal person can be taught to perform tasks successfully, if the unit of learning is small enough, arranged in hierarchical steps, and if the learner is appropriately reinforced. Reinforcement causes students to repeat behavior. In order for children to receive maximum amounts of stimulation and praise during a learning session, the teacher works with eight to ten children at a time and addresses most questions and praise to the group as a whole. Addressing the group is an attempt to keep all participants engaged at all times. Individual learning problems are diagnosed weekly, and students receive drill and practice necessary to learn required skills. Teachers initiate each stimulus and quickly reinforce or correct each response. They control students, keeping them on task through continuous interaction and positive reinforcement.

Early evaluation of direct instruction yielded mixed results. Some showed significant gains at first, but they later disappeared. However, in one study of long-term effects among fifth grade students in New York City who had been in a direct instruction program in basic skills for four years, it was found that students scored significantly higher than the control group. Evaluation of ninth graders who had been in a direct instruction program in kindergarten through third grade revealed that they were less likely to be retained, more likely to attend school, and more likely to graduate from high school. It appears that this approach can have a positive long-term effect upon student achievement and success (Myers & Myers, 1990).

Expository Teaching

Exposition means to make clear. This approach fits well with most grade levels. Material must be clear in order for students to grasp concepts, generalizations, and processes and see how these are interrelated. This means that students will understand different kinds of relationships, such as similarity, cause-effect, and means-end. The teacher plays a key role in exposition. Lectures and demonstrations are the most commonly used instructional techniques in expository teaching. Lectures can be very effective in dealing with abstract ideas. Use of media—television, video, dial-access equipment, and computers—could be included in this designation. Demonstrations, when appropriate, are more effective than lectures in clarifying concepts and ideas, provided they are accompanied by description and explanations. Effective demonstrations include models, drawings, photographs, and other visual aids.

This approach is an established method and a favorite with teachers. Its strength lies in its ability to communicate subject matter to students. It does little, however, for the affective goals of education (Charles et al., 1978).

Inquiry/Discovery

This approach is often referred to as discovery learning. It focuses more on thought process than on acquisition of knowledge. Its main purpose is to help students learn on their own. Learning on their own means observing, organizing, evaluating, arriving at concepts, generalizing, and making conclusions (Reisman & Payne, 1987). Although inquiry/discovery can enhance both inductive and deductive thinking, it emphasizes inductive thinking. Induction involves observing instances of related experiences and information and drawing conclusions about them—a part-to-whole relationship. In contrast, deduction is a process of reasoning from broad generalizations to specific instances—a whole-to-part thought progression.

Many educators and psychologists believe that inquiry and discovery produce learning that is more permanent and useful to the individual. Discovery learning was articulated by Bruner (1960), who believes that discovery is the best mode of learning and has done much to promote it as an approach to learning. He suggests that allowing the learner to discover and organize information is a necessary condition for learning to problem solve. Bruner also says that the most essential and basic component of any discipline is its structure, that is, the concepts and methods of inquiry. Instead of studying random facts, students should learn the principles constituting the heart of a discipline. The knowledge of fundamentals will enable a student to inquire into and solve problems in the area independently. Learning the structure of a discipline will enable students to transfer concepts from one situation to another. Teachers are encouraged to let students discover meanings for themselves. Instead of dominating the learning situation, teachers should create an open, nonthreatening environment that provides numerous opportunities to manipulate objects and materials. Teachers are discouraged from "telling" the answers. Rather, students are allowed to ask questions, face problems, and pose tentative answers themselves (Bruner, 1967; Cain & Evans, 1990).

The discovery approach is consistent with Piaget's view of how the child learns. Teachers often try to speed up the learning process. In so doing, a child may appear to have grasped an idea when in reality it may only be memorized. Children need time to interact directly with objects, ideas, and people. It also takes time to process, assimilate, and accommodate incoming stimuli. Active involvement is necessary for the child to acquire concepts. Active involvement can also provide experiential background for children from culturally different settings or with limited experience due to physical or sensory impairments. Hands-on, discovery learning is also useful for learners at any age who are encountering a new concept for which they have little background (Cain & Evans, 1990).

The arguments against the inquiry/discovery method focus on its inefficiency and difficulty in implementation. Advocates defend its ability to make learning more permanent and useful to the learner.

The teacher's role consists of helping students focus on a problem or topic, providing first-hand concrete activities and materials, knowing how to ask productive questions, clarifying thoughts, and examining answers. Students observe materials, discover trends, patterns, categories, and relationships, organize findings, and formulate and test hypotheses.

Simulations

Simulations are lifelike, reality-centered materials. Simulated instructional materials take many forms, such as enacting a dialogue about religion with friends. Movies or computers might simulate real situations, requiring religious content as part of the response. Some simulations are in the form of games, such as the "Ungame."[1] Such materials bring about a higher degree and longer duration of student involvement than any other method of teaching. They provide superior practice in group cooperation, resolving conflicts, and reconciling incompatibilities. They permit study in a form of role playing and bridge the gap between theory and practice.

Teachers select and prepare the simulations, introduce objectives and activities, interpret, guide, and assist students in identifying, organizing, and interpreting learnings. Students carry out the activities, follow rules, make decisions, solve problems, and analyze their own behavior. While simulations are good for promoting thinking processes and decision making, they are excellent for achieving the affective goals of improving self-concept, interpersonal relations, and effective group membership (Charles et al., 1978).

Questioning

Questioning is a teaching technique that has been used since the very beginning of education. Questioning strategies are among the oldest and most widely used methods of instruction. One of the most important aspects of teaching is the questions teachers ask. John Dewey once said that questions are the very core of teaching (Ryan & Cooper, 1988). It is difficult to think of a good teacher who does not ask good questions. Socrates was so proficient in questioning that his form of questioning is described as the Socratic method. Supposedly, Socrates used questioning as a total teaching method.

Questions are used to clarify procedures, determine if children understand assignments, and get feedback on the effectiveness of demonstrations. Questions may also be used to check comprehension of concepts, generalizations, or subject matter. Often questions require learners to reproduce or recall factual information. Berliner (1985) asserts that teachers more often ask questions that demand low-level thinking than questions requiring that students apply, analyze, synthesize, or evaluate information. Gall et al. (1978) found that teachers' questions could be categorized as recalling facts 60 percent of the time. He concluded that factual questions may be more effective for promoting achievement for young disadvantaged children, while higher cognitive questions may be more useful with older students of average and high ability.

When teaching complex cognitive content or trying to stimulate students to generalize, evaluate, or apply their learning, teachers need to raise questions that few students can answer. The data refute the frequently assumed notion that higher-level questions are categorically better than lower-level questions. Several studies indicate that lower-level questions facilitate learning, even learning of higher-level objectives (Brophy & Good, 1986).

Higher achievement occurs when teachers pause for about three seconds after the question to give students time to think before calling on one of them. The length of the pause following questions should vary directly with their difficulty level. Application questions require more time than do factual questions. The effectiveness of overt verbal participation varies according to grade, socio-economic level, and size of group. It is important that all students participate overtly in the early grades and in small-group lessons. Student verbalization usually correlates positively with achievement in low socio-economic classes but negatively in high socio-economic groups. Verbal participation does not seem to be an important achievement correlate in the upper grades (Brophy & Good, 1986). [See chapter six on ethnic differences in question answering.]

Rose (1973) found that just calling on low achievers often is not enough to insure learning. The "I don't know" or no response was often as high as 30 percent normally. He found that teachers can change this lack of responding pattern of low achievers by adding wait time, which correlates with the report of Brophy and Good (1986). Pausing for as much as three seconds resulted in:
1. increased length of student response
2. increased number of unsolicited but appropriate answers
3. increased contributions by slow students
4. increased student confidence
5. decreased failure to respond
6. decreased incidence of negative behaviors, such as restlessness, inattentiveness, and antisocial behaviors (Rose, 1973, chapter three).

Cummings (1983) stresses the importance of increasing participation of all students, including low achievers in question-and-answer sessions. To insure that expectations are not influencing who is called on, she suggests using techniques that guarantee randomness. These include using a can of popsicle sticks with each student's name written on a stick. When a question is asked, the teacher draws a stick out of the can to see whose name is called. Students soon learn that raising hands does not determine who is called on and that the teacher is not playing favorites or "picking" on someone. Teachers can use the same approach with 3x5 cards, using the back to record student participation. Another technique to ensure randomness is an adaptation of the army selection technique. Select a random number from one to ten. If the number is three, call out every third name. This approach has at least two advantages. Students know in advance they are likely to be called upon, and therefore, are more apt to listen. Teachers realize that a low achiever may be chosen and is, therefore, motivated to provide better instruction before asking questions.

In other studies of the technique of questioning, researchers concluded that it is better for teachers to ask questions that students can answer at least 75 percent of the time, that they should rely primarily upon direct questions in order to avoid irrelevant responses, and that they should spend most of their time asking questions rather than responding to pupil-initiated questions (Gage & Berliner, 1979; Fisher et al., 1980; Medley, 1977). Other researchers believe that teachers should use primarily lower-order cognitive questions (factual, knowledge, recall) rather than higher-order questions (analysis, synthesis, and evaluation) (Berliner, 1979; Gall et al., 1978; Medley, 1977; Soar & Soar, 1979). These conclusions contrast with the current emphasis on teaching the higher level thinking skills.

It was Bloom (1956) who first identified a hierarchy of six different levels of thinking skills, all of which are developed and promoted by questions and tasks required by the teacher. It was not until recently that questioning has been developed into what could legitimately be called a strategy of teaching. Questions have distinct characteristics. Some require factual recall. Others cause students to use other thought processes in forming an answer. Bloom's taxonomy is probably the best known system for classifying questions. The six levels of the taxonomy include knowledge, comprehension, application, analysis, synthesis, and evaluation.

Cooper (1986) provides a clear description of each of the six levels. The first level, *knowledge*, requires that students remember, recall, or recognize factual information. It has been fashionable to criticize questions which ask students to rely only on memory. College students often complain that exams require them to "spit back" information they have memorized from the text or lecture notes. However, remembering information is absolutely critical to the ability to function at all of the other levels of thinking. To say that the knowledge level is the lowest does not mean that it is the least important of the cognitive processes. On the contrary, it is the most essential, though not the ultimate level. Without basic knowledge, one has nothing with which to comprehend, analyze, apply, synthesize, or evaluate. One cannot process without content. Criticism comes because of the inordinate amount of teaching and learning time spent at the knowledge level compared to that spent at the other levels. The concern is for balance and the assurance that once children have a store of information they will then be able to do something with it at the other levels of thinking.

Use of knowledge questions promotes high success rates for students. Students from lower socio-economic levels achieve more in learning situations characterized by a high frequency of knowledge questioning. Effective

teachers provide both low and high ability students with many success opportunities. The use of knowledge questions plays a key role in establishing
this high success rate.

Comprehension is the second level of Bloom's taxonomy. Questions on
this level require students to demonstrate that they have enough understanding to organize and arrange material. They must go beyond recall of
information and show that they have a grasp of information by rephrasing,
putting it in their own words, identifying the main idea, summarizing, or giving an example. Comprehension questions require that students interpret
or translate ideas.

Application constitutes the third level of the hierarchy of thinking skills.
Such questions require students to apply previously learned information in
another similar situation. Application questions ask students to use prior
knowledge and understanding in order to solve a problem. After explaining what a proverb is, describing its pattern and reading one aloud, for example, the teacher may ask students to compose one of their own.

Analysis questions are the next level. They require students to think critically. These questions ask students to identify motives, reason, draw inferences, or make generalizations. Students are expected to examine and determine evidence to support or refute conclusions, inferences, or generalizations.
Students cannot answer an analysis question by repeating information, reor-
ganizing it, or putting it in their own words. They cannot rely directly on
instructional materials. Analysis questions require and promote critical thinking.

Synthesis questions are higher-order questions that ask students to perform
original and creative thinking. They require students to produce inventive outcomes, make predictions, and solve problems in which a number of answers
are feasible. Students must have a firm understanding of information and
factual background before being able to offer a logical response. Too often
teachers avoid analysis and synthesis activities because they are time-consuming and difficult to evaluate. While there may be appropriate information
to include, the way students formulate their responses would be very individualistic. There is no one right answer to synthesis questions.

Evaluation activities, like those at the synthesis level, do not have a single correct answer. They require students to judge the merit of an idea, evaluate solutions to problems, express an opinion, or give a rationale or criteria
for taking positions or holding certain values, beliefs, or attitudes. In evaluation questions, it is important to remember that some standard has to be
used. Different standards are acceptable and naturally result in different
answers (Cooper, 1986, pp. 140-156).

Below are some overt behavioral indicators that correspond to each level
of thought process and possible outcomes or products of each (Bloom, 1956;
Cooper, 1986, pp. 140-156):

	PROCESS	PRODUCT
KNOWLEDGE	List	Lists
	Label	Names
	Match	Dates
	Name	Recipe
	Recall	Facts
	Define	Definition
COMPREHENSION	Change	Summary
	Restate	Outline
	Summarize	Illustration
	Reorganize	Example
	Explain	Conclusion
	Translate	Main idea
	Interpret	Generalization
APPLICATION	Show	Diagram
	Make	Diorama
	Use	Collection
	Dramatize	Map
	Solve	Puzzle
	Construct	Lesson
	Demonstrate	Model
	Teach	Dramatization
ANALYSIS	Compare	Chart
	Contrast	Graph
	Dissect	Outline
	Differentiate	Diagram
	Deduce	Questionnaire
	Classify	Survey
	Order	Conclusion
SYNTHESIS	Imagine	Formula
	Hypothesize	Invention
	Create	Story
	Infer	Report
	Predict	Solution
	Forecast	Project
	Design	Advertisement

EVALUATION	Decide	Panel
	Dispute	Opinion
	Verify	Verdict
	Assess	Recommendation
	Rate	Editorial
	Judge	Scale
	Select	Advertisement

Modeling

Modeling or learning by imitation is the most subtle form of teaching, intentional or unintentional. It has been around since the beginning of time. Most of what children learn initially, especially in the affective domain, is learned through imitation of the dominant role models in their lives, usually parents. Television constitutes a most powerful force for shaping social behavior and values because of its pervasive presence in our society. Bandura (1971) is one of the first to develop the concept of modeling as an effective method of teaching which can be implemented by religious educators. Bandura and his colleagues identified traits of models that produce the most efficient learning in observers. It was found that models who are perceived as similar, nurturant, powerful, or prestigious are more apt to be imitated. Children who see a model being punished for aggression are less likely to imitate the behavior than those who see the model being rewarded or experiencing no consequences.

Models can be live, televised, filmed, or recorded. They can be real people, graphic presentations (cartoons, pictures, charts), verbal descriptions, or three-dimensional objects. Whatever the model, it must clearly present the process, concept, or behavior to be learned.

Teachers select the models, help focus student attention on the models, provide techniques for retention and application of principles learned, and give corrective feedback. Students carefully observe the models, identify and remember the goal behavior, and practice the application.

Modeling is relatively ineffective for teaching factual information and sequential skills but can contribute to the development of problem-solving skills. Its most effective use is for teaching complex social skills, values, and attitudes (Charles et al., 1978).

Projects

No teaching method allows for more intense pupil involvement than does the project method, and most children love it. They make choices, plan and organize their work, and best of all, they get to work with peers. In the end they have a tangible product to display. Projects can be short or long term and may be centered upon curriculum or some other source inside or outside the school. Projects focus on the process rather than the product and are appropriate for almost every area of study. This approach gets at all levels of educational objectives and thinking skills. Students grow in interpersonal skills, values, and attitude development. There are dozens of fascinating ideas for projects in religious education and at all grade levels.

The teacher's role in the project approach is to suggest appropriate topics and consult with students in identifying goals, procedures, materials, and activities. They arrange for projects to be shared and evaluated according to established criteria. Students are responsible for organizing work, producing an end product, and presenting it to others. Projects are an excellent means of including parents in the educational process.

Using projects is only moderately effective for acquisition of basic knowledge and skills. It is especially strong in developing social skills, attitudes, and values, as well as engaging students at all levels of the cognitive processes (Charles et al., (1978).

Group Process

This approach focuses primarily on group interactions, processes necessary to reach a common goal, resolution of conflicts, and leader-follower relationships. Group process helps students develop insights and skills involved in becoming a contributing member in a democratic society. It requires students to be actively involved in decision making which affects the welfare of the total group. Sessions may focus on social concerns or issues of justice and equality. The important goal of group process is to educate students about the nature of society and prepare them for responsible participation. No method is more difficult to implement than is group process. It often appears to waste a lot of time, given the amount of time and energy required for working through conflicts and arriving at consensus.

The teacher's main function is to participate in the group process, clarifying and counseling, but providing little or no other structure or direction. Students are active participants from beginning to end. They must examine their own roles, procedures, and contributions, and the learning comes from that process. Group process is very efficient in development of social interpersonal skills but not effective in acquiring subject area knowledge and information (Charles et al., 1978). The religious educator might adapt this process to teach religious perspectives on interpersonal relationships within the group context. [See also its application to discipline in chapter seven.]

Mastery Learning

Mastery learning is the fundamental belief that nearly all students can learn a basic curriculum, but some take longer than others. Bloom (1981) believes that most students can master what is to be taught and that it is the educator's responsibility to find the means which will enable students to master the material under consideration. In another publication, Bloom observes, "After forty years of intensive research on school learning in the United States as well as abroad, my major conclusion is, 'What any person in the world can learn, almost all persons can learn if provided with appropriate prior and current conditions of learning'" (Bloom, 1985, p.4). This does not apply to the 2 or 3 percent of individuals who have severe emotional or physical difficulties that impair their learning nor to the 1 or 2 percent who appear to learn in unusually capable ways. Given these possible exceptions, that leaves 95 percent of children who are very similar in terms of measurable achievement, learning ability, rate of learning, and motivation when provided with favorable learning conditions. One such favorable learning condition is mastery learning, in which students are helped to master each learning unit before proceeding to more advanced learning tasks. Generally, Bloom believes that the average student taught under mastery learning procedures achieves at a level above 85 percent of students taught under conventional learning conditions.

According to Bloom (1985), an even more extreme result has been obtained when tutoring was used as the primary method of instruction. Under tutoring, the average student performs better than 95 percent of students taught by conventional group instruction, even though both groups of students performed at similar levels in terms of relevant aptitude and achievement before the instruction began. This is good news for parents who elect to home-school their children, since the adult-child ratio in home schooling is generally the same as in tutoring, depending upon the number of children involved. This may account for the consistently higher achievement of home-schooled children as compared with their peers in typical public and private school classrooms (Moore, 1979).

Low ability students or slow learners would be expected to benefit most from a mastery learning approach. Clear instructional objectives are required for such programs. It is necessary to divide the subject or learning task into small discrete units of learning and arrange them hierarchically. This makes the task more conducive to close monitoring of student progress. Diagnostic tests are critical to a mastery learning program. Although the mastery-based program has been adopted by many educators around the world, efforts at evaluation have not been very consistent, well-organized, or planned (Stallings & Stipek, 1986).

Findings from several studies indicate a positive trend for mastery learning but have not shown that students are unusually superior on standardized achievement test scores. Proponents of mastery learning have claimed that competition would be eliminated by the highly individualized procedures. Yet informed observers suggest that competitiveness is not reduced by mastery methods, because children were observed creating competition within such settings (Crockenberg & Bryant, 1978). Other criticisms include the consuming of an inordinate amount of teacher time and that it may require some sacrifice in "waiting" on the part of high-ability students.

One of the most positive aspects of the approach is the basic belief that all students can learn. Given the significant relationship between teacher expectations and student achievement, mastery learning advocates make an important contribution to student learning by convincing teachers that all students can master the curriculum.

The main task of the teacher in mastery learning is to divide the material into sequenced, manageable parts. They decide what level of achievement constitutes mastery and provide ways of monitoring the progress of each student. One of the most difficult tasks is determining the variations in time requirement needed for each student. Students work at their assignments and seek teacher assistance when needed. Mastery learning especially promotes achievement in areas of knowledge and skills, but is not effective in promoting learning in the affective domain (Charles et al., 1978).

Cooperative Learning

Cooperative learning is an alternative learning format that has gained prominence in recent years. Cooperative learning programs have been designed to achieve at least four goals: 1) to raise the perceived value of cognitive achievement and encourage students to help and support peers in their group, 2) to increase understanding and encouragement in both high- and low-ability students through cooperative efforts and mutual assistance, 3) to insure that all students take ownership for and persist in contributing to the learning outcomes, and 4) to improve racial relations (Stallings & Stipek, 1986). Some educators maintain that cooperative learning changes the way students learn, their attitude toward what they are taught, and their perception of themselves and others (Ryan & Cooper, 1988).

Many cooperative learning programs have been studied. The following discussion will focus on three programs that stand out because of the amount of systematic development and research available.

Teams, Games, Tournaments. TGT is a supplement to the instructional approach already used by the teacher. New material is initially presented to the whole group in a lecture-discussion format. Students are then divided into four- or five-member teams, diverse in terms of level of achievement, race, and other variables. Practice sessions with teammates prepare students for game sessions in an ongoing tournament. DeVries and Slavin (1978, p. 29) describe how the tournament functions:

> In the tournament, which takes place once or twice each week, each student is assigned to a tournament table where he or she competes individually against students from other teams. The students at each table are roughly comparable in achievement level. The tournament tables are numbered, with Table 1 being the "top" table. At the end of the period, the

players at each table compare their scores to determine the top, middle, and low scorers at the various game tables. The top scorer at each table receives six points, the middle scorer four points, and the low scorer two points. Team scores are then calculated by simply adding the results for teammates. These scores are added to the team's tallies from previous game sessions in the tournament, creating a cumulative score. Team standings are then formed and shared with the students. . . . Skill exercise sessions which focus on the current subject matter are played during the tournament. At each three-person table, students answer questions posed on card sets or game sheets to demonstrate mastery of specific skills. A basic set of rules, including a challenge rule, dictates the form of play.

Student Teams and Achievement Divisions. STADs are similar to TGT programs. Teachers present new material by the lecture-discussion method, and students are divided into groups of four or five to help each other prepare to take quizzes rather than to participate in a tournament. They do not assist each other in taking the test. The groups are heterogeneous with regard to past performance. Rewards are contingent upon performance within a group of children organized into divisions composed of students equal in terms of past performance.

Jigsaw. The jigsaw method was designed to promote peer cooperation, tutoring, and positive race relations by creating interdependence among students. In models of Aronson's (et al., 1978) first jigsaw a different portion of a learning task is assigned to each of five or six members of a team. There may be several teams, each with the same number of members. Each team member is assigned the responsibility for mastering his assigned portion of a task for the purpose of teaching that portion to the rest of the team members. Members of different teams who have studied the same section meet in "expert groups" to discuss, rehearse, and review the most significant information needed by their teams. Students are dependent on other members of their team for sections they did not personally cover. They are, therefore, motivated to listen carefully to their teammates and to support their efforts. Teachers move around the room assisting, encouraging, and directing as needed. After team reports, students take quizzes. All group members are, therefore, ultimately responsible for learning all the curriculum material (DeVries & Slavin, 1978).

According to one evaluation of the method (Zigler & Muenchow, 1979), it was found that jigsaw children learned more and retained knowledge better than those in a control group. They also spent more time on task. Other studies of 493 fifth and sixth grade students resulted in superior performance for minority children, but not for Anglo children (Sharan, 1980). Still other assessments found positive effects of jigsaw methods on children's attitudes toward peers, self-esteem, and role taking (Blaney et al., 1977; Geffner, 1978;

Bridgeman, 1977). Augustine, Gruber, and Hanson (1989-1990) pointed out the benefits that mainstream children gained from cooperative learning. Many mainstream children lack social skills and have poor self-concepts. When they are assigned to small heterogeneous cooperative groups and given specific roles, their achievement generally increased, and their psychological health improved. They pointed out that such experiences also benefit high-achieving students who may lack certain social skills.

The incentive structure of cooperative learning experiences seems to play an important role in effectiveness. Slavin (1983) pointed out that working cooperatively with no incentive has not been found to increase student achievement more than instructions to work independently. Group rewards, depending on the mutual performance of each member, are likely to be motivating for students who under other conditions would likely fail.

Perhaps the most important outcomes of cooperative learning experiences are in the affective domain, such as mutual concern, friendships with students of other ethnic groups, and perceiving peer support. Neither mastery learning nor cooperative learning are appropriate for all teachers, children or religious education topics. Both emphasize motivation and provide opportunities for all children to succeed, including those who generally fail under individualized competitive conditions.

Microcomputers

At one time, blackboards and chalk were a new technology, a breakthrough, a new way of doing things. Today religious education is poised on the edge of an even greater technological breakthrough involving several technologies as learning tools. At its heart is the computer. The use of computers in religious education is advancing and will continue to advance. America is an information-based society. Churches need to help students acquire more and better information as well as skills for using that information (Ryan & Cooper, 1988).

Computers are classified into three groups—mainframes, minicomputers, and microcomputers. The microcomputer is the smallest and most adaptable. The microcomputer formats most used today are the Apple and the IBM-PC. Software designers have only begun to explore the computer's potential as an instructional aid for religious education curriculum. Drill and practice programs are the most common programs available, because they are the easiest to write. Simulated environments, in contrast, require advanced programing capability. Computers provide immediate, corrective feedback, which is an ingredient in effective learning. Creative use of microcomputers can generate enthusiasm among learning. Creative use of microcomputers can generate enthusiasm among learners. They often possess computer-related skills that surpass those of their teachers (Cain & Evans, 1990; Ryan & Cooper, 1988).

Decker Walker (1983) of Stanford University suggests the following ways in which microcomputers can contribute to learning:

1. They stimulate more active learning than traditional methods.
2. They can be linked with any device that generates or responds to an electronic signal, thus exhibiting their versatility.
3. They allow for pupil interaction.
4. They free the learner from many chores normally required for research, reducing mental exhaustion.
5. They individualize the process of learning, thus fulfilling the goal of individualized rate of learning tailored to student attention span and stage of learning.
6. They provide instant verification or detect and remedy more swiftly, fostering independent learning.
7. They can provide better aids to abstraction with use of graphics, simulations, and games.

Computers are used by students, preschool through college and beyond, in many different ways and for a variety of reasons. They can be used by one student at a time; groups of students can use a single computer; and teachers can use a computer to demonstrate concepts. Students sometimes have access to multiple computers in a lab setting. Computers can be applied to an infinite range of objectives. Preservice preparation of religious educators is probably needed to familiarize them with the basic knowledge and skills needed to operate and use a computer in the ongoing instructional program (Jarolimek, 1990).

PLANNING FOR INSTRUCTION

"Instruction is a process of deliberate decision making and action that makes learning more probable and successful than it would be without teaching" (Cummings, 1983). The three basic elements of instruction are planning, implementing, and evaluating. Of these three, planning is by far the most important.

Planning is one of the most difficult and time-consuming parts of the whole teaching process. During teacher preparation it is extremely important that students learn the elements of effective planning. Even though churches and parachurch groups may provide teachers with guides which include instructional activities and available resources for a content area for each grade level, these by no means are a substitute for their own personal planning. Some college and seminary instructors require preservice teachers to specify every step of their plans: long- and short-term goals, detailed lists of objectives, procedures and materials to match each objective, time scheduled for instruction, activities described for reteaching and remediation, planned enrichment for different learning styles, possible tasks for different levels of thinking, and evaluation procedures.

To some extent, highly detailed lesson plans are not generally carried into the real world of religious instruction. However, it is very crucial that the preservice teacher understand the complex nature of thorough planning without which very little learning will occur. Much evidence supports the contention that when teachers have planned well, clearly defined their objectives, and shared them with their students, better instruction occurs, more efficient learning results, and better evaluation by teachers and students takes place (Cooper, 1986). There is no better time or place to learn this than in college or seminary. Detailed planning may become more mental in actual process, but it is still required.

Long-Range and Short-Term Planning

Two types of planning are necessary: long-range and short-term planning. Long-range planning includes organizing the scope (content, process, skills, attitudes that will be taught) and sequence (in what order these will be taught for the quarter, semester, or year). Short-term planning is much more detailed and describes the sequential steps needed to proceed through the specific session activities necessary for reaching the goals of the long-range plans (Cain & Evans, 1990).

There are at least four different levels of planning: *curriculum guides*, which cover the whole range of instructional activities and goals from kindergarten through twelfth grade; *resource units*, which are sample units developed for a hypothetical group of students for given instructional periods of weeks, months, or perhaps a year; *teaching units*, which are created by the teacher for a specific group of students and are more detailed than resource units and cover smaller units of time; and *lesson plans*, which are usually developed for one to five group sessions. Lesson planning thus proceeds from the very general to the very specific. The progression might be illustrated as follows:

LONG-RANGE	SHORT-TERM
Curriculum guides - very general	Teaching units - specific
Resource units - general	Lesson plans - very specific
	(Reisman & Payne, 1987)

Curriculum guides and resource units are usually prepared by committees for use by the religious educators in the church or denomination. These may be revised periodically. On the other hand, religious educators are responsible for developing the teaching units and lesson plans for the curriculum. Good teachers use all kinds of resources in planning—ideas from other teachers, interests and needs of students, community concerns, parental expertise, current events, and their own specialized skills and knowledge (Cain & Evans, 1990).

Session-by-session planning is a necessary part of long-range planning. Although there are many formats for writing lesson plans, there are certain elements that all have in common. All lesson plans must have very specific objectives, procedures for accomplishing the objectives, and an evaluation to determine if the objectives have been accomplished. Jarolimek (1990) suggests that there are four essential components in a lesson plan: objectives, lesson development (readiness or interest-building procedures and work-study activities), summary and evaluation, and a list of instructional materials and resources.

Plans differ widely because they are written by individual teachers for a particular topic and group of students. At first, planning will be very detailed, but as teachers gain experience, they will need less time for the process.

For the purpose of providing guidelines for preparing lesson plans for an instructional session, the following components by Reisman and Payne (1987, pp. 81-87) are suggested:

A MODEL LESSON PLAN FORMAT

UNIT TITLE: Only a word or sentence describing the main idea of the unit is necessary.

GOALS AND
OBJECTIVES: Goals are usually stated in broad, nonbehavioral terms, while objectives need to be stated in specific, observable outcomes.

MATERIALS: Anything intended to supplement the lesson. Needs to be listed and at the fingertips before the lesson begins. All equipment should be in working order in advance of beginning the lesson.

PROCEDURES: Include a rationale in the lesson plan in order to help focus attention on the goals and objectives. Be specific about how the students' attention and interest is going to be obtained at the very beginning of the lesson.

Strategies, techniques, and activities should be listed with enough detail that they can be implemented without delay or uncertainty.

The content component of the lesson plan refers to what is to be taught—the facts, generalizations, and concepts. Be very specific about what is said and the order in which the information will be presented.

The ending of the lesson is just as important as the beginning and should be thoroughly planned. Students need to have opportunities to synthesize, summarize and evaluate.

EVALUATION: Assessing student learning is an ongoing process as well as a culminating event. Teachers need to be continually aware of the progress students are making toward mastering the goals and objectives of the lesson. The final evaluation tells the teacher if skills and concepts need to be retaught or if the students are ready to proceed to the next lesson.

CRITIQUE: This is the self-evaluation teachers do of themselves, the lesson and the response of students. Teachers should reflect back on the total experience and answer such questions as:

> Were objectives appropriate?
> Were directions easy to follow?
> Were students able to complete their assignment?
> What are some things that should be changed?
> How can it be better the next time?

Planning is an indispensable tool in helping teachers establish effective learning situations for students. Experienced teachers do not always write out detailed plans for every lesson they teach. However, competent teachers realize the necessity of careful planning and preparation.

The ITIP Model

In the last several years teachers have been encouraged to examine the Madeline Hunter approach, otherwise known as Instructional Theory into Practice (ITIP). This approach is an attempt to translate research-based knowledge into common language so that teachers can use it in their teaching experiences (Cain & Evans, 1990).

ITIP lessons incorporate Hunter's belief that the teaching process involves making a continual series of decisions. She categorizes decisions into three areas: those that involve the content, those that involve how students will achieve the learning, and those that involve specific teacher behaviors. ITIP provides teachers with a generic design and structure to be followed in each lesson. The lesson elements are anticipatory set, objective and purpose, input, modeling, check for understanding, guided practice, and independent practice.

Anticipatory Set. The anticipatory set captures the students' attention and serves to link the learning at hand with prior experience or knowledge. This may include novel, catchy attention-getting devices or simply a review of what went on in the previous lesson and an explanation of how it relates to the present activity. The object is to get students focused on the task at hand and to see it as a meaningful, purposeful extension of past learning or introduction to a new concept.

Objective and Purpose. The teacher tells the students what they are going to learn and how they will find it useful. This provides direction and focus for the students as well as tells them what it is they are expected to know, understand, or be able to do at the end of the lesson. If a lesson is like a trip, then the objective is the destination.

Input. The educator teaches the new material to the group. This can be done in a number of ways, such as lecturing, reading, student discovery, presentations, observing, and so on. The teacher sees that the students acquire the new information, knowledge, process, or skill. This should be clearly related to the achieving of the stated objectives of the lesson.

Modeling. This category consists of the visual, spatial activities involved in the lesson. The teacher provides concrete examples of the ideas, processes, or skills to be learned. Students learn better when all their senses are engaged. If students can see and hear what the teacher is talking about, they are more likely to understand and remember it. Modeling could include showing examples, using illustrations, making demonstrations, relating it to a current event, or relating a personal experience. When students see what the teacher means, they learn more quickly and understand more thoroughly, which gives greater assurance of success on the part of the student.

Check for Understanding. Frequent checks to see if students understand and are able to do the assigned activity tell the teacher when he or she needs to reteach, repeat, review, summarize, or proceed: Just asking, "Do you understand?" does not tell the teacher that learning has indeed occurred. Continual interaction with students at this stage is necessary in order to ensure that comprehension is occurring. This monitoring of student understanding can be accomplished in a variety of ways: asking for signals (show me where a king wears a crown), asking for a written response (jot down the four ways God speaks to people), or asking for a choral response from the group (tell me the name of the first martyr). By involving the whole group in similar responses, a clearer picture of how well they comprehend emerges. In addition, learning takes place at a faster rate than if attention is focused on one student at a time.

Guided Practice. Students practice their new knowledge or skills under teacher supervision. According to research, time spent in supervised seatwork activities is substantially more effective in promoting achievement than is unsupervised practice. During seatwork, the teacher should circulate to monitor progress and provide help when needed.

Independent Practice. Once the teacher is relatively sure that students have acquired the new knowledge or skill, they are assigned activities in which they practice independently what they have just learned. Working alone on seatwork is a common and frequent activity. Independent practice is necessary, but it has been found that the engagement rate or time on task goes down compared with teacher-directed practice (Rosenshine, 1980).

Therefore, it is important that teachers make every effort to maintain contact and interaction with the students during this time of independent work.

Hunter's method is very similar to many other teaching strategies that have been presented to teachers over the years. It was developed over twenty years ago and is based on established principles of educational psychology. Therefore, most educators support the basic sequence and techniques of the approach. Many public schools have designed teacher evaluation forms based on the model. School administrators are trained in the approach and use it to evaluate teachers. While religious educators might also use such evaluations, Hunter says that the model was "designed to help teachers plan. In no way can a teacher be judged by the inclusion of all those elements. . . . Any observer who used a checklist to make sure a teacher is using all seven elements does not understand the model" (Hunter, 1985, p. 57-60).

Research has not revealed that children score any better on achievement tests after being taught by the Hunter model. Nevertheless, many teachers like it. It is clear, easy to learn, provides a sensible framework for the teaching process, and offers a common vocabulary for labeling teaching strategies. The strength of the model lies in its organization, ease of use, language, and format. While it contains no new psychological principles, it does provide teachers with a systematized approach (Burns, Roe, & Ross, 1988).

CONCLUSION

Professional teachers in churches, parachurch organizations, and schools do not usually adopt any one method completely. They usually pick and choose elements from different approaches that fit their teaching style and use them in combination. Teachers may also adopt one method for one set of objectives or subject matter and an entirely different approach for another. This is reasonable and appropriate. The best teachers use a wide variety of instructional techniques and strategies (Charles et al., 1978). It is also well-known that there is no one best method for all time, teachers, students, or topics. Therefore, effective teachers will find what works best for them, their students, and under what circumstances. They will continue to grow in ability to recognize the best methods, remain open to continued research developments, and maintain an attitude of flexibility as they work with groups of students from year to year.

NOTE

1. It might be noted that the "Ungame" is available with religious questions—Ed.

REFERENCES

Anderson, R. C., Hiebert, E. H., Scott, J. A., & Wilkinson, I. A. G. (1985). *Becoming a nation of readers: The report of the commission on reading.* Washington, DC: The National Institute of Education, U. S. Department of Education.

Aronson, E., Stephan, C., Sikes, J., Blaney, N., & Snapp, M. (1978). *The jigsaw classroom.* Beverly Hills, CA: Sage.

Augustine, D. K., Gruber, K. D., & Hanson, L. (1989-1990). Cooperation works! *Educational Leadership, 47,* 4-7.

Bandura, A. (1971). *A social learning theory.* New York: General Learning Corporation.

Bennett, N. (1976). *Teaching styles and pupil progress.* London: Open Books.

Berliner, D. (1985). Effective classroom teaching: The necessary but not sufficient condition for developing exemplary schools. In G. R. Austin & H. Garber (Eds.), *Research on exemplary schools.* Orlando: Academic Press.

Berliner, D. (1986). In pursuit of the expert pedagogue. Presidential address at the 1986 annual meeting of the American Educational Research Association. *Educational Research, 15,* 5-13.

Berliner, D. (1979). Tempus Educare. In P. Petersen & H. Walberg (Eds.), *Research on teaching.* Berkeley, CA: McCutchan.

Berns, R. M. (1985). *Child, family, community.* New York: Holt, Rinehart and Winston.

Blair, T. R. (1984). Teacher effectiveness: The know-how to improve student learning. *The Reading Teacher, 38,* 138-142.

Blaney, J., Stephan, S., Rosenfield, D., Aronson, E., & Sikes, J. (1977). Interdependence in the classroom: A field study. *Journal of Educational Psychology, 69,* 121-128.

Bloom, B. S. (1956). *Taxonomy of educational objectives: Cognitive domain.* New York: David McKay.

Bloom, B. S. (1981). *All our children learning.* New York: McGraw-Hill.

Bloom, B. S. (1985). *Developing talent in young people.* New York: Ballantine Books.

Bridgeman, D. (1977). *The influence of cooperative, interdependent learning on role taking and moral reasoning: A theoretical and empirical field study with fifth grade students.* Unpublished doctoral dissertation, University of California, Santa Cruz.

Brophy, J. E. (1985). Classroom management as instruction: Socializing self-guidance in students. *Theory Into Practice, 24,* 233-240.

Brophy, J. E., & Good, T. L. (1986). Teacher behavior and student achievement. In Merlin C. Wittrock (Ed.), *Handbook of research on teaching* (3rd ed.). New York: Macmillan.

Bruner, J. (1960). *The process of education.* New York: Random House.

Bruner, J. (1967). *Toward a theory of instruction.* Cambridge, MA: Harvard University Press.

Burns, P. C., Roe, B. D., & Ross, E. P. (1988). *Teaching reading in today's elementary schools.* Boston: Houghton Mifflin.

Cain, S. E., & Evans, J. M. (1990). *Sciencing, an involvement approach to elementary science methods.* Columbus, OH: Merrill.

Carroll, J. (1963). A model of school learning. *Teachers College Record, 64,* 723-733.

Chambers, J. H. (1988). Teaching thinking throughout the curriculum—where else? *Educational Leadership, 45,* 4-6.

Charles, C. M., Gast, D. K., Servey, R. E., & Burnside, H. M. (1978). *Schooling, teaching, and learning American education.* St. Louis: Mosby.

Clark, C. M., & Petterson, P. L. (1986). Teachers' thought processes. In Merlin C. Wittrock (Ed.), *Handbook of research on teaching* (3rd ed.). New York: Macmillan.

Cooper, J. M. (Ed.) (1986). *Classroom teaching skills.* Lexington, MA: Heath.

Crockenberg, S., & Bryant, B. (1978). Socialization: The implicit curriculum of learning environment. *Journal of Research and Development in Education, 12,* 69-78.

Cummings, C. (1980). *Teaching makes a difference.* Edmonds, WA: Teaching, Inc.

Cummings, C. (1983). *Managing to teach.* Edmonds, WA: Teaching, Inc.

DeVries, D., & Slavin, R. (1978). *The systematic design of instruction.* Glenview, IL: Scott, Foresman.

Dunkin, M. J., & Biddle, B. J. (1974). *The study of teaching.* New York: Holt, Rinehart and Winston.

Fischer, B. B., & Fischer, L. (1979). Styles in teaching and learning. *Educational Leadership, 36,* 245-54.

Fisher, C., Berliner, D., Filby, N., Marliaru, R., Cohen, L., & Dishaw, M. (1980). Teaching behaviors, academic learning time and student achievement: An overview. In C. Denham and A. Lieberman (Eds.). *Time to Learn.* Washington, DC: National Institute of Education.

Flanders, N. (1965). *Teacher influence, pupil attitudes, and achievement* (Cooperative Research Monograph No. 12). Washington, DC: U. S. Office of Education.

Gage, N. L., & Berliner, D. C. (1979). *Educational psychology* (2nd ed.). Chicago: Rand McNally.

Gall, M., Ward, B., Berliner, D., Cohen, L., Winne, P., Eloshoff, J., & Stanton, G. (1978). Effects of questioning and recitation on student learning. *American Educational Research Journal, 15,* 175-199.

Gall, M., & Berliner, D. C. (1979). Synthesis of research on teachers' questioning. *Educational Leadership, 42,* 42.

Geffner, R., (1978). *The effects of interdependent learning on self-esteem, interethnic relations, and interethnic attitudes of elementary school children: A field experiment.* Unpublished doctoral dissertation, University of California, Santa Cruz.

Good, T. L., & Brophy, J. E. (1987). *Looking in classrooms* (4th ed.). New York: Harper & Row.

Good, T. L., & Grouws, D. A. (1977). Teaching effects: A process-product study in fourth grade mathematics classrooms. *Journal of Teacher Education, 28,* 49-54.

Harris, A. J. (1984). The effective teacher of reading, revisited. In J. Harris & E. R. Sipay (Eds.), *Readings on reading instruction.* New York: Longman.

Hunter, M. (1985). What's wrong with Madeline Hunter? *Educational Leadership, 42,* 57-60.

Jarolimek, J. (1990). *Social studies in elementary education.* New York: Macmillan.

Johnson, J. A., Collins, H. W., Supuis, V. L., & Johansen, J. H. (1985). *Introduction to the foundations of American education* (6th ed.). Boston: Allyn & Bacon.

Lehr, F. (1986). Direct instruction in reading. *The Reading Teacher, 39,* 706-708.

Lewin, L., Lippitt, R., & White, R. (1939). Patterns of aggressive behavior in experimentally created social climates. *Journal of Social Psychology, 10,* 231-299.

McKinney, K. (1987). *Five tips to improve teaching. Research in brief.* Office of Educational Research and Improvement. Washington, DC: U. S. Department of Education.

Medley, D. (1977). *Teacher competency and teacher effectiveness: A review of process-product research.* Washington, DC: American Association of Colleges for Teacher Education.

Medley, D. (1979). The effectiveness of teachers. In P. Peterson and H. Walberg (Eds.), *Research on teaching: Concepts, findings, and implications.* Berkeley, CA: McCutchan.

Moore, R. (1979). *School can wait.* Provo, UT: Brigham Young University Press.

Myers, C. B., & Myers, L. K. (1990). *An introduction to teaching and schools.* Chicago: Holt, Rinehart and Winston.

Nagel, J., & Richman, P. (1972). *Competency-based instruction.* Columbus, OH: Merrill.

Otto, W., Wolfe, A., & Eldridge, R. G. (1984). Managing instruction. In P. D. Pearson (Ed.), *Handbook of reading research.* New York: Longman.

Porter, A. C., & Brophy, J. (1988). Synthesis of research on good teaching: Insights from the work of the Institute for Research on Teaching.

Educational Leadership, 45, 74-83.

Reisman, F. K., & Payne, B. D. (1987). *Elementary education, a basic text.* Columbus, OH: Merrill.

Rose, M. (1973). *Teaching science as continuous inquiry.* New York: McGraw-Hill.

Rosenshine, B. V. (1971). *Teaching behaviors and student achievement.* London: National Foundation for Educational Research.

Rosenshine, B.V. (1976). Classroom instruction. In N. L. Gage (Ed.), *The psychology of teaching methods* (seventy-seventh yearbook of the National Society for the Study of Education). Chicago: University of Chicago Press.

Rosenshine, B. V. (1980). Direct instruction. In C. Denham and A. Lieberman, (Eds.), *Time to learn.* Washington, DC: National Institute of Education.

Rosenshine, B. V., & Stevens, R. (1984). Classroom instruction in reading. In D. F. Pearson (Ed.), *Handbook of reading research.* New York: Longman.

Rupley, W., Wise, B. S., & Logan, J. W. (1986). Research in effective teaching: An overview of its development. In J. V. Hoffman (Ed.). *Effective teaching of reading: Research and practice.* Newark, DE: International Reading Association.

Ryan, K., & Cooper, J. M. (1988). *Those who can, teach* (5th ed.). Boston: Houghton, Mifflin.

Ryans, D. (1960). *Characteristics of teachers.* Washington, DC: American Council on Education.

Shafer, C. (Ed.). (1985). *Excellence in teaching with the seven laws.* Grand Rapids, MI: Baker.

Sharan, S. (1980). Cooperative learning in small groups: Recent methods and effects on achievement, attitudes, and ethnic relations. *Review of Educational Research, 50*, 241-271.

Slavin, R. (1980). Effects of student teams and peer tutoring on academic achievement and time on task. *Journal of Experimental Education, 48*, 252-257.

Slavin, R. (1983). *Cooperative learning.* New York: Longman.

Smith, B. A. (1969). *Teachers for the real world.* Washington, DC: American Association of Colleges for Teacher Education.

Smith, L., & Sanders, K. (1981). The effects on student achievement and student perception of varying structure in social studies content. *Journal of Educational Research, 74*, 333-336.

Soar, R. S. (1977). An integration of findings from four studies of teacher effectiveness. In G. Barick & K. Fenton (Eds.), *The appraisal of teaching: Concepts and process.* Reading, MA: Addison Wesley.

Soar, R. S., & Soar, R. M. (1979). Emotional climate and management. In P. Peterson & H. Walberg (Eds.), *Research on teaching: Concepts, find-*

ings, and implications. Berkeley, CA: McCutchan.

Stallings, J. (1980). Allocated academic learning time revisited, or beyond time on task. *Educational Researcher*, *9*, 11-16.

Stallings, J., Cory, R., Fairweather, J., & Needels, M. (1978). *A study of basic reading skills taught in secondary schools*. Menlo Park, CA: SRI International.

Stallings, J. A., & Stipek, D. (1986). Research on early childhood and elementary school teaching programs. In Merlin C. Wittrock (Ed.). *Handbook of research on teaching* (3rd ed.). New York: Macmillan.

Stevens, B. (Ed.). (1985). S*chool effectiveness: Eight variables that make a difference*. Lansing, MI: Michigan State Board of Education.

The seven step lesson plan. (1986). *The mathematics publisher*. Menlo Park, CA: Addison Wesley.

Walker, D. (1983). Reflections on the educational potential and limitations of microcomputers. *Phi Delta Kappan*, *65*, 103-107.

Withall, J. (1949). The development of a technique for the measurement of social-emotional climate in classroom. *Journal of Experimental Education*, *17*, 347-361.

Wynn, R., & Wynn, J. L. (1988). *American education* (9th ed.). New York: Harper & Row.

Ziegler, S. (1981). The effectiveness of cooperative learning teams for increasing cross-ethnic friendship: Additional evidence. *Human Organization*, *40*, 264-268.

Zigler, E., & Muenchow, S. (1979). Mainstreaming: The proof is in the implementation. *American Psychology*, *34*, 993-996.

Chapter Ten

Assessment, Placement, and Evaluation

KALEVI TAMMINEN AND DONALD RATCLIFF

Religious education requires continual research and development to be maximally effective. In this case, research involves understanding the student and finding the best way to teach that student. Development is the religious understanding, attitudinal focusing, and spiritual direction of the student. But it also implies development of a program that accomplishes these tasks, a program that is dynamic, not static, continually adjusting to the needs of children.

While the heart of religious education in the local church or parish, from this perspective, is instruction and evaluation, too often antecedents of the educational process are ignored. The training of the teacher (preservice and inservice), the placement of the teacher (being assigned to a group of students), and the planning of instruction are important antecedents, yet they are beyond the scope of the present chapter (see chapters eight and nine). Here we will examine student-related antecedents and how these interface with religious instruction and evaluation (see Figure 1).

First, the child's readiness must be considered, comprised of various factors that constitute the child's adequacy (or lack thereof) for religious training. Second, some assessment (formal or informal) of the above areas yields important information for both placement decisions and lesson planning. Third, placement of the child generally occurs, often by age or grade but potentially by ability or interest. An alternative is no placement, such as intergenerational instructional contexts.

Instruction flows from these three antecedents, as well as instructional planning. Evaluation following instruction is threefold: evaluation of the individual student, the collective evaluation of the group (which is also an

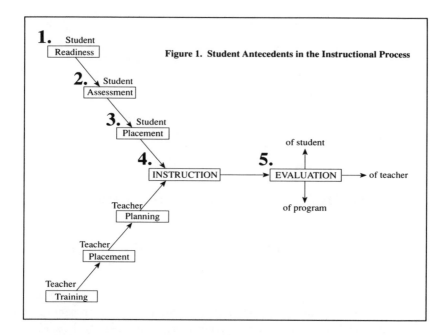

Figure 1. Student Antecedents in the Instructional Process

evaluation of the program), and evaluation of the instructor. Each of these, in turn, feeds back upon one or more of the antecedents, as will be examined near the end of this chapter.

READINESS

Religious education requires that the child be developmentally ready for religion. But in a sense readiness is a misnomer. "Reading readiness" has been replaced by the phrase "emergent literacy" in current educational nomenclature because the former implied that preschoolers were unable to understand language (Schickedanz, Hansen, & Forsyth, 1990). Recent research, in contrast, finds that young children know a great deal about reading and writing, but the manner in which they perform these tasks changes as they enter the elementary years. Likewise, readiness for religion may imply to some that a basic level of development must be attained for the child to become religious. In reality, religion like reading is emergent; religious thinking and activities can be observed very early in life (Tamminen, Vianello, Jaspard, & Ratcliff, 1988), but the *way* children think about and act upon religion changes as they get older. Religious educators can affirm the concept of readiness in relation to certain kinds of instruction as opposed to others, yet the gradual emergence of religious understanding, belief, and practice must not be overlooked.

Goldman's Research of Readiness

In the mid-1960s Ronald Goldman discussed the concept of readiness in his book *Readiness for Religion* (1965). Goldman built upon his prior work of the development of religious thinking in six- to sixteen-year-old British children and youth. On the basis of his research he created his well-known theory of religious development (Goldman, 1964).

Goldman initiated his work because surveys conducted in England indicated that the nationally sponsored religious education program produced weak results. Goldman (1965) encouraged religious educators to pay close attention to children's abilities in a manner they had not previously, to be sure children were indeed ready for religious instruction. Using Piaget's theory he asserted that the cognitive development of a child placed certain developmental limits on learning religious material. Most children are undeveloped in their thought and language; they are egocentric and concrete, while religion deals with abstract topics such as love, goodness, and spirit. Children use a lot of religious words, but Goldman believed they could not really grasp the concepts. Religious language makes extensive use of analogies and metaphors to communicate the nature of God and faith, language beyond the child's capabilities.

Likewise, Goldman held that the child's limited experience of life also impedes the understanding of religious expressions. Religious growth involves the interpretation of experience that relates to the divine. The child must have a wide range of experience from which to draw before experiences can be interpreted and related to a theological view. He warned that unless the child has adequate experience before learning about religion "much of what is taught may result in a mere religious vocabulary or the crystallizing of ideas too soon, which prevents a child reaching forward to higher levels of thought" (Goldman, 1964, p.44).

In *Readiness for Religion* (Goldman, 1965) distinguishes *intellectual* and *emotional* readiness. For Goldman, it is not until about age thirteen that a pupil is intellectually ready to apprehend an understanding of Christian faith. Prior to that Christian instruction must be connected to the pupil's own experience. For example, it is not yet possible to study the stories of the Bible systematically and chronologically.[1] Intellectual and emotional maturation are not separate but intrinsically connected with one another. During the early school years, children enter religion through personal fantasy rather than thinking their way into it intellectually.[2] They compensate for their limited religious intellect by playing, dramatizing, creative expression, and thinking imaginatively.

"Readiness for religion" (readiness for learning religion) is still a practical concept if it can be enlarged to incorporate a number of dimensions. Besides the intellectual and emotional dimensions suggested by Goldman we may add the attitudes a child has for or against religion and religious education, the salience of religious education to life, and formative religious influences. Each of these five areas of readiness varies in importance according to the age of the child.

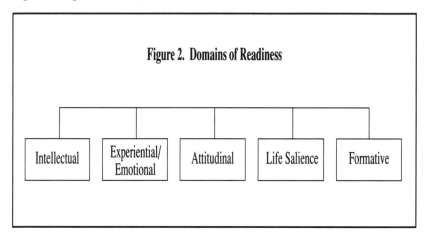

Figure 2. Domains of Readiness

Intellectual | Experiential/Emotional | Attitudinal | Life Salience | Formative

Intellectual Readiness

Building upon Goldman's semi-clinical research, Peatling (1973, 1974) created a paper-and-pencil instrument titled "Thinking about the Bible" to measure religious development. Peatling used Goldman's three biblical stories, Moses and the Burning Bush, Crossing the Red Sea, and the Temptations of Jesus. He added four questions after each story, each of which required the respondent to choose the most and least acceptable alternatives from four possible answers. The options were developed from a lengthy content analysis of open responses of children and adults in a preliminary study. These options represented very concrete, concrete, abstract, and very abstract levels of religious thinking.

The total score from the test items was placed on a scale of the four levels of thinking, from very concrete to very abstract, with two composite scores that combined the two concrete levels and two abstract levels. In addition each child or adult was asked if they thought the story actually happened, which resulted in a scale of literal versus nonliteral interpretation.

Peatling's (1973) initial testing of the instrument involved nearly 2000 students attending fourth to twelfth grades in North American Episcopal schools. Follow-up replications (Peatling & Laabs, 1975; Peatling, Laabs, & Newton, 1975) produced similar results. While the test scores generally confirmed Goldman's theory, a number of differences surfaced as well. Peatling's American students remained in a transition period between the concrete and abstract levels for a longer time than Goldman's British children (from age ten to fifteen). This discrepancy may in part be accounted for by the difference in research methodology (the semi-clinical interview versus items with fixed choices).

A number of later replications were conducted in several countries, including the United States, Finland, Northern Ireland, and the Republic of Ireland, representing a number of denominations including Lutheran, Methodist, Catholic, and Nazarene churches (Tamminen, 1976, 1983a, 1991; Hoge & Petrillo, 1978; Greer, 1980, 1981; McGrady, 1982; Degelman, Mullen, & Mullen, 1984). In all of these studies, the developmental progression is similar; children move from the concrete to the abstract levels gradually and consistently as they grow older.

There are, however, some differences between some of the populations tested: Missouri Synod Lutherans received lower scores on abstract thinking than the Episcopal students. Finnish and Irish children were also lower than Peatling's American subjects. Some of these differences may be due to differing views of the Bible held by different religious groups and nationalities. For example, a high score on the very abstract scale has a high positive correlation with a nonliteral interpretation of the Bible (the latter determined by response to the question, "Do you think the story really happened?"). The stories used by Peatling (as well as those used by Goldman) include accounts of miracles, resulting in hermeneutical issues that confound the assessment of religious thinking.

It should also be noted that there was considerable variation between children at a particular age. For example, on a scale that varied from 36 to 60, third graders studied by Tamminen (1990) scored from 40 to 57, while senior high students scored from 41 to 60. Variation was considerable even among pupils in the same school classroom.

Experiential/Emotional Readiness

Goldman's (1965) use of the phrase "emotional readiness" referred to the general life experiences of children. Affective experiences such as love, trust, and security are of great significance within Christianity, central aspects of the relationship between God and humankind. It is difficult for a child who has not experienced unconditional love at home and in other contexts to understand and accept the idea of God's love for the child.

An important aspect of emotional readiness is the experience of religion. Do children have actual religious experiences that provide a framework and integrating matrix for religious education? Researchers disagree on this point. From the beginning of this century, many researchers believed that only adolescents and adults could have genuine religious experiences, and these were highly unusual events such as conversion. In contrast to this tradition, Bovet (1929) asserted that all religious experiences typical of adolescents could also be found among children. According to Bovet, these experiences were not just superficial imitation, but deeply significant.

The question of whether children have religious experiences depends upon how religious experience is defined (this is considered at length by Tamminen, 1991). Christians generally affirm that religious experience involves a connecting to God and a transcendence that is vitally important.

Klingberg (1959) believed that religious experiences are common in childhood, basing his conclusions upon essays on the theme, "When I once thought about God" written by nine- to thirteen-year-old Swedish children. David and Sally Elkind (1962) found much the same result among American ninth graders when they were asked, "When do you feel closest to God?" and "Have you ever had a particular experience of feeling especially close to God?" Likewise, Tamminen (1983b, 1991) asked Finnish youngsters, "Have you at times felt particularly close to God?" which produced positive responses by most children seven to twelve years old, but negative responses by the majority of adolescents. Affirmative responses decreased the most between nine or ten and thirteen or fourteen. Older students may have been more questioning of the religious nature of their experiences because of the greater ability to reflect and critique.

Klingberg (1959) found that children regularly cite emergency situations such as being sick, having an accident, being in danger, being lonely, experiencing a thunderstorm, or having an encounter with death. In contrast, the Elkinds (1962) found children commonly had religious experiences in church. Tamminen (1983b, 1991), much like Klingberg, discovered that danger, illness, difficult situations, and death encounters were the most common circumstances for children's religious experiences, with loneliness and fear contexts taking second place (with seven- and eight-year-olds these were reversed). The third most important contexts were devotional and church situations. Very few reported feeling close to God in happy events.

Children may affectively experience and respond to God. Such experiences contribute to emotional readiness for religious instruction; children need constructs to help them understand these experiences, as well as affirmation for those experiences.

Attitudinal Readiness

Children's attitudes about religion are closely related to their motivation toward religion. Goldman (1965) concluded from his research that younger children are highly motivated toward religion, but that over time their attitudes move toward indifference and even negativism by the adolescent years. Other studies also indicate this negative movement, which may begin even in the very first years of school (Marklund, 1968; Hartman, 1971; Tamminen, 1969, 1975, 1991).

The clearest increase in negative attitudes toward religion occurs at about thirteen to fourteen (Hyde, 1963; Richmond, 1970; Mark, 1980; Turner, 1980), although Francis (1976, 1978, 1979) concluded that the trend is fairly uniform from age eight to sixteen. Irish children became more positive toward religion at about eight to ten, but then became more negative after that age (Greer, 1981). Tamminen (1985, 1991) in his study of Finnish youngsters ages seven to twenty found that children generally became more positive in their attitudes (for example, increased their trust in God) between seven or eight years and nine or ten years. After ten attitudes grew more negative, particularly between thirteen and fifteen. However, the attitude change was not uniform across all beliefs; only minor changes occurred in the belief in life after death.

The attitudes of girls at every age are generally more positive toward religious education than those of boys. This trend is not universal; not all individuals conform to the general pattern. Indeed, many youngsters become more favorable toward religion and religious education as they get older. It should also be noted that very few studies of younger children exist; indeed there are not many studies of children at any age, thus conclusions about the uniformity of the trend must remain tentative.

Why does this pattern of increased negativism exist? It may partly be because attitudes toward religion and attitudes toward religious education are closely related. Tamminen (1969, 1975) found that pupils who believe in God and who report an experience of God's presence were more likely to describe religious education as a pleasant experience. The trend toward negative attitudes is also significantly affected by general mental development and many aspects of their surroundings such as the religious views of parents, siblings, peers, and the religious education received at school and church.

Life Salience Readiness

It is crucial that religious education relates to an individual's life, here and now. What is relevant, or salient, at one age may not be as important at another time in life. The decreasing popularity of religious education among preteens (ten to twelve) was studied by Marklund (1968), who highlighted three major reasons for this attitudinal change; 1) preteens were more interested in the outside world than in religion, 2) the religious instruction was too abstract and thus too difficult, and 3) the methods used in teaching were not motivating. The first of these particularly implies a lack of life salience.

Tamminen (1982) considered the reasons given by Finnish nine- to eighteen-year-olds for religious education being pleasant or unpleasant. Younger students regularly stated that it was pleasant because religious education "tells about interesting things." Over half of the other youngsters also mentioned interesting topics making religious instruction pleasant, not just that good methods were used. Nine- to twelve-year-olds were convinced that good religious education drew them closer to God, but few older pupils agreed. The primary reasons given for religious education being unpleasant were dullness, monotony, and lack of interest in what was discussed. Many older students, in particular, commented that the teaching did not give answers to questions they believed to be important, and thus the instruction was not very useful (Tamminen & Vesa, 1982).

What topics were most interesting to students? From the responses of both children and teachers, Finnish pupils in the lowest grades were most interested in narratives from the Bible, especially the New Testament. However, this interest declines in higher grades. Youngsters of all ages are interested in fundamental questions of life such as, "Is there life after death?" Older students are concerned with personal problems and difficulties in human interrelationships, such as "the problem of violence," "my responsibility for friends," and global problems (Tamminen, 1975; Karttunen, 1976, 1977). Swedish youths did not report much interest in religious education but were concerned with fundamental questions in life that are basically religious or related to religion in some respect (Westling & Pettersson, 1972; Fagerlind, 1974).

In the last two decades Germany, England, and several other countries have attempted to reverse the lack of interest in religious education by using problem-oriented thematic religious education. By dealing with personal and other contemporary questions it was felt that pupils would become more interested in religious education and what religion has to offer.

One such study (Hartman, Pettersson, & Westling, 1973; Hartman, 1986), using problem check lists and projective photographs with unfinished short stories with nine- to twelve-year-olds, indicates that children frequently reflect upon profound existential questions with rich diversity in their thinking. Common themes include loneliness and the problems of war, violence, and suffering. In addition the future, guilt, life and death, and school worries were recurring issues. Older youngsters showed more concern with friends and school, yet societal and global questions increased with age. A replication of this study a decade later indicated that these issues continue to hold great interest for children in this age span (Ekstrom & Odenkrants, 1980).

Tamminen (1975, 1988) used similar measures with over 2700 Finnish students, ages seven to sixteen (including over a thousand in a 1986 replication). Seven- and eight-year-olds were more concerned with issues related to their immediate surroundings: school, home, and peers. They enjoyed acceptance, but feared rejection, teasing, or bullying. This age range was also more likely to describe fears, such as ghosts, prowlers, and so on. War was also a fear. By age nine and ten, children are worrying more about school concerns, although the previous concerns with peers remain. They are becoming concerned with problems in society and the world, such as war, poverty, hunger, violence, and crime. Children's religious interests included the suffering and death of Jesus, the existence of God and his creating the world, God's goodness and providence, and the miracles of Jesus. Youngsters were less likely to be concerned with fears at age eleven and twelve. They reflect more on the past and future, and their eventual vocation is of greater concern. War, hunger, poverty, and homelessness are frequently mentioned concerns, as well as life on other planets and how the world began. Religious questions decrease with age (although they still reflect upon the existence of God), but there is an increase in questions about the future, social issues, and global problems. The relationship between parents and children becomes increasingly important at puberty.

Formative Readiness

The ability and motivation of children in learning religious content also depends upon their home and cultural background. Evenshaug and Hallen (1988) point out that readiness is not only a result of development but also dependent upon socialization. Even within the same age group and mental ability, the differences between children are great and increase in older age ranges. This is in part because the family has socialized the child to a greater or lesser extent into religious values. Research indicates that the religious atmosphere and kind of child-rearing in the home influences the child's religious development and the attitudes manifested toward religious education (Argyle & Beit-Hallahmi, 1975; Gibson, 1989; Ozorak, 1989; Tamminen, 1991). This influence is not always what might be expected. For example Tamminen (1969) found that when first starting school some of the pupils most interested in the religious education lessons were from the least religious homes. Perhaps the lack of exposure made the religious education themes more interesting.

The family acts as a filter through which all other religious influences are modified (Evenshaug & Hallen, 1988). The religious practices of the family, such as experiencing God as a living Thou through prayer, hymns, and other religious rituals, significantly shapes not only the child's faith but also the receptivity to religious education external to the family. Evenshaug and Hallen comment that the presence of religious tradition in the family produces a propensity toward interpreting religious education meaningfully in school and church.

In addition to the home, all previous religious education in any context serves as a background that creates attitudinal and intellectual readiness for learning new religious content or serves as an obstacle to such learning. For example, extreme familiarity with a specific religious concept can produce indifference or boredom when that concept is brought up. Conversely, religious education judiciously introduced can create a readiness for other religious concepts or more advanced thinking about a given concept.

The importance of the religious background of the student is underscored in research conducted by Tamminen (1969). He studied the social and religious backgrounds of six- and seven-year-old Finnish children as they were beginning school, so these could be compared with their interest and achievement in religious education. The background of the students was assessed by sending a questionnaire to the parents, while the religious knowledge and attitudes were examined with a structured interview using pictures. Religious education activities by the children were observed throughout the year. The interest in religious education was again assessed at year's end by interview while tests were used to evaluate the amount of learning by the student. These measures, as well as grades given by the teacher, were strongly related to initial interest in religion at the beginning of the year, which in turn was strongly related to the children's social and religious background.

ASSESSMENT

The readiness of the student is evaluated through assessment, the measurement of one or more areas of readiness. It is important to bear in mind that assessment is only an approximate measure of readiness, as it can be influenced by the child's current motivational state, the circumstances surrounding the assessment, and many other factors. Ideally, multiple assessments separated by periods of time and conducted by multiple evaluators with multiple instruments would give a better estimate of readiness. Complete assessment of all five areas of readiness would also be ideal, but strictures in the specific context of instruction may delimit the amount of assessment possible. Partial assessment is better than none. The more complete, the better, so that a fuller understanding of the individual child, as well as the group as a whole, is possible.

Assessment may be formal or informal. These extremes lie on a continuum, however. At the more formal extreme would be paper and pencil tests of ability and knowledge, while casual observation is at the informal end. Formal and informal measures are complementary, providing a more complete picture taken together. Specific details on evaluation and measurement are provided by Starks and Ratcliff (1988), while details on performing surveys are summarized by Engel (1991).

In the final analysis, it is the religious education teacher who adapts the knowledge of the child's development to the instructional setting. Thus it is the instructor who should obtain and make use of assessment information. The instructor may have a general understanding of children's family backgrounds, a basic understanding of the religious capabilities at any given age, some broad ideas of what children think about religion and the fundamental questions of life, and so on. But this general understanding must be supplemented with specific information about his or her specific group, and about each individual child. Groups of the same age, church, geographical region, or denomination can differ considerably from one another, thus an overreliance on general characteristics may be an impediment to really understanding one's students. Specific development is individualized and unique, even though general patterns are observed. Within any specific group, wide differences between children are often the case. Age or developmental stage is not a sufficient indicator, as this neglects relevant past experiences. Here we will briefly outline possible means of assessment for each of the five domains of readiness.

Intellectual

Peatling's test of religion readiness would seem to be a good place to begin the assessment of religious cognition. His measure has been widely used in research of religious development but not for individual assessment by local churches. It may be that other kinds of measures could serve nearly as well. Peatling notes that mental age is a strong predictor of religious development scores, and thus some kind of ability test score might be sufficient.

While the religious abilities of children are important, specific religious information known by the child is also crucial. While developmentalists such as Piaget, Kohlberg, Fowler, and Peatling concentrate on cognitive structures, the cognitive content of those structures also demands attention. Evaluation of the child's knowledge of the Bible, theology, and religion is as important as religious thinking level.

With older children, the teacher could assign an essay on the topic of "My Idea of God" (Hilliard, 1960) or "What Is my God Like?" (Tamminen, 1991). With younger children similar questions might be asked in an interview format, with the answers tape recorded for later evaluation. Other possible formats include written or verbal open-ended sentences presented to the child, such as, "In my opinion prayer is ..." or "I think that in heaven ..." Projective photographs with or without accompanying explanations have also been used in research studies (see Goldman, 1964; Bassett et al., 1990; Tamminen, 1991).

Experiential/Emotional

An emphasis in this domain is the experience of religion by the child. This might be evaluated directly by questions such as, "Can you think of a specific time when you felt very close to God? Tell me what happened." The experiential component of religion could also be explored through questions such as, "When has religion or faith seemed most important to you?" Of course the exact wording of such questions must be tailored to the developmental stage of the child.

The measurement of the experiential/emotional area of religious education may not always be scorable, but one must be careful to not overvalue quantitative measures. While enumerated test results have the advantage of being statistically analyzable, they also require that one form of information (verbal or visual in most cases) be translated into another form (numbers), which introduces an additional source of error. In contrast, qualitative measures generally involve analysis of words or observations in their original form. Qualitative measures also can produce richer and deeper analysis and conclusions because they generally make use of fewer and more open-ended kinds of prompts.

It should be noted that many of the intellectual measures mentioned earlier can also elicit responses that relate to religious experience and emotions. When measurement is used, the evaluator should be sensitive to side comments and ideas related to domains of readiness other than the one being immediately considered. For example, a response to the question, "Who is God to you?" could result in responses in each of the five domains.

Attitudinal

Intellect is rarely separated from attitude in the school-aged child. When youngsters state their understanding of what God is, they are likely to give some indication of how important he is to them. The tone of voice and facial expressions are important clues to attitudinal readiness.

The studies cited earlier in this chapter indicate that the attitudes of children toward religion, in general, are less positive as they grow older. However, as noted, there are many exceptions to this trend, including some who become more positive with age. Thus it is imperative not to assume too quickly that preteens will be more negative toward religious instruction than younger children. Only assessment in a specific context can give definitive guidelines.

It may be possible to measure attitudes about religion and religious education by means of scaled responses. A number of aspects of religion can be listed, and the student mark a point on a scale denoting some level of agreement or disagreement. For example, one could ask, "Would you like to study the Bible more in junior church?" with five options: strongly agree, agree some, unsure, disagree some, strongly disagree. Another approach would be to give gradations on a scale from "enjoy" to "hate." With younger children, fewer gradations are better (for example, three options instead of five), and with the youngest children the measure may need to be read to them.

Life Salience

Measures of relevance are important, not only to determine important religious topics to consider, but also to find topics that can be related to religion. One can make a case that ultimately every topic can be related to religion, if religion is understood to pervade all of life. Relevant topics can be entering wedges with which to introduce religious views and values, or salient topics to be explored in their own right as a part of a broadly based system of religious education.

Life salience can be assessed by providing a box in which students deposit questions to be discussed, thereby providing insight to children's interests. This is most likely to be effective for older children. Assessment of how children spend their free time can also be useful. The books and magazines they read, the music they listen to, the television programs watched, new toys they have received, favorite hobbies, and other activities they participate in may be important clues to what is most relevant to the child at this point in life. These might be inventoried through formal protocols developed by religious educators or administrators, or they might be articulated by children through informal discussions or casual observations. Fortunately, children at this age are usually quite open about their interests.

Formative

The evaluation of the child's formative influences may be derived indirectly by some of the other measures suggested above. It may be more directly evaluated through questionnaires for parents to fill out or through discussions with parents, siblings, and school teachers. It is important to respect confidentiality at this point. To the extent possible, children and parents need to give informed consent to evaluation of any kind. While the evaluation should not be limited to religious topics, the most crucial issue will be to discover what kind of religious education has occurred in the home, if any, including the topics and methods used. The religious education provided by all churches attended from early childhood, as well as education provided outside the home and church, should be included.

While assessment is preparatory to placement, as indicated in the opening diagram of this chapter, it also should influence instructional planning as well. A full understanding of pupil readiness is crucial to the planning of religious education.

PLACEMENT

Placement is given surprisingly little attention in most churches. Children tend to be placed by age or grade level in school. Probably the latter is the most popular, since children can be easily promoted in church when they move to the next grade in school. Peatling (1973) found that grade level is a better predictor of religious development than age, which suggests that grade level is probably the better placement criterion of the two. In contrast, Tamminen (1991) found that specific course grades received were good predictors of religious development, particularly grades in upper-level courses requiring logical thinking or math.

Rather than using these placement criteria, Westerhoff (1976) encourages churches to use intergenerational religious education in which children and adults learn and worship at the same time in the same location. This idea, taken as offered by Westerhoff, would eliminate the need for individual placement. Many churches have instituted a variation of this idea by having children worship with adults for the first hymn or two and perhaps a children's sermon, then being excused for children's church. Westerhoff's insistence upon this approach to the exclusion of any separated experiences is too extreme — if a pastor or priest attempts to reach everyone simultaneously for an entire hour of worship, the net effect is likely to be boredom for adults (because the presentation is at a child's level) or boredom for children (because the content challenges adult intellects). Westerhoff's suggestions for intergenerational services are interesting and might be valuable if used occasionally but are not a substitute for developmentally individualized religious education.

In addition to placement by age or grade, religious educators might consider placement by religious developmental level. Peatling's test, should it become generally available, might be helpful, or ability testing is possible. Using Peatling's criteria, children could be separated into four groups: those who function at the simple concrete level, the concrete level, a few older children who are at the formal level, and the youngest children at the pre-concrete level (Peatling, 1977, 1979).

Another alternative for placement would be religious knowledge. This would provide remedial instruction for those children coming from a background deficient in religious instruction, while challenging other children who have a strong religious background. The problem here is the lack of standardized religious knowledge tests, although churches could develop their own instruments that are consistent with their doctrines and practices.

Great caution must be exercised in making a placement on the basis of any of the above criteria. Most tests have a standard error of measurement which must be taken into account; a difference of several points is possible purely by chance and such differences do not really indicate a significant difference between students. One must also consider the social consequences of differential placement. To illustrate, on the Peatling test the average scores of third graders differs from seniors in high school by seven points. The spread of scores from those two averages is considerable; many high schoolers have scores that are the same as many third graders! Using test criteria to place older teenagers with nine-year-olds could be extremely dysfunctional; what teenager would or could endure the social consequences? There is also the possibility that an individual student received a low score because of the circumstances of the test, being distracted by personal problems, or just having a bad day. Multiple measures are likely to help the religious educator avoid such difficulties, but again a placement determination must not be on the basis of minor differences in test scores.

One can make a case for placement by any of the readiness domains mentioned previously, or some combination of those domains. Yet we must also consider the potential value of having multiple levels of intellectual ability in the same learning context, a variety of children with different religious experiences, a spectrum of attitudes, multiple saliences, and youngsters with different kinds of religious backgrounds in a single group. Cannot those who are more able help those who are less able (peer teaching has been found to be of great value in some educational contexts)? Children who can describe their religious experiences may help other children articulate their experiences by providing descriptors and mutual understanding. Those with positive attitudes can be models for those with less positive attitudes (although the opposite could occur as well). Exposure to new ideas and interests could develop new saliences. The richness of one child's religious background could become a resource for other students. Developmentalists often suggest that children need exposure to others one level higher to encourage cognitive disequilibrium, dissatisfaction with one's current level, and consequent change in stage.

Another reason for heterogeneous groupings rather than homogeneity is seen in tracking theory. Sociologists of education have noted that when children are grouped by ability in school, several problems surface. Ability grouping tends to occur by race, ethnicity, or social class (Farley, 1990), and once a child is placed in a specific track it is unlikely he or she will move to another. Research indicates that children placed in lower tracks tend to do more poorly than comparable children in higher tracks. Farley cites studies in Catholic high schools indicating that racial and economic inequality might be decreased if tracking were eliminated. He concludes that if tracking is used, it should be very flexible, allowing for movement from level to level, and individual subjects should be tracked separately.

In spite of the dangers, dividing into groups makes sense. As has been noted, there are considerable differences in cognitive ability at any given age. But the differences between children's emotional backgrounds, attitudes, and experiences are likely to be even greater than their cognitive differences. Perhaps attitudinal grouping should be seriously considered with older children since it is essential that children participate in religious education willingly and older children are more likely to resist instruction (those not willing could be placed in a nonreligious education group or asked to stay with parents). But, again, there should be concern about social consequences of any placement decision made.

The individual church may want to experiment with different kinds of groupings to see what works best for their situation. Different populations of children and different goals held by religious educators may make different kinds of groupings more viable. It may well be that no group needs to be permanently divided into smaller groups but that certain religious instruction and activities are expedited through one or more kinds of groupings. It should also be noted that children change a great deal and the individual child's pace and direction of change may be different from an apparently similar child, thus requiring individualized instruction.

INSTRUCTION

After placement decisions have been made, the religious educator is now able to organize and implement instruction, making use of both assessment information and curriculum planning. The content and methods of teaching take priority at this phase (see chapters eight and nine on how teacher training and planning relate to instruction). Yet a knowledge of religious readiness in all of its five domains provides useful criteria in determining the goals of education; it helps the educator recognize what are sensible and achievable objectives for a specific group of children.

At the same time, those goals and objectives are also derived from a system of values that arise from the educational, philosophical, and theological orientation of a given agent of religious education (be that church, denomination, religious school, or other organization). The needs of the children must be cogently and creatively interfaced with the purpose of the group providing instruction. Evenshaug and Hallen (1988) noted that not only must the pupil be developmentally ready to learn religion, but also, "Is the religious instruction ready for the child?" This is another form of readiness, the readiness of the curriculum and the teacher. To accomplish the aim of being ready for the students, the teacher's preparation and interest in the teaching process is essential. The instructor must be able to face children's questions and to some extent live in their world. This will help in preparing instructional lessons that are interesting and appropriate for the children's level of development.

What makes for interesting and successful instruction? Several studies have been conducted on the methods and materials of good religious education (see Kerry, 1980, for example). Here we will cite only a few studies of this topic that clearly relate to readiness for religion (see chapters eight and nine of this book for other components of quality instruction).

Pupils in the third grade (nine and ten years old) in Finland preferred narration of the teacher to film or slide programs, while other grades preferred the media programs. From eleven years onward, open conversations, reasoning, and group work were preferred to narration, although the latter remained quite popular even into the higher grades (Tamminen & Vesa, 1982). Narration combined with open conversation is the method most used in the lower grades, according to teacher reports (Tölli, 1986; Rossi, 1986). Of course, the specific personality of the teacher, the character of the specific group of children, the nature of the content to be learned, and the cultural and social background of the children all have an impact upon what methods will be most useful and successful.

Teaching Parables

The importance of understanding developmental level in teaching religious education is particularly underscored in the teaching of parables, as these often require an understanding of metaphors, analogies, and allegories. Parables have sometimes been used to assess the development of religious thinking (for example, see Martinsson, 1968; Pettersson, 1969; Beechick, 1974; Murphy, 1977a, 1977b, 1979, and Tamminen, 1983, 1991). The understanding of parables has been found to increase with age. Indeed, Tamminen (1991) reports that the level of understanding parables is equivalent to the levels found by Peatling (1973) in his "Thinking about the Bible" instrument.

By the age of twelve or thirteen most pupils reach the abstract level of thinking necessary for understanding parables. But there are differences in children's understanding of different types of parables. For example, the Good Samaritan parable is easier to understand than the parable of the rich landowner or the mote and beam metaphors. Understanding depends upon the theme and content of the parable, as well as its familiarity to the child. Children understand the ethical message of parables more easily and earlier than they do the religious message, perhaps because the ethical message is more likely to relate to their own experiences. The religious experience and amount of religious activity also significantly correlate with the degree of understanding.

One of the difficulties in the parables research is that the studies tend to examine how children understand stories without any instruction in that form of understanding. With good instruction, their ability at interpreting parables might exceed what the extant research would indicate. Teaching methodology significantly impacts the potential understanding of parables.

A major study of teaching parabolic language (Fägerlind, 1974) focused on students who were ten to twelve years of age. The researchers analyzed children's predispositions toward religious instruction, and from that analysis developed and tested methods of teaching parables. This research, like Martinsson (1968) and Pettersson (1979), preceded the evaluation of parable understanding with a short instructional session. The results indicate that students at ten to twelve years are unable to directly interpret, analyze, and verbally explain the content of the parable. However, when taught at a concrete level, so that the instruction in a parable relates to their own experiences or situations, children are able to make meaning out of abstract and symbolic material. They are also able to make certain kinds of generalizations at this age, particularly in areas with which they are familiar. While not yet capable of adult understanding of a parable, with assistance they can abstract in familiar areas they deem important (Westling, Pettersson, & Fägerlind, 1973; Fägerlind, 1974). Eleven- to fourteen-year-olds learn to remember the central issues of parables and understand them better when taught by narrative than when they do their own reading of the material and discuss it afterward (Kangas & Salin, 1986; Heinilä, 1989).

It should be noted that existing research tends to look at the importance of parables by means of cognitive understanding. But it is also possible for children to value and participate in parables affectively long before those parables are fully understood (see Berryman, 1979 and chapter two of this book).

EVALUATION

As noted by Starks and Ratcliff (1988), the aim of religious education is to reach preset objectives. It is important for the teacher, the pupil and the organization to know to what extent goals have been reached. This is important, not only for the purpose of feedback, but also so proper changes can be made in the religious education process.

Evaluation, like assessment, can be formal or informal. Also like assessment, evaluation involves analysis of student performance. Unlike assessment, the instructor should also be evaluated (by students, other teachers, administrators, self-evaluation, or some combination of these). Besides student and teacher evaluation, the overall program should be analyzed by examining a composite of the individual students' performance. This summative evaluation, an evaluation of overall student performance, is also a reflection of the teacher's abilities and performance.

Inadequate performance by only one student may call for repetition of the instruction, different methods of teaching, tutorial or other compensatory instruction, or in some cases alternative placement of the child. However, if a pattern of inadequate performance in the group of children is found, this suggests a faulty program. This could either be due to insufficient planning because of inadequate use of the initial assessment of readiness, inadequate training or placement of the teacher, or insufficient time for preparation. The kind of placement (by age, grade, ability, and so on) may also need to be evaluated. Substandard results from evaluations of the teacher may require alternative placement at a different grade level, inservice training of the instructor, adding assistant teachers, or dismissal.

Evaluation in religious education is often problematic because objectives are often multilayered. The intellectual or cognitive consequences are the easiest to measure, but that is only one aspect of religious education and not necessarily the most important one. Of the other domains of readiness, the experiential/emotional and attitudinal areas would seem to be the most likely to need evaluation. Yet there are other aspects of religious education that may be difficult, if not impossible, to evaluate. For example, teachers need to empathically help students understand their individually distinctive relationship with God. This kind of objective is impossible to operationalize precisely in advance, and evaluating its accomplishment would be just as difficult. Finding one's own niche spiritually is often a lifelong quest, not amenable to an annual objective. The development of personal religion is not always a smooth, planned, predictable process for children or adults.

Unexpected cognitive or emotional conflicts can result in derailment from spiritual development, or be a starting point for adopting a deeper or completely different variety of faith.

It is important that evaluation occur regularly throughout the instructional unit, not just at its termination. Both students and teacher need to know how they are doing, so that any needed adjustments can occur prior to the end of the unit. This also encourages all participants in the instruction to see learning as a dynamic process, not a static product. Good teachers constantly monitor their ongoing effectiveness, making adjustments as needed.

The results of evaluation (as well as the entire process developed in this chapter) should not just be used by a single teacher but should be a catalyst for broader research projects by churches, denominations, and other providers of religious education. The individual religious educator needs to both feed into, and benefit from, broader research into instructional effectiveness, so that maximal benefit can be apprehended.

NOTES

1. This conclusion flows from Goldman's assumption that most biblical content is formal operational because it is to be understood metaphorically, not literally. This presumes a theology that not everyone would accept. He also asserts that children under thirteen have no sense of chronology or systematic thought, a serious mistake as can been seen by even a cursory view of elementary school curriculum (also see Hall, Lamb, & Perlmutter, 1986, on children's understanding of time).

2. We agree with Goldman that teachers should link pupils' experience to instruction: Formal operational understandings must be built upon prior concrete operational experiences. Direct experience with religion and/or religious objects (preoperational content, regardless of age) precedes thinking about such experiences (concrete operational), both of which are foundational to understanding abstract theology (formal operational). Thus Goldman (1965) suggests that children learn about shepherds and sheep in preparation for later formal instruction on the Good Shepherd. But children's ability to think concretely about experience would indicate that they should be given terminology by which they can understand their personal religious experiences. This would be a theology that would be too abstract for children, according to Goldman. Some of his pedagogical advice is helpful, yet his view of religious education for children seems truncated.

REFERENCES

Argyle, M., & Beit-Hallahmi, B. (1975). *The social psychology of religion.* London - Boston: Routledge & Kegan Paul.

Bassett, R., Miller, S., Anstey, K., Crafts, K., Harman, T., Lee, Y., Parks, T., Robinson, M., Smid, H., Sternes, W., Stephens, C., Wheeler, B., & Stevenson, D. (1990). Picturing God. *Journal of Psychology and Christianity, 9*, 73-81.

Beechick, R.A. (1974). *Children's understanding of parables: A developmental study.* Unpublished Ph.D. Dissertation, Arizona State University.

Berryman, J. (1979). Being in parables with children. *Religious Education, 14*, 271-285.

Bovet, P. (1929). *Le sentiment religieux et la psychologie de l'enfant.* Neuchatel - Paris.

Degelman, D., Mullen, P., & Mullen, N. (1984). Development of abstract religious thinking. *Journal of Psychology & Christianity, 3*, 44-49.

Ekström, U., & Odenkrants, J. (1980). *Livsfragor och attityder hos barn i aldrarna 9-13 ar.* Rapport 13/1980. Stockholm: Institute of Education. Stockholm School for Teaching Training.

Elkind, D., & Elkind, S.F. (1962). Varieties of religious experience in young adolescents. *Journal for Scientific Study of Religion, 2*, 103-111.

Engel, T. (1991). Conducting a needs analysis and the research process. In D. Ratcliff (Ed.), *Handbook of youth ministry.* Birmingham, AL: Religious Education Press.

Evenshaug, O., & Hallen, D. (1988). Readiness for religion - an educational perspective. In M. Pyysiainen (Ed.), *Kasvatus ja uskonto.* Porvoo - Helsinki - Juva: WSOY, 201-212.

Fägerlind, I. (1974). Research on religious education in the Swedish school system. *Character Potential: A Record of Research, 7*: 1, 38-47.

Farley, I. (1990). *Sociology.* Englewood Cliffs, NJ: Prentice-Hall.

Francis, L. (1976). *An inquiry into the concept "readiness for religion."* Unpublished Ph.D. Dissertation, University of Cambridge.

Francis, L. (1978). Attitude and longitude: A study on measurement. *Character Potential: A Record of Research, 8*, 119-130.

Francis., L. (1979). Measurement reapplied: Research into the child's attitude towards religion. *British Journal of Religious Education, 1*, 45-51.

Francis, L. (1988). Monitoring attitude toward Christianity during childhood and adolescence. In M. Pyysiainen (Ed.), *Kasvatus ja uskonto.* Porvoo - Helsinki - Juva: WSOY, 230-246.

Gibson, H.M. (1989). Attitudes to religion and science among schoolchildren aged 11 to 16 years in a Scottish city. *Journal of Empirical Theology, 2*, 5-26.

Goldman, R. (1964). *Religious thinking from childhood to adolescence.* London: Routledge & Kegan Paul.

Goldman, R. (1965). *Readiness for religion.* London: Routledge & Kegan Paul.

Greer, J. (1980). Stages in the development of religious thinking. *British*

Journal of Religious Education, 3, 24-28.

Greer, J. (1981). Religious attitudes and thinking in Belfast pupils. *Educational Research, 23,* 177-189.

Hall, E., Lamb, M., & Perlmutter, M. (1986). *Child psychology today* (2nd ed.). New York: Random House.

Hartman, S.G. (1971). *Eleverna och skolans religioinsundervisning.* Stockholm: Stockholm School of Education.

Hartman, S.G. (1986). Children's philosophy of life. *Studies in Education and Philosophy, 22.* Stockholm: CWK Gleerup.

Hartman, S.G., Pettersson, S., & Westling, G. (1973). *Vad funderar barn pa?* Stockholm: Utbildningsforlaget.

Heinilä, P. (1989). *Narratiivinen menetelma peruskoulun uskonnonopetukessa.* Unpublished Master Thesis in Rel. Education, Faculty of Theology, University of Helsinki.

Hilliard, F.H. (1960). Ideas of God among secondary school children. *Religion in Education, 27,* 14-19.

Hoge, D.R., & Petrillo, G.H. (1978). Development in religious thinking in adolescence: A test of Goldman's theories. *Journal for Scientific Study of Religion, 172,* 139-154.

Hyde, K.E. (1963). Religious concepts and religious attitudes I and II. Educational review. *Journal of Institute of Education.* University of Birmingham, 15, 132-141, 217-226.

Kangas, S., & Salin, P. (1986). *Kerronta tyotapana uskonnonopetuksessa.* Tutkimus tyotavan vaikutuksista vertauskertomusten ymmärtämiseen 5.-6. luokalla. Unpublished project study report, Teacher Training Institute, University of Turku.

Karttunen, P. (1976). *Uskonnonopetus opettajien arvioimana.* Evankelis-luterilaisen uskonnon opetussuunnitelmista saatuja kokemuksia kartoittavan projektin kokoava raportti. Uskonnonpedagogiikan julkaisuja A 16/1983. Institute of Practical Theology, University of Helsinki.

Karttunen, P. (1977) *Peruskoulun uskonnonopetus opettajan nakokulmasta.* Tutkimus opettajien tavoite- ja oppianinespreferensseista seka opetuskaytannosta ja opetusvaikeuksien kokemisesta. Uskonnonpedagogiikan julkaisuja A 20/1983. Institute of Practical Theology, University of Helsinki.

Kerry, T. (1980). The demands made by RE on pupils' thinking. *British Journal of Religious Education, 3,* 46-52.

Klingberg, G. (1959). A study of religious experience from 9 to 13 years of age. *Religious Education, 54,* 211-216.

Lee, J.M. (1985). *The content of religious instruction.* Birmingham, AL: Religious Education Press.

Lee, J.M. (1988). How to teach? In D. Ratcliff (Ed.), *Handbook of Preschool Religious Education.* Birmingham, AL: Religious Education Press.

Mark, T.J. (1980). *A study of religious attitudes, religious behavior, and religious cognition.* Paper presented at ISREV 2 in Schenectady 7-11.7.1980.

Marklund, B. (1968). *Intresse for kristendomsamnet pa grundskolans lag- och mellanstadier.* Stockholm: Stockholm School of Education.

Martinsson, E. (1968). *Religionsundervisning och mognad.* En jamforande studie av formagan att tanka abstrakt, forsta liknelser och religiosa begrepp hos barn i arskursarna 2, 4 och 6. Stockholm: School for Teacher Training. (Unpublished)

McGrady, (1982). *Establishing the level of religious thinking as a prerequisite to facilitating growth.* A paper presented at ISREV 3 in Driebergen.

Murphy, R.J.L. (1977a). Does children's understanding of parables develop in stages? *Learning for Living, 16,* 168-172.

Murphy, R.J.L. (1977b). The development of religious thinking in children in three easy stages? *Learning for Living, 17,* 16-19.

Murphy, R.J.L. (1979). *An investigation into some aspects of the development of religious thinking in children aged between six and eleven years.* Unpublished Ph.D. Dissertation, Department of Psychology, St. Andrews University.

Ozorak, E.W. (1989). Social and cognitive influences on the development of religious beliefs and commitment in adolescence. *Journal for the Scientific Study of Religion, 28,* 448-463.

Peatling, J.H. (1973). *The incidence of concrete and abstract religious thinking in the interpretation of three bible stories by pupils enrolled in grades four through twelve in selected schools in the Episcopal church in the United States of America.* Unpublished Ph.D. Dissertation, School of Education, New York University.

Peatling, J.H. (1974). Cognitive development in pupils in grades four through twelve: The incidence of concrete and abstract religious thinking in American children. *Character Potential: A Record of Research, 7,* 52-61.

Peatling, J.H. (1977). On beyond Goldman: Religious thinking and the 1970s. *Learning for Living, 16,* 220-225.

Peatling, J.H. (1979). The particularity of potential: Religious thinking as an example of a developmental problem. *Character Potential: A Record of Research, 9,* 45-55.

Peatling, J.H., & Laabs, C.W. (1975). Cognitive development of pupils in grades four through twelve: A comparative study of Lutheran and Episcopalian children and youth. *Character Potential: A Record of Research, 7,* 107-115.

Peatling, J.H., Laabs, C.W., & Newton, T.B. (1975). Cognitive development: A three-sample comparison of means on the Peatling scale of religious thinking. *Character Potential: A Record of Research, 7,* 159-162.

Pettersson, S. (1969). *Mognad och abstrakt stoff.* En studie av barns satt att uppfatta visst abstrakt stoff vid en lektionsserie i religionskunskap i arskurs fyra. Pedagogisk-psykologiska institutionen. Lararhogskolan i Stockholm (Institute of Education and Psychology, Stockholm School for Training of Teachers).

Richmond, R.C. (1970). *Maturity of religious judgments and differences of religious attitudes between the ages of 13 and 16 years.* Unpublished Diploma in Psychology of Childhood, University of Birmingham.

Rossi, J. (1986). *Peruskoulun 5. ja 6. luokkien opettajien kasitykset uskon-nonopetuksen apuvalineista.* Unpublished Master Thesis in Religious Education, Faculty of Theology, University of Helsinki.

Schickedanz, T., Hansen, K., & Forsyth, P. (1990). *Understanding children.* Mountainview, CA: Mayfield.

Starks, D., & Ratcliff, D. (1988). Planning, evaluation, and research. In D. Ratcliff (Ed.), *Handbook of preschool religious education.* Birmingham, AL: Religious Education Press.

Tamminen, K. (1969). *Koulutulokkaat ja uskonnonopetus.* Tutkimuksia n:o 7. Institute of Education, University of Helsinki.

Tamminen, K. (1975). *Lasten ja nuorten elamankysymykset uskontokas-vatuksessa.* Suomalaisen teologisen kirjallisuusseuran julkaisuja 99. Helsinki.

Tamminen, K. (1976). Research concerning the development of religious thinking in Finnish students: A report of results. *Character Potential: A Record of Research,* 7:4, 206-219.

Tamminen, K. (1982). In K. Tamminen & L. Vesa (Eds.), *Miten opetan uskontoa.* Vammala: Kirjapaja.

Tamminen, K. (1983a). *Lasten ja nuorten uskonnolliset kasitteet kouluias-sa 1: Ajattelu ja kasitys Raamatusta.* Uskonnonpedagogiikan julkaisuja B 9/1983. Institute of Practical Theology, University of Helsinki.

Tamminen, K. (1983b). *Religious experiences of children and young people.* Research Reports on Religious Education C 2/1983. Institute of Practical Theology, University of Helsinki.

Tamminen, K. (1985). *Mihin koululaiset ja heidan vanhempansa uskovat?* Uskonnonpedagogiikan julkaisuja B 149/1985. Institute of Practical Theology, University of Helsinki.

Tamminen, K. (1988). *Existential questions in early youth and adolescence.* Research Reports on Religious Education C 5/1983. Institute of Practical Theology, University of Helsinki.

Tamminen, K. (1991). *Religious development in childhood and youth.* Helsinki: Finnish Academy of Science.

Tamminen, K., & Vesa, L. (1982). *Miten opetan uskontoa.* Vammala: Kirjapaja.

Tamminen, K., Vianello, R., Jaspard, J.M., & Ratcliff, D. (1988). The religious concepts of preschoolers. In D. Ratcliff (Ed.), *Handbook of preschool religious education*. Birmingham, AL: Religious Education Press.

Tölli, L. (1986). *Peruskoulun ala-asteen 1.ja 2. luokan opettajat uskonnon oppimateriaalin kayttajina*. Unpublished Master Thesis in Religious Education, Faculty of Theology, University of Helsinki.

Turner, E.B. (1980). General cognitive ability and religious attitudes in two school systems. *British Journal of Religious Education, 2*, 136-141.

Westerhoff, J. (1976). *Will our children have faith?* New York: Seabury.

Westling, G., & Pettersson, S. (1972). *Undervisning i religionskunskap pa mellanstadiet - nägra metodiska synpunkter*. Stockholm: Stockholm School of Education.

Westling, G., Pettersson, S., & Fägerlind, I. (1973). *Mognad och undervisning i religions kunskap*. Stockholm: Utbildningsforlaget.

Contributors

JERRY ALDRIDGE teaches in the School of Education at the University of Alabama at Birmingham. Previous teaching experiences include first and fourth grades, special education, and college level at Livingston University, Samford University, and Furman University. He has a doctoral degree in special education as well as Masters degrees in special education and early childhood education and an Educational Specialist degree in special education with a concentration in school psychometry. Dr. Aldridge has written a text for the National Education Association on early elementary classrooms, three instructor's manuals for developmental psychology textbooks, chapters in two books on exceptionality, and more than twenty articles in professional journals. He is also a popular conference speaker and consultant.

JEROME BERRYMAN serves as Canon Educator at Christ Church Cathedral in Houston, Texas, as well as Adjunct Assistant Professor of Pediatric Pastoral Care at Baylor College of Medicine and Adjunct Professor of Christian Education at The Houston Graduate School of Theology. He possesses a J.D. degree from the University of Tulsa Law School, as well as an M.Div. from Princeton Theological Seminary. Dr. Berryman studied at Oxford University and acquired a one-year diploma at The Center for Advanced Montessori Studies in Bergamo, Italy. He has served on numerous occasions as a consultant on religious education and child development for many colleges, medical facilities, seminaries, and denominations. A popular conference speaker, He is a member of the American Bar Association and has been a guest speaker at several law conferences. His most recent book is *Godly Play* (Harper & Row). He coauthored *Children in Worship* (Westminster Press) and edited *Life Maps* (Word), a cooperative effort with James Fowler and Sam Keen. In addition he has authored numerous journal articles and book chapters.

JEAN BOX teaches in the School of Education at Samford University and serves as coordinator of early childhood programs at Samford. Previous teaching experiences include first grade and kindergarten. Dr. Box holds a

Ph.D. in early childhood education and development from the University of Alabama at Birmingham where she also received Masters and Educational Specialist degrees in the same field. Dr. Box has conducted research on literacy development in Head Start children.

CARY A. BUZZELLI is currently Assistant Professor in Early Childhood Education and Development in the Department of Curriculum and Instruction at the University of Alabama at Birmingham. He received an M.A. in child development and early childhood education from Purdue University and a Ph.D. from Georgia State University. He has published articles and presented papers in the areas of children's friendships and moral development of young children.

JAMES MICHAEL LEE is Professor of Education at the University of Alabama at Birmingham, and publisher of Religious Education Press. He acquired a doctoral degree at Columbia University. He served as Director of the Religious Education program at the University of Notre Dame. In addition to writing numerous chapters in scholarly books, he is acknowledged as the leading proponent of the social-science theory of religious education. Perhaps his finest work to date is *The Content of Religious Education*, the culmination of his massive trilogy documenting how research in the social sciences is the only adequate foundation for teaching religious education.

BLAKE NEFF is the Director of the School of Communication at Toccoa Falls College. He possesses an M.Div. degree from Asbury Theological Seminary and a Ph.D. in interpersonal and public communication from Bowling Green State University. He also pastors a United Methodist Church. He is a popular speaker and has conducted numerous family enrichment seminars. He was a visiting lecturer at Winebrenner Theological Seminary and served on the editorial advisory board of Roxbury Publishing Company. Neff authored a chapter in the *Handbook of Youth Ministry*.

JOLENE PEARL is the Coordinator of Elementary Education in the Teacher Education Department at Spring Arbor College. She has also taught at Mobile College, Southeastern Louisiana University, and the University of South Alabama. She spent many years as an elementary public school teacher and principal in Michigan, as well as supervising student teachers. She has a Ph.D. in elementary education from North Texas State University and an M.A. in elementary education from Northwestern Louisiana State University. Dr. Pearl was named to *Who's Who in American Education* for 1989-1990.

DONALD RATCLIFF is Assistant Professor of Psychology and Sociology at Toccoa Falls College, and has an M.A. from Michigan State University and an Ed.S. from the University of Georgia, both in educational psychology. He has published numerous articles on psychology and sociology in scholarly journals. Ratcliff is the author of *Using Psychology in the Church*, a coauthor of *Introduction to Psychology and Counseling*, edited the *Handbook of Preschool Religious Education*, and coedited the *Handbook of Youth Ministry*. He is listed in *Who's Who in Religion*.

JUDITH SEAVER is working with the Center for the Ministry of Teaching at Virginia Seminary and Morehouse Publishing in developing the Episcopal Children's Curriculum. Dr. Seaver was formerly the Director of Children's Ministries at St. Columba's Episcopal Church in Washington, D.C. Previous experience includes teaching early childhood education at the Pennsylvania State University, serving as a child care consultant to several organizations, and being a public school teacher. She has coauthored two books and written several articles in professional journals.

KALEVI TAMMINEN is Professor of Religious Education at the University of Helsinki in Finland. He holds both Ph.D. and Th.D. degrees. His research work has related to a wide variety of topics, including history of religious education, didactics, and moral and religious development. He has published many books and journal articles, has served as president of the Church Education Center, and recently authored a comprehensive book on religious development titled *Religious Development in Childhood and Youth*.

RENZO VIANELLO is Professor of Developmental Psychology at the University of Padova in Italy. His research has concentrated upon children's concepts of religion, magic, and death, as well as handicapped children. He possesses a degree in pedagogy and specialization in psychology. He was recently elected Vice President of the European Association for Special Education. Dr. Vianello has authored numerous journal articles and several books, including a major treatise on children's religious concepts.

KEVIN WALSH is Associate Professor of Education at the University of Alabama at Birmingham. He is the eleven-time recipient of the University's Excellence in Teaching award. He has also taught at the University of Pittsburgh and Rutgers University, as well as teaching children and serving as a principal. Dr. Walsh received his Ph.D. from the University of Pittsburgh in Elementary and Early Childhood Education. He is the originator of nationally recognized Developmental Discipline approach, has authored numerous articles and programs, and coauthored *Taming the Young Savage* and *Developmental Discipline*.

Index of Names

*This index was prepared with the assistance of
John Wesley Ratcliff, age 10*

Index of Subjects